ISLAM AND WOMEN

ENCYCLOPAEDIA OF WOMEN SOCIETY AND CULTURE SERIES-5

Islam and Women

RAJ PRUTHI
&
BELA RANI SHARMA

ANMOL PUBLICATIONS PVT LTD
New Delhi-110 002

ANMOL PUBLICATIONS PVT LTD
4374/4B, Ansari Road, Daryaganj
New Delhi-110 002

Islam and Women

First Edition 1995
ISBN 81-7488-086-0

PRINTED IN INDIA

Published by J.L. Kumar for Anmol Publications Pvt. Ltd., New Delhi and Printed at Mehra Offset Press, Delhi.

Acknowledgement

Some good work has been published on the otherwise neglected area of gender studies in the recent past. While compiling the present series we have collated relevant information to answer some of the present day queries pertaining to women studies. In doing so many distinguished contributors have earned our gratitude and we are deeply indebted to them.

Prof. Sheik Ali, Prof. G.C. Pande, Prof. M.N. Das, Prof. Romila Thapar, Prof. Aparna Basu, Prof. Vina Majumdar, Prof. Suvra Jaiswal, Prof. Leela Dubey, Prof. Devaki Jain, Prof. Sardamani have constantly inspired us. We are obliged to them.

Dr. (Mrs.) S. Pruthi, Dr. M. Lakshman and Dr. Neelam Khurana have facilitated the preparation of this series and we are sincerely grateful to them too.

Last but not the least, we are thankful to Shri J.L. Kumar without whose help and cooperation this series would not have seen the light of the day.

Editors

Preface

Of late, the women's question has attracted the attention of social scientists who find plenty of areas still unexplored for research. Women and their problems have acquired growing importance in our social milieu.

The present volume *Islam and Women* comprising of eight chapters is an attempt to collect and collate informations from various sources on Islamic modernisation in India and the role of Muslim women in Indian society which becomes an integral part of the popular Indian cultural milieu.

We hope that the present volume will be of immense value not only to the masses but also to the students, research scholars, teachers who are interested in women studies.

Editors

Contents

1

The Story of Islam

After the "Farewell Pilgrimage" the Arabs scattered to their homes carrying with them the memories of their journey to Medina and Mecca and of the glorious message of Muhammad. They all realised that Muhammad's mission was now fulfilled and Muhammad himself knew that his end was not far off. But he was not the man to think of resting on his laurels or on his achievements. His paradise was the welfare on his people. The Arabs had become Muslims, but what about Syria, Iraq, Egypt, and Abyssinia? These countries must also hear the Voice of God repeated five times a day.

The Kesra of Persia had torn Muhammad's letter. The Governor of Syria had scorned his message and threatened to attack him; and at Muta three Muslim generals had sacrificed their lives for the cause of Islam. Their martyrdom was a challenge to the Muslims, and Muhammad began to make his preparations to turn the tables on the Romans. But before he could do so, new dangers threatened him in Arabia. They say "imitation is the sincerest form of flattery" and many a clever poet and speaker thought of imitating Muhammad and declaring himself to be a prophet. One of these self-styled prophets was Tulaiha Za'im bin Asad of Nejd. He claimed to be a prophet and a messenger. But he was afraid of Muhammad and waited to declare himself till after Muhammad's demise. It was then that Khalid bin Walid defeated him and he became a Muslim.

But Musailma (the Liar) was more daring. He sent word to Muhammad that he (Musailma) was also a prophet like Muhammad and that half of the earth belonged to him and half to the Quraish.

The Prophet replied to Musailma: "From Muhammad the Prophet of God to Musailma the Liar. The earth belongs to God and He causes it to be inherited by whom He pleases from His virtuous servants and peace be on him who follows the guidance."

Aswad 'Ansi of Yemen was the third claimant. He claimed to be a magician and practised his art in secret till he had a big following. He expelled Muhammad's agents from Yemen, advanced towards Najran, killed Ibn Badhan the late ruler of Yemen and married his widow. His power spread in Yemen. He imprisoned or killed Muhammad's new agents sent to Yemen. But God delivered the Muslims from his atrocities. His own wife killed him as a revenge for the murder of her first husband, Ibn Badhan. Yemen was rid of the pretended sorcerer and tyrant.

Muhammad and the Romans knew that the clash between the Muslims and the Christians was inevitable. The Romans would have invaded Muhammad's territory long ago had it not been for their fear of these terrible warriors who did not fight to win or to conquer but to die. The Romans being men of experience and skilled in the arts of government knew how dangerous it was to stir up the Muslims. Muhammad also knew that the enemy was only waiting till his own followers became weak and lazy when they would be an easy prey to the trained legions of Byzantium.

With characteristic energy he immediately ordered an army to proceed to Syria under Usama, son of Zaid bin Harith. Zaid was Muhammad's freed slave but Muhammad had put him above all his kinsmen and above all his most intimate companions in the Battle of Muta. He did the same now with regard to Usama who was barely 20 years old.

He ordered Abu-Bakr and 'Omar to follow Usama and they willingly accepted to follow a mere youth at Muhammad's bidding. "We hear and we obey" that was their contract with God and they carried it out. If Muslims did the same thing to-day they would again become great. But the leaders and followers must all be actuated by the same spirit of one for all and all for one as animated Muhammad and his fullowers. And it must be remembered that Zaid and Usama did not accept the office of a leader for the sake of honour only. They undertook the leadership to lay down their lives in the cause of Islam.

And Muhammad ordered Usama to go by the boundaries of Balqa' and to enter the enemy's territory *via* Palestine close to Muta where his father had been killed and to attack God's enemies early in the morning and to carry the war to its bitter end and when God gave him the victory not to stop there but to come home immediately.

As has been previously pointed out in this book it is the custom with Arabs to choose a place outside the town where caravans gather before they start on a journey, and in case of war or a big gathering it takes some days before the caravan and its provisions are ready for the start.

In accordance with this custom, Usama took up his station at Jurf, not in far from Medina, in order to collect his arms and army.

Muhammad's Last Sickness

Whilst preparations for the collection of the army were going on Muhammad fell ill. People did not know what to do, and the army remained at Jurf awaiting the turn of events. Muhammad's sickness started in the month of Safar (the 2nd month) of 11 A.H. He was suffering from the effects of the poison administered to him at Khaibar by his Jewish hostess. He had fever and headache. In spite of his sickness he went on with his duties, going to the mosque and leading the prayers. He himself, however, knew that his end was near.

He could not sleep at night. The effect of the poison was disturbing his nervous system. On or about the fourth night of his sickness, he got up and accompanied by his attendant he went to the graveyard of the Muslim martyrs to pay them his last visit. He told his attendant: "I have been ordered to ask God's forgiveness for the souls of the departed, accompany me". They went and he prayed to God for their forgiveness. Muhammad never forgot any of his followers—not even the dead. He was the best of friends that mankind ever had and though now sick unto his death he was doing his duty to his departed companions. When he had finished, he told his attendant: "I was given the keys of the treasures of the world and lasting assurance of their enjoyment, and then of Paradise. I chose the meeting of my Lord and Paradise."

The next morning, Muhammad went to 'Aisha's house and complained of severe headache and told her he was feeling great pain and constantly said: "O my head! my head!" But still he would not lie down on bed, and continued to attend to his wives. Five days more passed like this. When he was in the house of Maimuna he became so weak that he could hardly get up. He called all his wives and asked them in whose house he should pass his days of sickness. Such was his regard for the feelings of his wives and of all men. They all consented to the house of 'Aisha. Supported by 'Ali bin Abu-Talib and his uncle 'Abbas he moved to 'Aisha's place with great difficulty.

His condition became worse. But he would still go to the mosque to lead the prayers. More days passed and he heard people say that he had appointed a boy to lead the Ansar and Muhajirin to war with the Romans. He was now hardly able to move, so great was his pain and his headache. He would, however, not let people be in doubt. He ordered his wives to pour seven skinfuls of cold water on his head till it was cooled when he said: "It is enough, it is enough". He put on his clothes, tied his head with a band, went to the mosque and took his seat on the pulpit. He praised God, said prayers for the martyrs of Ohod and others and asked God's forgiveness for their souls and lengthened his prayers on their behalf and then said: "Ye men! carry out the mission of Usama. By my life, if you have been saying anything against his leadership you said the same about his father before, whilst he is the fittest person for this leadership as was his father."

Then he remained silent for a while and continued: "There was a servant of God whom God gave the choice of this life and of the hereafter against what was with Him and the servant chose what was with God". He again became silent and the people were puzzled but Abu-Bakr understood that the person spoken of was Muhammad himself. Abu-Bakr could control himself no longer. He wept and said: "Nay, we will offer our lives and our sons for thee". Muhammad made a sign to Abu-Bakr to hold his peace and then said: "Let all doors opening on the mosque be locked except the door of Abu-Bakr". When that had been done he said: "I know no one who has been a better companion to me than he (Abu Bakr), and if I was to take any man as my *Khalil* (the most intimate friend) I would choose Abu-Bakr. But his companionship and brotherhood in faith is enough till God join us with Himself."

Muhammad now wanted to return to the house of 'Aisha but went on saying:

"Ye Muhajirin, I command you to help the Ansar in all good things, because men will increase (as time passes) but the Ansar, under the circumstances will decrease. They gave me shelter. Therefore, return their good deeds with good deeds and pass over their mistakes."

He then left and entered 'Aisha's house but the speech, only parts of which are given above, had been a terrible strain on his nerves which had been artificially cooled down by the effect of cold water. His condition now became serious. He still wanted to go to the mosque and speak to men about Usama's expedition, about the necessity of union amongst Muslims when he had expired and about a great many other things but each time he tried to get up he fainted. This happened three times and then he ordered that Abu-Bakr should lead the prayers in his stead. This together with the previous sermon was a clear indication from him that he wanted Abu-Bakr to be the leader of the Muslims after his death.

'Aisha, daughter of Abu-Bakr, asked the Prophet three times to excuse him (Abu-Bakr) as he was too tender-hearted and given to weeping when reciting the Qur-an and, three times, the Prophet repeated his command. Abu-Bakr, therefore, became his deputy.

One day when Abu-Bakr was absent, 'Omar led the prayers. The Prophet recognised his voice from his place and said: "Where is Abu-Bakr"? People understood that he (Muhammad) wanted Abu-Bakr to be the *Khalifah* after him.

More than a fortnight had passed since Muhammad fell sick and his condition was now very grave indeed. His daughter Fatimah visited him daily and he used to kiss her. When he was dangerously ill, she came one day. He kissed her as usual and whispered to her something and she cried. Then he whispered to her again and she laughed.

'Aisha questioned her, after the Prophet's death, as to this weeping and laughing and Fatimah replied: "The first time he told me that he would not recover from this illness and I cried. The second time he told me that I would be the first of the family to join him and I laughed". So that, not only men but women in Islam also loved to die.

It is also stated that in the early days of his illness the prophet said to 'Aisha: "How would you like dying in my life-time so that I might say prayers over your body and bury you?" She replied: "If I were sure of that, I would immediately go to my parents' house and come back dressed as a bride."

He was now being consumed by the fire of the poison and its fever and had to dip his hands in cold water and wash his face constantly to keep the heat down.

One day, while he was in this condition and his companions came to see him, he said: "Come here, I will cause you to write something so that you will never fall into error." Some of those present said: "The Prophet of God is suffering from pain and you have the Qur-an with you and the Book of God is sufficient unto us." Others wanted the writing to be carried out. When Muhammad saw them quarrelling over it, he said, "God and leave me alone."

Usama and his army now returned to Medina as the prophet was in an extremely dangerous condition. Usama came to see him.

the Prophet raised his hand and prayed for him and then put his hand on Usama's head to show his approval of him.

The prophet's family thought he was suffering from pneumonia and prepared some medicine for him but he refused to take it. When he was unconscious they poured the medicine down his throat. On his regaining consciousness he asked all the people in the house to take the same medicine as a punishment for disobeying his orders.

Muhammad had seven *dinars* in his possession and being afraid that they might be left behind he had them distributed to the poor. He did not want to meet his Lord and have it said that he had any wealth left behind him.

Muhammad's Shortlived Recovery

This was the last night of Muhammad's life, Sunday 11th of Rabi ul-Awwal, 11 A.H. The fever seemed to leave him a bit and in the morning he was able to tie his head and supported by 'Ali and 'Abbas he ventured out from 'Aisha's house into the mosque ('Aisha's house was practically part of the mosque and separated from it by a mud partition). Abu-Bakr was leading the prayer.

The Muslims were in their prayers and when they saw him come out they were so happy that they very nearly broke their prayers. Abu-Bakr felt what was happening and wished to retire from the leadership but Muhammad touched him from behind as a sign to go on with his business and himself said his prayers by the side of Abu-Bakr. The Prophet said his prayers sitting down whilst Abu-Bakr led the prayers.

When the prayers were over he addressed the people loud enough to be heard outside:

"Ye men! the fire (of hell) is blazing and persecutions (or disturbances) in Faith are coming like a piece of dark night. And I tell you, by God, do not attribute to me anything (which does not belong to me). Surely, by God, I have not declared anything lawful which the Qur-an has not made lawful nor have I made anything unlawful which the Qur-an has not made unlawful. And God disapproves of those people who make their tombs as their mosques."

The Muslims thought that the Prophet had recovered and that there was no more danger. Usama came and asked his permission to go with his army to Syria, Abu-Bakr congratulated him saying, "I see thee, O Prophet of God, in good health by the grace of God and His blessing as we wish thee to recover!" and asked his permission to go out of Medina to bring his wife and he got the permission of the Prophet to go to Sunh where his wife lived. `Omar and `Ali also left to attend to their affairs and the Muslims dispersed well pleased and happy after they had despaired of the life of the Prophet the previous day. Muhammad returned to the house of `Aisha exhausted more than ever.

His head was resting on the lap of 'Aisha when he saw someone coming with a tooth-brush. He pointed towards it. 'Aisha took it and made it soft for him. The prophet cleaned his mouth and said:

"O God, help me in the agony of death."

'Aisha says: "I felt as if he was getting heavier in my lap. I looked at his face when his eyes looked up in a stare and he said:

" 'Nay, (I choose) the Companion on High in Heaven (or Paradise).' You say, `Have I made my choice'? "Yes, I have, and I swear by Him Who has sent thee with the truth'."

This is the conversation between Muhammad and the Angel of Death. Muhammad is being offered the choice of recovery or the meeting of his Lord and he chooses to meet his Lord in Heaven.

The choice was accepted by God and lo! the praised one, Muhammad, was with the One Who Is Always Praised!

"All praise belongs to God, Lord of all the worlds" !

2

Life of Muhammad

European biographers are amazed at the success of Muhammad's mission and his victorious march as a leader of mankind. No reformer, no king, no warrior, has ever been able to influence mankind as did Muhammad. In twenty-three years he transformed the savage Arabs into the best organized body of men, although circumstances were heavily against him. That is admitted even by the writer in the *Encyclopaedia Britannica.*

"At the time of Muhammad's birth and youth nothing seemed less likely than that the Arabs should presently make their triumphal entrance into the history of the world as victors over Greeks and Persians."

The facts of Muhammad's life and his unique conquest over the hearts of his followers are unquestionable. The other conquests over the Greeks and Persians followed as a consequence of his conquest of hearts.

Such a fascinating, honourable, charming and lovable man commands the respect and obedience of all mankind. But European writers are born anti-everything that is not European. The colour prejudice nourishes itself in their vitals.

For centuries they have called themselves Christians, but they have never been Christians. They have always been nationalists or Europeans, and nothing else. They despise all non-Europeans. Each country in Europe has modified Christianity to suit its own nationalism. Religion is, and has been, with the Europeans, a mere matter of expediency.

We see in our own day that Russia, under the Bolsheviks, has cast off Christianity and become an atheist country. Germany under Hilter is anti-Jewish, and anti-Catholic. The religion of Germany is Germanism. The religion of Italy is Mussolini-ism, and of France nothing but love of France. England has always been a self-loving country. America is a land where kidnapping of Lindberg baby is the pastime of its underworld, and sensational posters the delight of its upperworld.

It is only natural for writers of European countries to throw mud on those who do not belong to them and who are not of the same colour as they are. This is a malady for which there is no cure.

> In their hearts there is a disease,
> And this disease does God increase to them;
> And for them is a painful agony,
> On account of what they lied.
>
> (Qur-an, 2 : 10)

For three centuries, they have cried themselves hoarse over their accusations of Muhammad being a licentious man, an imposter, a murderer, a liar and all other vile epithets which their imaginations could suggest and their hearts could accept. And they go on repeating these lying accusations believing that some of the mud they throw may stick. But they might, just as well, spit at the moon fancying that their spitting will reach the upper regions. Muhammad requires no defence. God is his Defender. The Europeans may soon be throwing mud at the holy persons of Jesus and Virgin Mary.

And what proof have these writers of Muhammad being a licentious man? Nothing but the fact that after he was 53 years old, he gradually contracted a number of marriages which they dislike, and the further fact that whilst he limited the number of wives to his followers at a maximum of four he made an exception of the law in his own case.

The fact that Muhammad had many wives at a certain stage of his life, namely, after his Emigration to Medina is undisputed but Abraham, David, Solomon and many other prophets and saints of the Old Testaments had many wives. Were they all licentious men? God forbid such as accusation!

As to the law, the limitation of the number of wives was fixed at the end of the Eighth year of the Hegira and Muhammad had married all his wives before that period. He was told by God to keep those whom he had married but was forbidden to marry any more. If he divorced his wives, or if they became widows as the majority of them did, they could not be remarried. Out of respect for the prophet, they were called "Ummhat ul-Muminin" or "Mothers of the Faithful". This was all the special legislation allowed to him.

He was the Ruler of the State of Arabia when the Revelation came in favour not of Muhammad but of his wives—that they need not be divorced, and also against them that they must not remarry after his death. And all of them remained widows till their death.

The question is: "Should there be any special privileges regarding the family of a ruler of a country?" It was published the other day in the newspapers that the will of King George V was not subject to the laws governing the wills of his subjects, and that is as it should be. If subjects begin to scrutinize the personal wills of their rulers, the relationship of ruler and the subject must become strained. The very fact that a man is ruler over others gives him a status different from his subjects. Muhammad was subject to law but it was God's Law, not the law of his European biographers. Rulers always had and must have special privilege and the writer could mention scores of such privileges. But let that suffice. The accusation that Muhammad was a licentious man because he married so many wives is absolutely false and without foundation of fact. Muhammad's marriages were all marriages that were forced upon him, or marriages of protection of the females whose husbands had died in the Cause of God and whom he took into his household or, lastly, marriages especially contracted to cement the bonds of love with those who could by their position and influence be of service to Islam. In every single case, it was a personal sacrifice on the part of Muhammad to have contracted the marriage, or circumstances obliged him to do so whilst there was as yet no law limiting the number of wives.

His marriages will now be considered seriatum.

First Marriage with Khadijah

Muhammad's first marriage with Khadijah has been fully described. He was then in the full strength of his manhood and had lived an exemplary chaste life. His age then was 25. She was 40 and a widow twice over. The proposal of marriage came from her. She was rich and he was poor. And his guardian-uncle, abu-Talib, was burdened with a big family and was also poor. Muhammad accepted the proposal and it turned out to be a most happy marriage. For twenty-five years thereafter they lived together till she died at the age of 65. And during these 25 years he never thought of marrying again in spite of the fact that during the last 15 years of their marriage she was old, past child-bearing age and he was still a strong man. He always cherished her memory in the most loving terms, so much so that 'Aisha was jealous of her as she never was jealous of his other wives who were alive. She used to say to Muhammad, "Why do you mention an old woman so often when God has given you better wives"? And his reply was: "No, she loved me and was the first to believe and I loved her."

Is that consistent with the accusation of Muhammad being a licentious man? For a strong and comparatively young man to live with an old wife and not to think of marrying another was possible for Muhammad because he was devoted to the service of God. There was no *purdah* amongst the Arabs then. There was no law or custom restricting Muhammad to marry another woman. He never even raised his eyes towards another woman. He was content and controlled his desires for another woman. He was content and controlled his desires for full 15 years between the age of 35 and 50. During these years, Muhammad had sacrificed his personal comfort a thousand times for the sake of Islam. That he lived and prospered was due to God only. He had killed his evil passions and all worldly desires. He was a man possessed of the purest heart.

Muhammad's Second Marriage with Sauda bint Zama

When Khadijah died, Muhammad had a family of two unmarried daughters on his hand. He was still in full manly power and could have chosen a young wife. He was single. But the wife he chose was a widow—Sauda *bint* Zama. Sauda was a Muslim and had emigrated with her first husband Sakran bin 'Amr to Abyssinia. She also had a son named Abd ur Rahman. Was this the act of a licentious man—marrying a widow of one of his faithfull followers with a son as an encumbrance?

Marriages with 'Aisha and Hafsa

These marriages were contracted to cement his relations with his ministers, Abu-Bakr and 'Omar, just as he gave his own daughters to 'Othman and 'Ali. All this was done for the sake of Islam and not for the sake of satisfying any personal desires. Hafsa was also a widow of one of the martyrs of Badr named Khanais. 'Omar offered her hand to Abu-Bakr and 'Othman but they refused. Hafsa, like her father, was a strongminded woman and not quite young. Muhammad was now over 54 years old. There is no evidence of a holy man having been content with one wife and turning suddenly licentious after the age of 53. And Muhammad had led an exemplary life and was always legally married. He was the man who proclaimed adultery as a capital sin. European writers condone adultery but condemn marriage.

Marriages with Zainab bint Khuzaima Umm ul-Masakin and Umm-Salama

Zainab Umm ul-Masakin (the mother of the poor) was a widow of 'Abdullah bin Jahash, a martyr of Ohod. Muhammad took her under his protection but she died soon afterwards.

Umm-Salama was also a widow of Abu-Salama who had been

dangerously wounded at Ohod and died in 4 A.H. Muhammad was 57 years of age when this marriage was contracted.

It must be remembered that the death-role at Badr, Ohod and the murder of 77 teachers of religion by the treachery of the Arabs had widowed nearly half the Muslim women at Medina, and Muhammad was not the only man who was contracting these marriages of protection and necessity. He was setting an example to his companions and they all had to take this extra burden on their heads. Those were not marriages of pleasure but of absolute and dire necessity. Abu-Bakr, 'Omar, 'Othman, and all the rest had their share of this burden. Women could not be left to look after themselves and the punishment for fornication and adultery was respectively 100 strokes of the leather in public and death. What Muhammad was doing for the preservation of the morality of his people is interpreted as licentiousness by his opponents. Truly none are so blind as those who won't see.

Marriage with Zainab bint Jahash

Muhammad's marriage with this lady (Zainab bint Jahash) provides the Western scandal-mongers with the most fanciful stories. She was on her mother's side, daughter of Umaimah bint 'Abd ul-Muttalib and so a cousin of Muhammad. She had been like a sister to him and Muhammad had known her and seen her all his life. There was no *purdah* and no secrecy between them. If she was a model of beauty as European writers allege, her charms were known to Muhammad for a long time past.

The Arabs were a most proud race and had always treated their slaves with great harshness, and they looked upon them with great contempt even when they were emancipated. In fact, a slave was always a slave, just as a *Sudra* amongst the Hindus always remained a low caste, no matter what his personal merits were. He was born low. Muhammad had come to abolish this inequality for ever. Slaves and free men were all equal in the eyes of God and he alone was most honourable who was most reverent to God. (*Inna akramakum 'ind-Allahzi-atqakum*—Qur-an, 50:13).

No one, amongst the Arabs, dare make himself the equal of his slaves though emancipated.

Muhammad set the example as he did in all other cases.

He asked his emancipated slave, Zaid bin Harith, to marry Zainab bint Jahash and grand-daughter of the great 'Abd ul-Muttalib.

Zaid was afraid to do it. Zainab would not have it, but Muhammad insisted because he had to abolish the unjust rules as to the inequalities amongst men.

God approved of Muhammad's proposal. God had His own plans as yet unknown even to Muhammad himself. The plans of God spread wide and sure and no man can escape therefrom. God revealed to Muhammad about this proposed marriage. "And it is not fit for a believing man or a believing woman, when God, as well as His messenger, has decided an affair, that they should have any choice in their affair."

Hence neither Zaid nor Zainab had any choice. They were married. But forced marriages are seldom lasting. And it was so in this case. Zainab boasted of her nobility to Zaid and was a woman gifted with the power of speech. Zaid could not bear it. He complained to the prophet. The Prophet advised patience. In matrimonial matters, however, the advice of superiors is seldom of much effect. At last, Zaid divorced her. It was not Zaid who did so but it was the Will of god. God ordered Muhammad to marry her. Muhammad thought that Zaid was his adopted son and was often called Zaid bin Muhammad instead of Zaid bin Harith and it was against Arab custom to marry an adopted son's widow or divorced wife. What could Muhammad do? But God's commands must be obeyed. God said that an adopted son was not a real son and his wife had not the status of a real daughter-in-law. The Arab custom must be abolished once for ever and Muhammad himself was chosen to be God's first agent to do so. Says God:

> Nor has He made your adopted sons your (real) sons;

> There are your words spoken with your mouths:
> But God speaks the truth and He guides in the (right) path.
> Call them by their (real) father's names, that is more equitable in the sight of God.
>
> (Qur-an, 33 : 4.5).

So that Zaid could no longer be called bin Muhammad. As to marrying his divorced wife God was also explicitly clear:

> And when thou didst say to him whom God had blessed and whom thou hadst blessed: "Keep thou thy wife and reverence God."
> And thou wast concealing in thy mind what God was going to disclose and thou wast afraid of the people.
> And it is more righteous that thou shouldst be afraid of God.
> Therefore when Zaid had had his want of her, We married her to thee that there might be no barrier upon the Faithful in the marriage of the wives of their adopted sons when they have had their want.
> And God's order was bound to be carried out.
>
> (Qur-an, 33 : 37)

He sacrificed his will to the Will of God. He was a Muslim. These are the facts about this marriage.

Marriages with Juwairiya and Safia

Both these marriages and the circumstances under which they took place have been mentioned in the body of this book. Juwairiya was the daughter of Harith bin Darar and was a captive of war. Her father married her to Muhammad as an honour to himself and his daughter and this was the cause of the freedom of all the war prisoners of banu Mustaliq. This marriage might rightly be called a marriage for the sake of Charity and Brotherly Love. It was by such deeds that Muhammad won the hearts of the Arabs.

As to Safia she was the daughter of a Jewish chief (Huyyai bin Akhtab) and the widow of another Jewish chief Kinana (killed at Khaibar). It was not fit for any Muslim to take a lady of such rank as a captive of war and though the Prophet gave her to Dihya bin Kalbi he was obliged to take her back to himself. She was a Jew by birth but Muhammad loved her as much as he loved any Arab wife of his. Once when Hafsa or 'Aisha called her the daughter of a Jew and not equal to an Arab lady, she complained to the prophet. The Prophet told her: "Why did not you say 'Harun is my (fore) father, Moses my uncle and Muhammad my husband, how can you be better that I ?" Safia loved the Prophet dearly and he returned her love.

Marriages with Umm-Habiba and Maria

The first of these two marriages was a marriage of necessity as Umm-Habiba was a widow of 'Abdullah bin Jahash who had emigrated to Abyssinia and died there. Muhammad married her by proxy, and this also was a marriage to win over the unbelieving quraish as she was the daughter of Abu-Sufyan, the chief of the Quraish. In fact, it may be said that the conversion of Khalid and the weakening of Abu-Sufyan's opposition to Muhammad was greatly influenced by this marriage. It showed them that Muhammad was not their enemy but one who wished them well and it was a folly to fight such a good and honourable kinsman.

Maria was sent to Muhammad as a gift by the Ruler of Egypt and he could not possibly hand her over to another as it was against all kingly rules.

Marriage with Maimuna

There only remains one more marriage to explain, *viz.*, that of Maimuna. She was divorced by her first husband Harith. She then married one Abu-Rahm and was widowed. She made a gift of her person to the Prophet and lived up to 51 A.H.

This finishes the whole list of the Prophet's marriages. Up to the age of 53 he had only one wife. Then in seven years he contracted all his other marriages. When he was sixty years old, at the end of the Eighth year of Hegira, God sent the Revelation about the limit of marriages:

> And if you fear that you will not be able to do justice to the orphan (girls)
>
> (By taking them in marriage),
> Then marry whom you like
> From amongst other women,
> Two at a time, or three, or four;
>
> But if you are afraid that even then you will not be able to keep equality
>
> (Amongst your wives),
> Then (marry) only one
> Or that which your right hands have possessed:
> This is nearer to keeping you from doing an injustice.
>
> (Qur-an, 4 : 3)

The Arabs, like most other people, used to take rich orphan girls under their control as their wives. God asks them to do these girls justice and if they fear they cannot do justice by marrying them, they should choose other women as wives. According to this commandment, Muslims who had more than four wives at that time were forced to divorce the extra ones. But what about Muhammad? If he divorced his wives, who was to marry them? There would be rivalries and bloodshed, and rival families would be fighting each other till the end of the world. New causes for war might arise amongst Muslims and people might boast of their descent from the Prophet's wives.

God made the retention of his married wives lawful for Muhammad but commanded him to marry no more in any event whatsoever.

> Hereafter no more wives are allowed thee nor (is it allowed to thee) to change them for other wives even though their beauty surprise thee—excepting what thy right hand possesses:
> For God is Guardian over all things.
>
> (Qur-an, 33 : 52)

This is the truth about Muhammad's marriages. He left nine widows and each of them led an exemplary chaste life till her death. They were collectively called *Ummahat ul-Muminin* or "Mothers of the Faithful." May God bless them all and His Noble Prophet Muhammad for ever and for ever!

3

Maulana Abu'l Kalam Azad on Islam

The entire message of the *Quran* is based on love and mercy. There are over three hundred places in the *Quran,* dealing with divine mercy and love. If we take into account all these verses which deal with other attributes related to mercy and love, then we can say that the *Quran* is nothing but a message of Divine mercy. Whenever it addresses the sinners, says Maulana Azad, it addresses them with love and affection. "Say : O My bond servants who have been prodigal to their own hurt, despair not of the mercy of God, who forgiveth all sins. He is forgiving, the Merciful."

And in this verse also He calls them my bond servants: "And on the day when He will assemble them and that which they worship instead of God and will say: was it ye who misled these my bond servants or did they (themselves) wander from the way?"

God addresses with all this affection no more than twenty occasions in the *Quran.* Maulana Azad asks, 'what more can a message of Mercy be?" He points out that the *Quran* stresses on its mission to reunite all mankind. It has not brought a new message, and it does not favour any exclusive group or nation. On the other hand, its mission is to put an end to all conflicts and differences in groups and to show all mankind the one path, the path of rectitude and truth. And that is the same path, as the one that has been shown by prophets from time immemorial. "He hath ordained for you that religion which He commended unto Noah, and that which we inspire in thee (Mohammed), and that which we commanded unto Abraham and Moses and Jesus, saying : Establish the religion, and be not divided therein. Dreadful for the idolaters is that unto which thou callest them. God chooseth for Himself whom He will and guideth unto Himself him who turneth."

Again, He says:

"Verily we have revealed to thee as we revealed to Noah and the prophets after him, and as we revealed to Abraham and Ishmael and Isaac, and Jacob, and the tribes and Jesus, and Job and Jonah, Aaron and Soloman, and to David. Of some apostles we have told thee before, of other apostles we have not told thee—Apostles charged to announce and to warn, that man, after those apostles, might have no plea against God." (4: 162 to 165)

"O Ye apostles! Truly this your religion is the one Religion, and I am your Lord."

Maulana Azad maintains that for the *Quran,* the oneness of God implies the oneness of His truth, however different might have been the languages in which His message was conveyed. If you believe in one prophet and do not believe in other prophets, it means you accept a reality at one place and reject the same reality at another. The *Quran* calls upon every one to accept all the prophets and their books without any discrimination.

"The apostle believeth in that which has been sent down from his Lord, as do the faithful also. They all believe in God and His angles and His Books, and His apostles: We make no distinction between any of His apostles. And they say We have heard and obeyed. Thy mercy, Lord! for unto thee must we return."

For the *Quran* , the divine truth is an universal gift from God. It is not the monopoly of any race or religious group. Man may be divided into geographical and racial boundaries. But divine truth knows none. It cannot be divided. It bears no national or racial imprint. You should, therefore, seek this truth and follow it. This Truth of God is man's treasure, no matter in whatever form it is found and man is heir to it. The Quran invites man to follow this truth and avoid every form of groupism, nationalism, and racialism. The *Quran* calls the path of denial, the path of division and distinction.

It says, the path of rectitude lies in the belief in all the prophets, because the acceptance of one and rejection of other means rejection of all.

"Of a truth they who believe not in God and His apostles, and seek to separate God from His apostles, and say `some we believe and some we believe not", and desire to take a middle course : These ! they are veritable disbelievers! and for the disbelievers have we prepared shameful punishment. And they who believe in God and his apostles and make no difference between them— these! We will bestow on them their reward and God is gracious, Merciful!'

In the following lines the *Quran* points out the path of true believers: "who believe in the unseen and establish worship, and spend of that we have bestowed upon them; and who believe in that which is revealed unto thee (Mohammed) and that which was revealed before thee, and are certain of the hereafter. These depend on Guidance from their Lord. These are the successful."

The *Quran* asks : Why are there conflicts and tension in the name of God and religion when God is one and the same and His message has been identical? Repeatedly it calls upon man to have faith in one God and to live a righteous life in conformity with that belief without condemning any religion or its founder. The *Quran* confirms the basic message of all religions. The *Quran,* points out Maulana Azad, never claimed to be a new religion. It was the same religion of God appearing at different times. It asked the people to return to their own religions by clearing them of the accretions which had gathered around them. Had they done it they would have found no conflict between this message and the message they had received before.

Says the *Quran:* "Establish worship and enjoin kindness and forbid iniquity."

Maulana Azad observes that the *Quran's* message is that there are deeds which are universally accepted as good and there are also acts which are wicked in the eyes of one and all. For instance, all are of one accord that truth is good and mendacity is evil. All agree that honesty is a virtue and dishonesty is a vice. All hold that kindliness towards every one, service to parents, care of the poor and assistance of the oppressed and needy are things really good.

All agree that cruelty and ill treatment are evil acts. When all religions of the world, all moral philosophers and all communities, in spite of differences in other matters, hold similar views in respect of these matters, why then should there be any hostility to the message of the *Quran?* In other words, the message of the *Quran* has been accepted universally. It is in vogue everywhere. It is another matter that some people are not aware of the fact that they are following the same path shown to mankind fourteen hundred years ago. Thus, the mission of the *Quran* has been fulfilled to a great extent.

The *Quran* says that natural laws never change. So, the way of God or the right religion, cannot be altered for any one.

The *Quran* calls upon man to do whatever is good and to avoid whatever is evil.

This is the same message which was brought by Abraham and it is Islam. "Turn steadfastly to the path of devotion, to the ways of God, for which he hath fitted man. There is no altering of the ways of God.

That is the right religion; but most people know it not. And ye be turned to Him and fear Him and observe prayer, and be not of those who unite Gods with God, or of those who have split up their religion and have become sects, where every party rejoices in what is their own."

The *Quran* holds that if all the people resolve to return to the path of devotion to God and righteous living then the purpose of the *Quran* is fulfilled.

The beauty of the Quranic message, according to Maulana Azad, is that it approves all the religions in their original form. It calls upon the followers of all the religions to assemble on one platform, and declares that all religions of the world are the branches of one great tree. The *Quran* presented to mankind the principle of the universal truth of religion.

1. The *Quran* proclaimed the unity of religion.
2. It is opposed to all groupisms.
3. It made it clear that salvation can be achieved through devotion to God and righteous living.

No racial or religious group can claim itself to be the only heir. The *Quran* made it clear that as the physical laws of nature are necessary for man's physical development, so spiritual laws of nature are essential for his spiritual progress. Quranic revelation was delivered to remind mankind of the spiritual laws of nature and to weld them in a single brotherhood, under one banner, and to lead them towards peace, progress and prosperity. Dr. Latif says: "To the student of the *Quran,* not one word, in the preamble or in the objectives of the charter and not a single article in the text of the universal declaration of Human rights, will seem unfamiliar. Under a creed, which places man next to God, and brushes aside all distinctions of race, colour and birth and calls upon all mankind to live together as a family of God, the Universal Declaration of Human Rights must follow as a basic corollary, or an extension of the Quranic programme." The *Quran* stands for Internationalism for which modern social scientists and philosophers are striving.

Summing up, we may say that the basic teaching of all the prophets is the same and the *Quran* was delivered when the followers of the former prophets had, disregarding the original teaching, strayed away from the right path. The Prophet Muhammad came and brought the same message, though in a different language and style. Thus, the *Quran* reiterates the same teaching and shows the same path which had already been pointed out many times on previous occasions. It enjoins men to act in ways which have universally been admitted to be right. It forbids all those acts which are universally considered to be wrong. "Thus the *Quran' says* Maulana Azad, `calls upon man to follow this universally recognised path of rectitude and to shun all other path, which lead to differences and divisions.'

This path of rectitude, a true path or common religion of all the prophets, is termed Islam in the *Quran.*

4

European Views on Islam

Sincere and not an Impostor

"The question of the imposture of Mahomet is one which may best be left to the candid reader, who, from the records of his life, will judge how far he has laid himself open to so grave an imputation. That he was the imposter pictured by some writers is refuted alike by his unwavering belief in the Truth of his own mission, by the loyalty and unshaken confidence of his companions, who had ample opportunities of forming a right estimate of his sincerity, and finally, by the magnitude of the task which he brought to so successful an issue. No imposter, it may safely be said, could have accomplished so mighty a work. No one unsupported by a living faith in the reality of his commission, in the goodness of his cause, could have maintained the same consistent attitude through long years of adverse fortune, alike in the day of victory and the hour of defeat, in the plenitude of his power and at the moment of death."

The Glory of Muhammad

"Judged by the smallness of the means at his disposal, and the extent and permanence of the work he accomplished, no name in the world's story shines with a more specious lustre than that of the Prophet of Mecca. To the impulse which he gave, numberless dynasties have owed their existence, fair cities and stately palaces and temples have arisen, and wide provinces became obedient to the Faith. And beyond all this, his words have governed the belief of generations, been accepted as their rule in life and their certain guide to the world to come. At a thousand shrines the voices of the Faithful invoke blessing on him, whom they esteem the very Prophet of God, the seal of Apostles, now passed into the highest heaven as their intercessor with the All-Merciful Allah. Judged by the standard of human renown, the glory of what mortal can compare with his?"

The Excellent Morals of the Qur-an

"Thus the duty of helping the poor, of relieving the needy traveller, and of doing justice to the orphan, is insisted on. The love and honour due to parents from their children, the performance of covenants, and the use of just weights, form part of the believer's duty. Liberality is commended, profuseness condemned. The Prophet points out, how, at the end of the world, our words, our thoughts, nay, the very use of our eye-sight, will be brought into account and he states, how desirable it is for the true believer to love God, to pray to Him, and to walk humbly in His Sight (Sura XVII)."

Miracles

"On this head it may be remarked that Mahomet always disclaimed the power of working miracles, and assumed no higher honour than that of being a Prophet sent by God—'a warner,' an apostle—the instrument of communicating God's will to men; and the honesty of his conduct in this respect speaks well for him, and implies a perfect reliance on the goodness of his cause.

To those who demanded from him some miraculous proof of the truth of his claims, he pointed to the Koran—a book revealed to 'an ignorant and unlearned man', as the greatest of miracles, and he assured the objectors that if not convinced by it, no sign, however, stupendous, would have power to compel their belief."

Salvation

"The Koran, as above explained, however, much its followers may have departed from its teachings, repudiates the idea of any vicarious sacrifice for sin, teaches expressly that each soul must account for itself to God, and denying the truth of the Christian redemption, lays upon each individual the task of atoning for his sin, of securing pardon, and of rendering himself meet for admission to Paradise. Self-righteousness, the merit of good works, and of a rigid attention to the prescribed formularies and ceremonies of their faith, with God's mercy to supply any possible deficiency, these constitute the scheme of salvation prescribed by Islam."

Marriages

"Mohammed's numerous marriages after Khadijah's death have been attributed by many European writers to gross passion, but they would seem to have been mainly dictated by motives of a less coarse kind. Several of his alliances were political in character, the Prophet being anxious to bind his chief followers more and more closely to himself. This was doubtless his object in marrying the daughters of Abu-Bakr and Omar; while a political motive of a different sort is to be found in his alliances with the daughters of political opponents or fallen enemies. Victory over an enemy would seem to have been consummated only when the enemy's daughter was introduced into the conqueror's harem. The remainder are to be explained by his extreme anxiety to have a son."

The above extract from one of Muhammad's most vicious critics is of great value as rebuttal of the views of other equally vicious critics.

His Work

"His political work was not left half finished at his death: he had founded an empire with a religious and a political capital; he had made a nation of a loose agglomeration of tribes. He had given them a rallying-point in their common religion, and therein discovered a bond more permanent than a dynasty. The old faiths which had survived so long in secluded Arabia had been given their death-blow."

It is, however, very pleasant to come across a most learned Christian author named Dr. Henry Stubbe, M.A., of Christ Church, Oxford, born on the 28th of February 1631, and who died on 12th July 1676, whose Manuscript was copied by Charles Hornsby of Pipe Office, in 1705 and was published in 1911 under the auspices of the Islamic Society by Luzac & Co., London, under the name of

"An account of the Rise and Progress of Mahomedanism with the Life of Mahomed."

This early author refutes the Christian accusations against Muhammad and Islam. A few extracts from this work are given below but the book must be read to be enjoyed.

The Muslim Wars

"It is a vulgar Opinion that `Mahomet propagated his Doctrine by the Sword,' and not only compelled the Arabians at first to receive his Religion but obliged his Successors by a perpetual Vow or Precept to endeavour the Extirpation of Christianity and all other Religions, thereby to render his own universal. But how generally soever this be believed, and how great men soever they be who support it, yet is it no other than a palpable mistake. It is very true that Mahomet did levy warr in Arabia, but it was with the object of restoring an old Religion, not to introduce a new one. He taught his followers to abolish idolatry everywhere, and that all the World was obliged to the profession of these truths, that there was one God, that he had no Associates, that there was a Providence, and a Retribution hereafter proportionate to the good or ill Actions of Men, just as the Jews thought themselves obliged to bring all Mankind (as far as in them lay) under the observation of the Law of Nature contained in the seven precepts of Noah. But that all Mankind were to be forced to the profession of his Religion, or that he compelled any thereto, is a falsehood. Yet had it been so, it is plain that many Christian Doctors have held that Christianity may be enforced, and that it is a just Cause for one Prince to invade and conquer another's Territories, to propagate the true Religion thereby. They say that if one King may chastise and reduce under obedience the subjects of another, they may do as much for the Lord paramount of the Universe. That Kings are the Ministers of God to execute Wrath upon such as do Evil, and that being the Viceroys of the Almighty they ought to assert the Glory, Cause, and Sovereignty of God, that it may be everywhere submitted to. We are not without many Examples of such Actings. Amongst the Jews Hyrcanus compelled the Idumaens to be circumcised and turned Jews, and all the Christian Histories furnish us with instances of the like Nature. It is also true that several Christian Doctors teach that a Nation guilty of enormous Crimes may be invaded, and that it is a just pretence of war to reclaim them from notorious wickedness, it being lawful to compel them to observe those laws of Nature whereto God hath originally subjected them.

"These and sundry other Titles of War are treated of and maintained by the Divines who write concerning the Spanish Rights over the Indians. But tho' the Christian Doctors and some Popes have urged them, and thereby prepared Apologies for Mahometans, I do not find that Mahomet proceeded any further in Arabia the desert than to exterminate Idolatry, but not force Men to profession of Islamism. He himself gave Letters of security and protection to the Jews and Christians in Arabia, and never used any Violence to them upon the Account of Religion. At Medina such Jews as peaceably paid Tribute continued unmolested (tho' mortally hated), until the days of Omar, the son of Alchittabi, who expell'd them out of Arabia, he being told that Mahomet had prohibited that two different Religions should be tolerated within that Country, the Seat of Empire. But tho' they were thereupon expell'd thence (which was rather an Act of Civil produce than Religion), yet were they not compelled to Mahometanism, nor banished his other Territories.

"The same Omar gave the Christians the following security upon the taking of Jerusalem: `In the name of God, merciful and gracious, from Omar, the son of Alchittabi, to the inhabitants of the City of Aelia. Security and protection is granted as to their persons, Children, Wives, estates and all their Churches, that they be neither destroyed, alienated, nor prohibited the Christians to resort to.—And when Amurus, the Saracen General, under Abubecr, beseiged Gaza. He made this declaration to the Christian Governour thereof: Our Lord hath commanded us to fight and Conquer you, except you will embrace our Religion, and so become our Friends and Brethren, pursuing the same Comon Interest with us, so you will have us your faithful Allies: but if you will not accept of these terms, then submitt to pay us Tribute yearly, yourselves and your Posterity for ever, to us and our Successors, and we will protect you against all opposition whatsoever, and you shall be in League with us; if you agree not hereunto, then the Sword must decide our Rights, and we will not desist until we have subdued you, and put in Execution the Will of God.

"By this Declaration it is manifest that the Mahometans did propagate their Empire, but not their Religion, by force of Arms." (Pages 180-82).

The Articles of Faith

"Let us now lay aside our prejudices and see what there is a miss in the Mahometan Religion. Their Articles of Faith are few and plain, whereby they are preserved from Schisms and Heresies, for altho' they have great diversity of opinions in the explication of their law, yet, agreeing in the fundamentals, their differences in opinion do not reach to that breach of Charity so common among the Christians, who thereby become a scandal to all other Religions in the world. Their Notions of God are great and noble, their opinions of the Future State, as I have shewn, are consonant to those of the Jews and Christians. As to the moral part of their Religion, if we consult Hottinger, who has taken the pains to transcribe a great many of their precepts out of the books of the Mahometans, we shall see that it is not inferiour to that of the Christians. And lastly, their Religious Duties are plainly laid down, which is the cause that they are duly observed, and are in themselves very rational, tho' perhaps some of them were retained or instituted partly upon a political Account, as has been don by the wisest Legislators in all Ages.

"Thus, two of the five Articles before mentioned seem to be established upon prudential Reasons, I mean the Pilgrimage to Meccha and the Fast of Ramadan. For tho' Mahomet retain'd many Arabian usages (and such I have shewed this pilgrimage and Fast to have been), his aim being only to perform the old Religion, and not to introduce a new one, yet I believe he the rather continued these two points upon a prudent foresight that they would be of great use in a military Empire such as he designed, to the support whereof valiant and hardy Soldiers were necessary, and nothing could more conduce to the successive generation and education of such than these two institutions; for how active, laborious, and abstinent must the Women as well as the Men render themselves, to be able to endure the fatigue of the pilgrimage or the hunger of the Fast. The Pilgrimage I have described largely; the Fast is movable and every year happens a Month later in the year preceding so that it falls sometimes in Summer, other times in Winter, in the hottest and coldest seasons, the longest as well as the shortest dayes, and is observed so strictly that from day-break to star-light not one (except travellers and sick persons) doth eat or drink anything, or so much as wash his Mouth with a little Water; nay, the most dissolute persons who at other times adventure to drink Wine, will not then so much as smell to it. It is true that at night when the Emaum or Priest declares it to be time to eat, they feed plentifully, even to excess, and even this hath its reason upon Account of health, for this fasting and feasting in such extreams contributes to their health during the whole year. It is commended by Celsus to the healthy, not to live by rule, but use a variety in Diet, lest they contract a Custom, the change whereof would be as dangerous as the continuance inconvenient and inconsistent with daily Action and business.

"I also believe that the third Precept, concerning Alms, was political in its Original, for Mahomet having persuaded his followers into such a Parsimony as was requisite to the making of them hardy, and to the making of them welcome in their quarters, that they might not lapse from his Institutions, and be debauched by riches, he obliged them to those extraordinary Alms, which was a kind of Grecian levelling Law. Mahomet calls it Zacot (Zacat), which signifies as much as Increase, as if the giving alms to the needy were the principal means to augment their Riches, and this he inculcated to them that they might not grow effeminate through Luxury or mutinous by means of their Riches.

"Neither was there less Prudence in the precept concerning Prayers, for the injunction of the Sallah five times in twenty-four hours obliged them to a diligence and sobriety which, perhaps, no other contrivance could have engaged them to, and doth also imprint in them a sense of their Religion which without Apostacy nothing can obliterate. Besides it is a part of that precept never to mention any Prophet or Person whom they reverence but with this Eulogy, God's Peace be with him! of glorious memory, etc.; nor any Enemy of their Religion, but thus, God's Curse be upon him! God keep him from hurting us, etc., which saying did fix them more and more in their Religion and estrange them more and more from their adversaries."

Christianity at the Time of Muhammad's Birth

"This was the Condition of Christianity in which Justinian found it about the year 540. He by his Conquests subdued the Arrian Goths and Vandals in Italy and Affrick, and by severe Laws established and enforced the Trinitarian Religion, and suppressed the different Sects and Religions in the Empire, abusing the Jews, persecuting the Arrians and all other Hereticks (except it be true that he favoured the Eretychians), he raigned thirty-nine years. After him succeeded Justinus the Second, Tiberius, Mauritius Phocas, and Heraclius, in whose dayes arose Mahomet. It is observable that in all these times there was such a general Corruption of Manners, and Christianity was so depraved, that the Church of England and other Protestants in general reject the authority of them, and admit no general Councils after that of Chalcedon, under the Emperor Martianus. Their Reigns suggest nothing considerable to the subsequent Discourse, but that Christianity was then degenerated into such a kind of Paganism as wanted nothing but the ancient Sacrifices and profess'd Polytheism, and even as to the latter there wanted not some who made three Gods of the Trinity, others made a Goddess of the Virgin Mary, the Reverence to the Saints differed little from that of the Pagans to their Heroes and lesser Gods, and then were Images brought into Churches, tho' not by public authority."

The Romance of Islam

"The end was evidently rapidly approaching, sick in body, and emaciated in frame, it remained for Muhammad only `to busy himself in the praises of his Lord, and to seek for pardon." Such, in his own words, was *now* his mission. No longer able to visit in turn the homes of his numerous wives, he announced his intention of betaking himself to the abode of Ayisha, who had from the first possessed an inscrutable hold over the affections of her husband. Faithful to her charge, the youthful wife—she was at this time but twenty years of age—watched and tended the bedside of her aged lord and master; the affection of so young and beautiful a damsel for the aged and infirm Prophet was touching and pathetic. It was the *romance* of Islam. Prostrate with fever, and scarce able to move from his couch, the Apostle of God felt that his end was at hand; so repairing, though with tottering steps, to the Mosque, he there, amidst the tears and sobs of his faithful followers, addressed them in accents of mingled pride and affection. But the excitement of the occasion was too much for his exhausted strength, and for some days the flame of existence flickered in the socket; at length, however, the paroxysm of pain passed away, and finding a slight return of strength, the prophet again appeared before the congregation. It was a striking scene—the Mosque, at all times full when Muhammad was present, was on this occasion, the memorable 8th June, 632, thronged to suffocation, for the dangerous condition of his illness had become known throughout the city. With slow and weary steps the venerable Prophet, supported by two attendants, repaired to his accustomed spot; too weak to lead the devotions, the task devolved upon the faithful Abu Bakr; yet `the Lord verily had granted unto Muhammad refreshment in prayer', and mustering the feeble remnants of his decaying strength, he spoke with emotion as to the single-mindedness of his actions, and his belief in his mission. But the effort severely taxed his emaciated frame and feeble energies, and on reaching his apartments he was seized with an attack of delirium. Ayisha thereupon lifted his right hand, and rubbed it to restore animation, repeating at the same time an invocation which the Prophet himself had been wont to use when visiting the sick. It may well be imagined his weak body could ill bear such rough, though affectionate usage; so, on recovering his consciousness, he begged that he might be left quiet. He then muttered a scarce audible prayer: `Lord, grant me pardon, and join me to the companionship on high.' Too weak to continue his devotions, he lay back on his bed, and there was stillness, interrupted at times with ejaculations, `Eternity in Paradise. Pardon! Yes, the blessed companionship on high!' Grand, noble expressions were these, the last words which hung on the lips of the dying Muslim. After a few moments, perceiving a change, Ayisha, with her arms around her lord, looked up as the grey head grew heavy on her breast. It needed not the instinct of a ministering angel to realize that the soul of the Prophet of Arabia had winged its way to the Mansion in the skies..... Such was Muhammad: such his life, such his death!"

The Miracle of the Qur-an

"It is asserted by the Muslims that each Prophet who has appeared in the world, has performed miracles in that department of skill or science which flourished in his particular age; thus, Moses was a magician, Jesus healed the sick, while Muhammad produced a work which, for its eloquence and beauty of diction, was unrivalled by any of the compositions of its time. This circumstance is deemed to stamp the Quran as having a divine origin, and indeed to this miracle, for such it is considered in Islam, Muhammad himself appealed for the confirmation of his mission, publicly challenging the most learned and gifted men of the day to produce a single chapter to compare with the book which he alleged God had whispered into his ear. The challenge was accepted, and a poem written by Labid Ibn Rabia, one of the greatest wits in Arabia, being fixed up on the gate of the temple of Mecca, an honour allowed to none but the most esteemed performances, none of the other poets durst offer anything of their own in competition with it. But the second chapter of the Quran being placed by its side soon after, Labid himself (then an idolator) on reading the first verses only, was struck with admiration, and immediately professed the religion taught thereby, declaring that such words could only proceed from an inspired person.

"That Muhammad's boast as to the literary excellence of the Quran was not unfounded, is further evidenced by a circumstance, which occurred about a century after the establishment of Islam. The story runs that in those days a body of religious `Nihilists', by seeing the enormous power which the Quran exercised over the hearts of the Faithful, commissioned a certain Ibn al Muqaffa, a man of profound learning, unsurpassable eloquence and vivid imagination, to produce a book to rival the emanation of Muhammad's pen. Ibn al Muqaffa agreed, but stipulated that he should be allowed a period of twelve months wherein to accomplish his task, during which time all his bodily wants should be supplied, so that the might be enabled to concentrate his mind on the task which he had undertaken. At the expiration of half the allotted interval his friends, on coming to make inquiries as to his progress, found him sitting, pen in hand, deeply absorbed in study, while before him was a blank sheet of paper, and around his desk a wild confusion of closely-written manuscripts torn into pieces, and scattered indiscriminately over the apartment. In good truth he had tried to write a single verse equalling the Quran in excellence, and failed; and he confessed with confusion and shame that a solitary line had baffled all his efforts for six months, so he retired from the task hopeless and crest-fallen."

Smith on Islam

Bosworth Smith, M.A., was Assistant Master in Harrow School, England, and a Fellow of Trinity College, Oxford. In February and March 1874, he delivered a series of four long lectures before the Royal Institution of Great Britain which were afterwards published under the name of "Mohammed and Mohammedanism".

Bosworth Smith has taken such pains in studying Islam and has been so fair-minded that, in spite of his Christian bias, he deserves the heartfelt gratitude of all Muslims for ever. It may, therefore, be hoped that the reader who is not already acquainted with him (be he Muslim or non-Muslim) will persue the following excerpts from the book above named (published 1876 London: Smith, Elder and Co., 15 Waterloo Place) with great interest and advantage to himself.

(A) Christianity and Islam in Africa

"As to the rapid spread of Islam, Dr. Barth says that `great part of the Berbers of the Desert were once Christians, and that they afterwards changed their religion and adopted Islam; and he describes `that continual struggle which, always extending further and further, seems destined to overpower the nations at the very Equator if Christianity does not presently step in to dispute the ground with it.' He remarks in another place, that Mohammedans alone seem able to maintain any sort of government in Africa; and, what is more important, that there `is a vital principle in Islam which has only to be brought out by a reformer to accomplish great things'.

"On the other hand, the Rev. Edward Blyden, a native African of the purest Negro blood, a Christian missionary who has given the energies of his life to extending education and founding schools in the interior of Liberia, and who has learned by experience to deal with Mohammedan prejudices against Christianity, writes to me as follows. It may be worthwhile to add that he is now Principal of the Presbyterian High School in Monrovia, West Africa, that he was quite unknown to me before, and is known to me now only by his writings and his reputation.

> It is curious, how at a distance from the scene and only from 'the study of books in the European languages, and from reflection upon the materials they supply,' you have arrived at precisely the same conclusions with regard to the character and influences of Mohammedanism in Africa which I have reached after years of travel among, and intercourse with, the people. Your remarks as to the superiority of the Mohammedan Negro are quite in accordance with any own observation and experience. If those Christians who, are so unmeasured in their denunciations of Mohammedianism could travel, as I have travelled, through those countries in the interior of West Africa, and witness, as I have witnessed, the vast contrast between the Pagan and Mohammedan communities—the habitual listlessness and continued

deterioration of the one, and the activity and growth, physical and mental, of the other; the capricious and unsettled administration of law, or rather absence of law, in the one, and the tendency to order and regularity in the other; the increasing prevalence of ardent spirits in the one, and rigid sobriety and conservative abstemiousness of the other—they would cease to regard the Musalman system as an unmitigated evil in the interior of Africa.

"It is melancholy to contrast with widespread beneficial influences of Mohammedanism, on which I have insisted, the little that has been done for Africa, till very lately, by the Christian nations that have settled in it, and the still narrower limits within which it has been confined. Till a few years ago the good effects produced beyond the immediate territories occupied by them were absolutely nothing. The achievement of Vasco de Gama, for which Te Deums were sung in Europe, proved for centuries to be nothing but the direct curse to Africa. If the Oceanic slave trade has been, to the eternal credit of England in particular, at last abolished by Christian nations, it cannot be forgotten that Africa owes also to them its origin, and on the West Coast, at all events, its long continuance. The message that European traders have carried for centuries to Africa has been one of rapacity, of cruelty, of selfishness, and of bad faith. It is a remark of Dr. Livingstone's that the only art that the natives of Africa have acquired from their five hundred years' acquaintance with the Portuguese, has been the art of distilling spirits from a gun-barrel; and that the only permanent belief they owe to them is the belief that man may sell his brother man; for this, he says emphatically, is not a native belief but is one to be found in the track of Portuguese."

(B) Explanation of Muhammad's Marriages

"It should be remembered, however, that most of Mohammed's marriages may be explained, at least, as much by his pity for the forlorn condition of the persons concerned, as by other motives. They were almost all of them with widows who were not remarkable either for their beauty or their wealth, but quite the reverse. May not this fact, and his undoubted faithfulness to Khadijah till her dying day and till he himself was fifty years of age, give us additional ground to hope that calumny or misconception has been at work in the story of Zeinab? There are some indications on the face of it, besides those mentioned in the text, that this is the case. For example, Zeinab was the Prophet's cousin, and there was nothing to prevent his having married her himself when both he and she were younger, instead of giving her in marriage to his freed-man." (P. 136, Note.)

(C) The Consistency of Muhammad's Life

"Rigid consistency in itself is no great merit rather the reverse: what one has a right to demand in a great man is that the intensity of the central truth he has to deliver should become, not less, but more intense; that flame shall burn so clear as to throw into the shade other objects which shine with a less brilliant light; that the essence shall be pure even if some of the surroundings be alloyed; and this, I think, if not more than this, with all his faults, we may affirm of Mohammed. On the whole the wonder is to me not how much, but how little, under different circumstances, Mohammed differed from himself. In the shepherd of the desert, in the Syrian trader, in the solitary of Mount Hira, in the reformer in the minority of one, in the exile of Medina, in the acknowledged conqueror, in the equal of Persian Chosroes and the Greek Heraclius, we can still trace a substantial unity. I doubt whether any other man, whose external conditions changed so much, ever himself changed less to meet them; the accidents are changed, the essence seems to me to be the same in all.

"Power, as the saying is, no doubt put the man to the test. It brought new temptations and therefore new failures, from which the shepherd of the desert might have remained free. But happy is the man who, living

'In the fierce light that beats upon a throne,
And blackens every blots,'
can stand the test as well as did Mohammed."

(D) Magnanimity of Muhammad after the Conquest of Mecca

"There was now other left in Mecca that could thwart his pleasure. if ever he had worn a mask at all, he would now, at all events, have thrown it off; if lower aims had gradually sapped the higher, or his moderation had been directed, as Gibbon supposes, by his selfish interests, we should now have seen the effect; now would have been the moment to gratify his ambition, to satiate his lust, to glut his revenge. Is there anything of the kind? Read the account of the entry of Mohammad into Mecca, side by side with that of Marius or Sulla into Rome. Compare all the attendant circumstances, the outrages that preceded, and the use made by each of his recovered power, and we shall then be in a position better to appreciate the magnanimity and moderation of the Prophet of Arabia. There were no proscription lists; no plunder, no wanton revenge."

(E) Muhammad's Reliance on God

"The spell of his untaught eloquence recalled them to themselves, and we are assured that his defeat at Ohud advanced his cause as much as did his victory at Bedr.

"Here is a story which illustrates the nature of the revenge which the Prophet lived to take. He was one day sleeping under a tree alone, and at a distance from his camp, when he awoke and beheld Durthur, his deadly foe, standing over him with a drawn sword. `O Mohammed', cried he, `who is there now to save thee?" `God', said the Prophet. Struck with awe, Durthur dropped his sword; Mohammed seized it, and exclaimed in his turn, `Oh Durthur, who is there now to save thee?' `No one', replied Durthur. `Then learn from me to be merciful'; and with these words he gave him back his sword, and made him his firmest friend."

(F) What Muhammad swept away

R.B. Smith referring to the useless dogmas and disputations of the Christians and the empty claims of the Jews says:

"The sceptre departed from Judah, but the Jewish exiles in Arabia still clung desperately to the phantom of those proud religious privileges when all which had given some claim to them had disappeared. Christians too, such Christians as Mohammed had ever met, had forgotten at once the faith of the Jews, and that higher revelation of God given to them by Christ which the Jews rejected. Homoousians and Homoiousians, Monothelites and Monophysites, Jacobites and Eutychians, making hard dogmas of things wherein the sacred writers themselves had made no dogma, disputing fiercely whether what was mathematically false could be metaphysically true, and nicely discriminating the shades of truth and falsehood in the views suggested to bridge over the abysmal gulf between them; turning figures into facts, rhetoric into logic, and poetry into prose, had forgotten the unity of God, while they were disputing about it most loudly with their lips. They busied themselves with every question about Christ except those which might have led them to initiate Christ's life. Now Mohammed came to make a clean sweep of such unrealities. Images: what are they? `Bits of black wood, pretending to be God;' philosophical theories and theological cobwebs. Away with them all! God is great, and there is nothing else great. This is the Musalman Creed. `Islam', that is, man must resign his will to God's, and find his highest happiness in so doing. This is the Musalman life.

(G) Muhammad not a Fatalist

"He (Muhammad) inculcates hope in adversity, and humility in success, on the ground that there is a supreme Ruler who never leaves the helm; who knows what is really best for man when man himself does not; and whose supreme will and power, where He asserts them, cannot be crossed by the efforts of the creatures of His hand. But this is not the only side to his teaching. he asserts that man is a free agent; free to refuse or to accept the Divine message, responsible for his acts, and therefore deserving, now of punishment, now of reward. The future, in fact, is in his own hands, and Mohammed incessantly urges him to use his opportunities. Ali, the most saintly, I would almost say the most Christian, of all Musalmans, pronounces those who say the will is not free to be heretics."

(H) Muslim and Christian Wars Compared

"The sword may silence, it cannot convince: it may enforce

hypocrisy, it can never force belief. But this has not always seemed so self-evident; and I say it deliberately and with all the force of conviction, compared with the war of the Confederate States in the nineteenth century for the perpetuation of slavery, compared with our own Japanese wars for the extension of our trade, our Chinese wars for the sale of opium, and our miserable African wars waged for the possession of a territory which we brought, and had no moral right to buy, from those who sold what they had no moral right to sell, the Mohammedan wars for the propagation of a comparatively pure religion and a higher morality were, in their time and according to their light, inasmuch as they were purely selfish, I do not say excusable, but they were at least intelligble and natural."

(I) The Unity of Islam

"'A Musalman first and a Turk, an Afghan or an Arab afterwards,' is no mere formula or figure of speech with that vast assemblage of peoples and of tongues to whom the Prophet of Arabia, by teaching them to worship the one true God, has given a bond of union stronger than any tie of blood or nation; and that, by means which were nobler and with objects that were higher than those which Papal Rome is striving, in these latter days, to implant a similar feeling in the Catholic. Sublime and Eternal and Unchangeable as its God, Islam appears to its votaries a religion worthy at once of the worshipper and of the Being that he worships; and is it for us to say that it is not so?"

(J) Muhammad the very Prophet of God

"Mohammed to the end of his life claimed for himself that title only with which he had begun and which the highest philosophy and the truest Christianity will one day, I venture to believe, agree in yielding to him—that of a Prophet, a very Prophet of God."

Extracts from Major Arthur Glyn Leonard's "Islam, Her Moral and Spiritual Value" published by Luzac and Co. 1909.

(A) The Genius of Muhammad

"But in the case of Islam there can be no mistake. True, the

Arabs in themselves were a great and virile people. But it was the genius of Mohammed, the spirit he breathed into them through the soul of Islam, that exalted them. That raised them out of the lethargy and low level of tribal stagnation, up to the high water-mark of national unity and Empire. It was in the sublimity of Mohammed's deism, the simplicity, the sobriety and purity it inculcated, the fidelity of its founder to his own tenets, that acted on their moral and intellectual fibre with all the magnetism of true inspiration. To them Islam was the Faith—the Faith of God."

(B) Light and Truth

"To thoroughly comprehend the spirit of Mohammed or the soul of Islam, the student himself must be thoroughly in earnest and sincere. He must in addition possess that moral, mental and intellectual sympathy which gives the ego an insight into human subtleties as well as simplicities. He must take Mohammed and Islam as he finds them—in the same intensely sincere spirit that constituted the one and inculcated the other. He must at the outset recognize that Mohammed was no mere spiritual pedlar, no vulgar time-serving vagrant, but one of the most profoundly sincere and earnest spirits of any age or epoch. A man not only great, but one of the greatest—*i.e.*, truest—men that Humanity has ever produced. Great, *i.e.*, not simply as a prophet, but as a patriot and statesman: a material as well as a spiritual builder who constructed a great nation, a great empire, and more even than all these, a still greater Faith. True, moreover, because he was true to himself, to his people, and above all to his God. Recognizing this, he will thus acknowledge that Islam is a profound and true cult, which strives to uplift its votaries from the depths of human darkness upwards into the higher realm of Light and Truth."

(C) The Design of Muhammad

"Personal ambition and aggrandizement never for a moment entered his head or formed part of it. The national good,—to one and only by a national or universal God-the one and only God of the universe—was the one great ambition that inspired and impelled him. Because although every one for himself and God for us all is presumably a natural law, Mohammed managed to evade it. But in evading it he was not revolutionary. On the contrary, in this way he rose one step upward above the lower human level towards that higher humanity which approaches the divine.

"This design, as I have just said, originated from the doctrine of divine unity attributed to Moses and Abraham. Indeed, as one reads the Koran carefully and steadily through from beginning to end, it is manifested in every surah—almost in fact on every page. The whole work, in fact, is saturated with the one idea, inspired by the one thought. Everywhere there is evidence of the final object in view, the unconquerable will, the inflexible resolve, the fixed purpose, the indomitable perseverance, the unyielding persistency, the infinite and interminable patience, the calm endurance, the irresistible courage, and the grim tenacity of the ego."

(D) God and Muhammad

"An idea is a spark falling upon straw" ...(quoting Dumas). "Thus it was with Mohammed. God was the spark, the vital spark of spiritual flame, and this humble but honest Arab trader was the straw that after twenty years of silent but tenacious smouldering, God had set a light to."

(E) Good and Evil

"But of all the passage in the Koran, the following is, in many ways, one of the most significant : "Whatever good befalleth thee, O man, it is from God; and whatever evil befalleth thee, it is from thyself." It is obvious from this that the Prophet believed evil to be a human weakness with man as an active and self-willed agent. Sale in a note thereon says: "These words are not to be understood as contradicting the preceding verse, that all is from God, since the evil that befalls mankind, though ordered by God, is yet the consequence of their own wicked actions.

"But as Mohammed regarded the sublime divinity of God, it would be more accurate to interpret the *evil* not as being ordained or even sanctioned by God, but as being permitted, or rather not prevented by Him as a thing inevitable. To him the purity, sanctity and inviolability of God was of such vast moment, that it was unjust—a mortal sin—to devise even a lie against Him. `And who is more unjust than he who deviseth a lie against God, that he may seduce men without understanding.'"

(F) The Practical Nature of Islam

"Mohammed's sincerity and fixity of purpose is fact we cannot get away from. It is this which has chained his followers as with the sure cord of God to the Faith. Islam, in a word, is a creed of practice, not theory. By practice it was formed. On practice it lived. It was because mohammed practised what he preached, that the small seed of his original idea blossomed at last into the mighty `Igdrasil' of the East—the great banyan tree of existence. Verily this sun-burnt son of Arabian Petraea was a tangible reality and no desert simulacrum. A reality that lives in the soul of Islam. A reality that will endure until the end of all things human. It is not manners that maketh the man. It is the man that makes the manners. It is the nature that is around him, the nature that is in him, and that comes out of him as mental and moral energies, that makes the man. Town bred as he was, it was the desert in all its naked and silent grandeur that made Mohammed, that inspired him with all the might and majesty of God, and turned him into a Prophet. Yet it was his career as a trader and the inherent tribal instinct that developed the political element in him. As Longfellow says : `Glorious indeed is the world of God around us, but more glorious is the world of God within us. There lies the land of song, there lies the poet's native land.' But in Mohammed's case, as in the case of all great workers and thinkers, the world that is around us, is the world of our inner consciousness. The two are synonymous if not one. Only with him the native earth was religion, and he was the Prophet, not the Poet of it. "It is Nature's highest reward to a true, simple, great soul, that he gets thus to be a *part of herself.*

"It was thus with Mohammed. Thought, though changeable, is eternal. It never dies. So the one idea that possessed Mohammed not possesses (differing only in merely superficial degrees) some two hundred and fifty millions."

(G) True Muslims

"In speaking of Islam and of Moslems as I have done, I have spoken of them as I have found them. Apart from a careful study of the Koran, my knowledge of both is based on personal facts and experiences as varied as they are extensive. In every clime and under a variety of conditions, I have been in touch with Moslems of all classes and shades, and have always found them animated by the same spirit—for race or colour makes no difference to the spirit of Islam. Always consistent and devout, always God-fearing and incerse as regards their Faith. Before all things religious, their cult, the creed of Mohammed — *i.e.* El Islam or self-surrender. Afghan, Arab, Baluchi, Hindustani, Somali, Turk, Egyptian, Hadendowa, Berber, Senegalese, Fulani, Hausa, Yoruba, Mandingo, Malay, I have found them in the main Islamic to the every core. In peace or war, in camp and cantonment, working and fighting with or against them, my experience of their moral consistency and spiritual stamina has been the same. Brave to a fault, endowed with the reckless courage of the Fatalist, fearless and contemptuous of death, their fidelity to their Faith, their belief in the greatness of Mohammed, and their veneration of God, is something that once it is rightly understood, can only be respected and appreciated at its true value. For my part, seeing as I have their splendid heroism in their own cause, and their touching devotion to those whose salt they have eaten, my feelings towards them is not only one of unmixed admiration and respect, but also of deep esteem and regard. Such men are worthy of Islam, as Islam indeed is worthy of them. Only the soul—the moral and spiritual essence — of Islam could have made them what they are, could have turned out of the dregs of barbarism a human material so truly splendid."

Extracts from Rodwell's Preface to His Translation of the Qur-an

(A) Muhammad

"Muhammad's career is a wonderful instance of the force and life that resides in him who possesses an intense Faith in God and in the unseen world; ... he will always be regarded as one of those who have had that influence over the faith, morals, and whole earthly life of their fellow-men, which none but a really great man ever did, or can exercise; and ... whose efforts to propagate a great verity will prosper ...

"The more insight we obtain, from undoubted historical sources, into the actual character of Muhammad, the less do we find to justify the strong vituperative language of Maracci, Prideaux, and others ..."

(B) Qur-an

"It must be acknowledged, too, that the Koran deserves the highest praise for its conceptions of the Divine nature, in reference to the attributes of Power, Knowledge and universal Providence and Unity—that its belief and trust in the One God of Heaven and Earth is deep and fervent.

(C) The Qur-an and Muslims; Islam an unquestionable blessing

"It is due to the Koran that the occupants... of an arid peninsula, whose poverty was only equalled by their ignorance, became not only the fervent and sincere votaries of a new creed, but, like Amru and many more, its warlike propagators.

"The simple shepherds and wandering Beduins of Arabia, are transformed, as if by a magician's wand, into the founders of empires, the builders of cities, the collectors of more libraries than they at first destroyed, while cities like Fostat, Baghdad, Cordova, and Delhi, attest the power at which Christian Europe trembled. And thus, while the Koran, which underlays this vast energy and contains the principles which are its springs of action, reflects to a great extent the mixed character of its author, its merits as a code of laws, and as a system of religious teaching, must always be estimated by the changes which it introduced into the customs and beliefs of those who willingly or by compulsion received it. In the suppression of their idolatries, in the substitution of the worship of Allah for that of the powers of nature and genii with Him, in the abolition of child murder, in the extinction of manifold superstitious usages, in the reduction of the number of wives to a fixed standard, it was to the Arabians an unquestionable blessing, and an accession of .... Truth."

Excerpts from Stanley Lane—Poole's "The speeches and Table-Talk of the prophet Mohammad"

(A) The Sayings of Muhammad Concerning Goodness

"Say not, if people do good to us, we will do good to them, and if people oppress them; but resolve that if people do good to you, you will do good to them, and if they oppress you, oppress them not again.

"God saith : Whoso doth one good act, for him are ten rewards, and I also give more to whomsoever I will; and whoso doth ill, its retaliation is equal to it, or else I forgive him; and he who seeketh to approach me one cubit, I will seek to approach him two fathoms; and he who walketh towards me, I will run towards him; and he who cometh before me with the earth full of sins, but joineth no Partner to me, I will come before him with an equal front of forgiveness.

"There are seven people whom God will draw under His own shadow, on that Day when there will be no other shadow; one a just king; another, who hath employed himself in devotion from his youth; the third, who fixeth his heart on the Mosque till he return to it; the fourth, two men whose friendship is to please God, whether together or separate; the fifth, a man who remembereth God when he is alone, and weepeth; the sixth, a man who is tempted by a rich and beautiful woman, and saith, Verily I fear God! the seventh, a man who hath given alms and concealed it, so that his left hand knoweth not what his right hand doeth.

"The most excellent of all actions is to befriend any one on God's account, and to be at enmity with whosoever is the enemy of God."

(B) Concerning Prayer

"No neglect of duty is imputable during sleep; for neglect can only take place when one is awake: therefore, when any of you forget your prayers, say them when ye recollect.

"When any one of you goeth to sleep, the Devil tieth three

knots upon his neck; and saith over every knot, `The night is long, sleep.' Therefore, if a servant awake and remember God, it openeth one knot, and if he perform the ablution, it openeth another : and if he say prayers it openeth the other; and he riseth in the morning in gladness and purity : otherwise he riseth in a lethargic state.

"When a Muslim performeth the ablution, it washeth from his face those faults which he may have cast his eyes upon, and when he washeth his hands it removeth the faults they may have committed, and when he washeth his feet, it dispelleth the faults towards which they may have carried him; so that he will rise up in purity from the place of ablution."

(C) Concerning Charity

"When God created the earth, it began to shake and tremble; then God created mountains, and put them upon the earth, and the land became firm and fixed; and the angels were astonished at the hardness of the hills, and said, `O God, is there anything of Thy creation harder than the hills? and God said, `Yes, water is harder than the hills, because it breaketh them?' Then the angles said, `O Lord, is there anything of Thy creation harder than water? He said, `Yes, wind overcometh water: it doth agitate it and put it in motion.' They said, `O our Lord! is there anything of Thy creation harder than wind?" He said, `Yes, the children of Adam giving alms: those who give with their right hand, and conceal from their left, overcome all.'

"The liberal man is near the pleasure of God and is near Paradise, which he shall enter into, and is near the Learts of men as a friend, and he is distant from hell; but the niggard is far from God's pleasure and from paradise, and far from the hearts of men, and near the Fire; and verily a liberal ignorant man is more beloved by God than a niggardly worshipper."

(D) Concerning Fasts

"A keeper of fasts, who doth not abandon lying and slandering, God careth not about his leaving of eating and drinking.

"Keep fast and eat also, stay awake at night and sleep also, because verily there is a duty on you to your body, not to labour overmuch, so that ye may not get ill and destroy yourself; and verily there is a duty on you to your eyes, ye must sometimes sleep and give them rest; and verily there is a duty on you to your wife, and to your visitors and guests that come to see you; ye must talk to them; and nobody hath kept fast who fasted always; the fast of three days in every month is equal to constant fasting; then keep three days' fast in every month."

(E) Concerning the Qur-an

"Read the Koran constantly; I sevear by Him in the hands of whose might is my life, verily the Koran runneth away faster than a camel which is not tied by the leg."

(F) Concerning Labour and Work

"A man came to the Prophet, begging of him something, and the Prophet said, `Have you nothing at home?' He said, `Yes, there is a large carpet, with one part of which I cover myself, and spread the other, and there is a wooden cup in which I drink water.' Then the Prophet said, `Bring me the carpet and the cup.' And the man brought them, and the Prophet took them in his hand and said, `Who will buy them?' A man said, "I will take them at one silver piece.' He said, `Who will give more?' This he repeated twice or thrice. Another man said, `I will take them for two pieces of silver. Then the Prophet gave the carpet and cup to that man, and took the two pieces of silver, and gave them to the helper, and said, `Buy food with one of these pieces, and give it to your family, that they may make it their sustenance for a few days; and buy a hatchet with the other piece and bring it to me. And the man brought it; and the Prophet put a handle to it with his own hands, and then said, `Go, cut wood, and sell it, and let me not see you for fifteen days.' Then the man went cutting wood, and selling it; and he came to the Prophet, when verily he had got ten pieces of silver, and he bought a garment with part of it, and food with part. Then the Prophet said, 'This cutting and selling of wood, and making your livelihood by it, is better for you than coming on the day of Resurrection with black marks on your face."

(G) Concerning Women and Slaves

"The world and all things in it are valuable, but the most valuable thing in the world is a virtuous women

"I have not left any calamity more hurtful to man than woman.

"A Muslim cannot obtain (after righteousness) anything better than a well-disposed, beautiful wife: such a wife as, when ordered by her husband to do anything, obeyeth; and if her husband look at her, is happy; and if her husband swear by her to do a thing, she doth it to make his oath true; and if he be absent from her, she wisheth him well in her own person by guarding herself from inchastity, and taketh care of his property.

"Verily the best of women are those who are content with little."

"He who beateth his slave without fault, or slappeth him in the face, his atonement for this is freeing him.

"A man who behaveth ill to his slave will not enter into paradise.

"Forgive thy servant seventy times a day."

(H) Concerning himself

"I am no more than man : when I order you anything with respect to religion, receive it, and when I order you about the affairs of the world then I am nothing more than man."

Description of Muhammad's Person and Characteristics

"Mohammad was of the middle height, rather thin, but broad of shoulders, wide of chest, strong of bone and muscle. His head was massive, strongly developed. Dark hair, slightly curled, flowed in a dense mass almost to his shoulders; even in advanced age it was sprinkled with only about twenty gray hairs, produced by the agonies of his `Revelations. His face was oval-shaped, slightly tawny of colour. Fine, long arched eye-brows were divided by a vein, which throbbed visibly in moments of passion. Great, black, restless eyes shone out from under long heavy eyelashes. His nose was large, slightly aquiline. His teeth, upon which he bestowed great care, were well set, dazzling white. A full beard framed his manly face. His skin was clear and soft, his complexion `red and white,' his hands were as `silk and satin,' even as those of a woman. His step was quick and elastic, yet firm as that of one who steps from a high to a low place.' In turning his face he would also turn his whole body. His whole gait and presence were dignified and imposing. His countenance was mild and pensive. His laugh was rarely more than a smile.

"In his habits he was extremely simple, though he bestowed great care on his person. His eating and drinking, his dress and his furniture retained, even when he had reached the fulness of power, their almost primitive nature. The only luxuries he indulged in were, besides arms, which he highly prized, a pair of yellow boots, a present from the Negus of Abyssinia. Perfumes, however, he loved passionately, being most sensitive to smells. Strong drink he abhorred.

"His constitution was extremely delicate. He was nervously afraid of bodily pain; he would sob and roar under it. Eminently unpractical in all common things of life, he was gifted with mighty powers of imagination, elevation of mind, delicacy and refinement of feeling. `He is more modest than a virgin behind her curtain,' it was said of him. He was most indulgent to his inferiors, and would never allow his awkward little page to be scolded whatever he did. `Ten years,' said Anas his servant, `was I about the Prophet, and he never said as much as "uff" to me.' He was very affectionate towards his family. One of his boys died on his breast in the smoky house of the nurse, a blacksmith's wife. He was very fond of children; he would stop them in the streets and pat their little heads. He never struck any one in his life. The worst expression he ever made use of in conversation was, `What has come to him? May his forehead be darkened with mud!' When asked to curse someone, he replied, `I have not been sent to curse, but to be a mercy to mankind.' He visited the sick, followed any bier he met, accepted the invitation of a slave to dinner, mended his own clothes, milked the goats, and waited upon himself,' Relates summarily another tradition. He never first withdrew his hand out of another man's palm, and turned not before the other had turned.

"He was the most painful protector of those he protected, the sweetest and most agreable in conversation. Those who saw him were suddenly filled with reverence; those who came near him loved him; they who described him would say, `I have never seen his like either before or after.' He was of great taciturnity, but when he spoke it was with emphasis and deliberation, and no one could forget what he said. He was, however, very nervous and restless withal; often low-spirited, downcast, as to heart and eyes. Yet he would at times suddenly break through these broodings, become gay, talkative, jocular, chiefly among his own. He would then delight in telling little stories, fairy tales, and the like. He would romp with the children and play with their toys.

"He lived with his wives in a row of humble cottages, separated from one another by palm branches, cemented together with mud. He would kindle the fire, sweep the floor, and milk the goats himself. The little food he had was always shared with those who dropped in to partake of it. Indeed, outside the Prophet's house was a bench or gallery, on which were always to be found a number of poor, who lived entirely upon his generosity, and were hence called `the people of the bench.' His ordinary food was dates and water, or barley bread; milk and honey were luxuries of which he was fond, but which he rarely allowed himself. The fare of the desert seemed most congenial to him, even when he was sovereign of Arabia."

5

Main Tanents of Islam

Faith

The very first book of the *Sahih Muslim* is the "Book of Faith" *(Kitab al-I man)*. It contains 431 traditions *(ahadis)* divided into ninety-two chapters. It discusses question regarding faith. Someone comes to Muhammad from a great distance, yet without any sign of fatigue, and says: "Muhammad, inform me about *al-Islam*." The Messenger of Allah replies : *"Al-Islām* implies that you testify that there is no god but Allah and that Muhammad is the Messenger of Allah, and you establish prayer, pay *Zakat*, observe the fast of *Ramzan* [Ramadan] and perform pilgrimage." Later on, when the inquirer is gone, Muhammad tells 'Umar: "He was Gabriel. He came to you in order to instruct you in matters of religion." This is the very first *hadis* narrated by 'Umar, the future Khalifa, through several chains of narrators.

This theme runs through hundreds of *ahadis*. *Al-Islam* is faith in Allah, faith in Muhammad as His Messenger, faith in His Book in His angels, in the resurrection, in the hereafter, and in the payment of the poor tax *(zakat)* and the observance of fast *(Ramzan)* and pilgrimage.

Allah is not Enough

Belief in Allah alone in not sufficient. It must be accompanied by belief in the apostleship of Muhammad. A delegation of the tribe or Rabi'a visit Muhammad. He tells the delegates: "I direct you to affirm belief in Allah alone," and then asks them: "Do you know what belief in Allah really implies?" Then he himself answers:

"It implies testimony to the fact that there is no god but Allah, and the Muhammad is the Messenger of Allah." Other things mentioned are prayer, *zakat, Ramzan,* and "that you pay one-fifth of the booty." We shall hear more about war booty in its proper place.

In the same vein, Muhammad tells Mu'az, whom he sends out as governor of Yemen; "First call them to testify that there is no good but Allah, that I [Muhammad] am the Messenger of Allah; and if they accept this, then tell them that Allah has made *Zakat* obligatory for them."

There is a still clearer statement of Muhammad's mission. " I have been commanded to fight against people till they testify that there is no god but Allah, that Muhammad is the Messenger of Allah, and they establish prayer, and pay *Zakat* and if they do it, their blood and property are guaranteed protection on my behalf."

Muhammad retails the word "Allah profusely, but there are times when even Allah occupies a backseat. "None of you is a believer till I am dearer to him than his child, his father and the whole mankind," Muhammad tells the believers.

Allah and his Messenger—rather, Muhammad and his God—prayer, *zakat, Ramzan,* and pilgrimage are sometimes called the "Five pillars" of Islam, but there are other beliefs and institutions no less important which recur again and again in the *Hadis*. These are, to name the more important ones, Paradise, Hell, Doomsday, *jihad* (holy war against polytheists,) *jizya* (the poll tax paid by polytheists), war booty *(ghanimah),* and *khums* (the holy one-fifth). These are the staples of the religion preached by Muhammad. Allah becomes concrete in His threats and punishments of Hell, and in his promises and rewards of Paradise. Similarly, in the history of Islam, *jihad* and war booty have played a more important role then even pilgrimage or *zakar*. All of these concepts will come up for review in this study in their proper places.

Good and Evil Deeds

What are good deeds and what are bad deeds? These questions

have been the concern of many religions, many philosophies, and many teachers. Islam too has provided its characteristic answers. It tells us that good deeds are not a matter of indifference but must be coupled with the choice of the right religion. Abdul Hamid Siddiqi, the translator of the *Sahih Muslim,* gives the Islamic view in the following words: "The good deeds performed in the state of ignorance (outside the fold of Islam) are indicative of the fact that a man is inclined towards piety. But to be truly pious and virtuous it is quite essential to have the correct understanding of the Will of God. This can be confidently known only through the Prophets and is embodied in Islam. Thus without having faith in Islam we cannot serve our Master and Lord according to His Will . . . The acts of virtue may be good in their own way but it is by coming within the fold of Islam that these become significant and meaningful in the eyes of the Lord."

In the eyes of Muhammad, a wrong theology is worse than wicked deeds. When asked, "Which sin is the gravest in the eyes of Allah?" he replies: "That you associate a partner with Allah. "To kill your child and to commit adultery with the wife of your neighbour are second and third in gravity according to Muhammad.

In fact, only a wrong theology can keep a Muslim out of Paradise. But no morally wicked act—not even adultery and theft —can prevent his entry. Muhammad tells us: "Gabriel came to me and gave me tidings: Verily he who died amongs your *Ummah* [sect, nation, group] without associating anything with Allah would enter paradise." In clarification, Abu Zarr, the narrator of the *hadis,* asks Muhammad whether this is true even if the man committed adultery and theft. Muhammad replies: "Yes, even if he committed adultery and theft." The translator clarifies the point further: He says that adultery and theft "are both serious offences in Islam .... but these do not doom the offender to the eternal hell," but polytheism or associating any god "with the Lord is an unpardonable crime and the man who commits it is doomed to Hell."

If polytheism is the worst of crimes, monotheism, by the same token, is the best of virtues. Muhammad is asked about "the best of deeds." He replies: "Belief of Allah." "What next?" he is asked. *"Jihad,"* he replies. In Muslim theology the formula "belief in Allah" of course means "belief of Allah and His Messenger."

Once one accepts the theological belief in Allah and His Messenger, one's past crimes are obliterated, and future ones hold no great terror. Muhammad gave this assurance to some polytheists who "had committed a large number of murders and had excessively indulged in fornication," but who were ready to join him. To another person who felt a sense of guilt about his past, Muhammad said: "Are you not aware of the fact that Islam wipes out all the previous misdeeds?"

Moral Values

Muhammad's religion is predominantly theological, but moral values are not altogether neglected. The pre-Muslim Arabs believed in many moral values common to all mankind. Muhammad retained these values but gave them a sectarian twist. A muslim owes everything to the *ummah,* very little to others. He has no obligations, moral or spiritual, toward non-Muslims as part of the human race, except to convert them by sword, spoils, and *jizya.* For example, sincerity is a universal human value, and we should exercise it in our relations with one another irrespective of creed and nationality. But in Islam, it is limited to Muslims. Muhammad at one place defines *al-din* (*"the* religion," i.e., Islam) as "sincerity and well-wishing," which should be a good definition for any religion. But on being asked, "Sincerity and well-wishing for whom?" he replies: "for Allah, His Book, His messenger and for the leaders and general Muslims." Jarir b. 'Abdullah reports that he "pledged allegiance to the Apostle of Allah on sincerity and well-wishing for every Muslim."

Again, other moral values are given the same twist, and the universal is turned into the sectarian. Muhammad tells his followers: "Abusing a Muslim is an outrage and fighting against him is unbelief."

Theology Distorts Morals

No wonder that such a sectarian and preponderantly theological approach should now and then teach us topsy-turvy morals. Thanks to this approach, despoiling a whole people is meritorious if they are polytheists, but stealing booty once it is in the possession of Muslims is a mortal sin. A slave of Muhammad died in a holy war, thus automatically carning a place in Paradise as a martyr. But Muhammad saw "him in the Fire for the garment or cloak that he had stolen from the booty." On hearing this, some people were greatly perturbed. One of them who had presumably committed a similar act of pilfering, came to Muhammad "with a lace or two laces and said: Messenger of Allah, I found them on the day of Khaibar [name of a þattle]. The Holy Prophet remarked: This is a lace of fire or two laces of fire." This means, as another text puts it, hat like the two pieces of lace the man had stolen, there will be two columns of fire like unto these waiting for him in the hereafter.

To rob a whole people is piety, but to remove a paltry something from a looted treasure is moral depravity of a magnitude that deserves eternal fire. Men driven by ordinary temptations indulge only in petty crimes and small lapses, but committing real enormities needs the aid of an ideology, a revelation, a God-ordained mission.

The Pre-Muslim Areas

Muslim theologians and writers are in the habit of painting a very dark picture of pre-Islamic Arabia. They describe it as morally depraved and utterly lacking in any sense of chivalry and generosity, referring to this period of history as the "state of ignorance or bar barism" *(jahiliyya)*. Everything good began with Muhammad. But there are many *ahadis* which prove the contrary. We are told that one Hakim b. Hizam did "many deeds of religious purification ... in the state of ignorance." Another *hadis* tells us that he "freed one hundred salves and donated one hundred camels" in this state.

Ordinarily such good acts do not avail a polytheist; but if he embraces Islam, it is a different story, and the whole complexion of his acts is changed., They are no longer wasted; they become furitful and are credited to his account. Muhammad assures Hakim:

"you have accepted Islam with all the previous virtues that you had practised."

Evil Thoughts and Evil Deeds

A Muslim is Allah's prodigal son as well as His spoiled child. His past is forgotten unless it is good, his future is assured, and many things are permissible for him that are not permissible for a polytheist or even for a Jew or a Christian, the Peoples of the Book. Jesus spoke of "lusting with the eyes" regarding it as bad as lust in its more visible form. But Muhammad gave greater latitude to his followers: "verily Allah forgave my people the evil promptings which arise within their hearts as long as they did not speak about them or did not act upon them." This idea is expressed with less partiality and in more universal terms in the Indian spiritual tradition. God knows that man is weak and forgives his lapses and failure but supports his strength and multiplies his good. The less theistic but not less exalted yogic systems would put this idea somewhat differently and in more psychological terms— we should not harp too obsessively on our lapses, but should dwell more lovingly on the Divine within us.

Muhammad Has the Largest Following on the Day of Judgment

Muhammad tells us that he "will have the greatest following on the Day of Resurrection." And understandably so, for the hellfire is on his side. The hellfire will be busy consuming the opponents of Muhammad, and there will be no one left for Paradise to receive except the Muslims.

Muhammad tells us : "He who amongst the community of Jews and Christians hears about me, but does not affirm his belief in that with which I have been sent and dies in this state of disbelief, he shall be but one of the denizens of Hell-Fire." The Jews and Christians will suffer in hell not only for their own unbelief in Muhammad, they will also act as proxies for any Muslims who happen to be sent there. "There would come people amongst the Muslim on the Day of Resurrection with as heavy sins as a mountain, and Allah would forgive them and he would place in their stead the Jews and the Christians," Muhammad tells us. This would also, incidentally, solve the problem of space in heaven: "Space in paradise would be provided by Christians and Jews being thrown into Hell-Fire," the translator tells us.

Another important segment of the infernal population is made up of women. Muhammad says, "O womenfolk.... I saw you in bulk amongst the dwellers of Hell." When a woman asks him why it should be so, Muhammad tells her: "You curse too much and are ungrateful to your spouses. I have seen none [like them] lacking in common sense and failing in religion but robbing the wisdom of the wise." The "proof of the lack of common sense" in them is the fact that in Allah's law promulgated by Muhammad himself, "the evidence of two women is equal to one man;" and the proof of their failing in religion, as he tells them, is that "you spend some nights and days in which you do not offer prayer and in the month of *Ramzan* you do not observe fast." Women sometimes abstained from voluntary fasts because the Prophet had commanded that it was more meritorious for them to do their duty by their husbands than to fast. 'Aisha, the Prophet's wife, did not observe some fasts "due to the regards for the Apostle of Allah." But, it seems, the very merit of women turns into its opposite: predestined damnation.

The Day of Judgment

The Day of Judgment *(qiyamat)*, the Last Day *(yaumu'l-akhir)*, is an indispensable prop of Muslim theology. In the Quran, the word *qiyamat* appears seventy times and in addition has seventy-five synonyms, as shown by Mirza Hairat in his *Mukaddma Tafsiru'l Farqan.* Along with its attendant concepts, Paradise and Hell, it pops up from practically every page of the *Hadis* too. The dreaded day *(yaum)*, colourfully described as the day of "reckoning" *(hisab)*, or of "separation" *(fasl)*, or of "standing up" *(qiyamah)*, is mentioned over three hundred times in the Quran.

The arrival of the Last Day will be announced by many signs. "When you see a slave woman giving birth to her master—that is one sign; when you see barefooted, naked, deaf and dumb as the rulers of the earth—that is one of the signs of Doom. And when you see the shepherds of the black camels exult in buildings— that is one of the signs of Doom." In short, when the poor and the deprived inherit the earth that is the end of it according to Muhammad.

There is a vivid account of the Day of Resurrection in eighty-two *ahadis* at the end of the "Book of Faith." Muhammad tells us that on this day, Allah "will gather people" a "bridge would be set over the hell," and "I [Muhammad] and my *Ummah* would be the first pass over it."

Unbelievers, of course, will be thoroughly miserable on this day but even the Jews and the Christians—the Peoples of the Book — will fare no better. For example Christians will be summoned and asked, "What did you worship?" When they reply, "Jesus, the son of Allah," Allah will tell them, "You tell a lie; Allah did not take for himself either a spouse or a son." Then they will be asked what they want. They will say: "Thirsty we are, O our Lord! Quench our thirst." They will be given a certain direction, and Allah will ask: "Why don't you go there to drink water?" When they go there, they will find that they have been misguided; the water is no more than a mirage, and it is really hell. Then they will "fall into the Fire" and perish.

On this day, no other prophet or savior will avail except Muhammad. People will come to Adam and say: "Intercede for your progeny." He will reply: "I am not fit to do this, but go to Ibrahim, for he is the friend of Allah." They will go to Ibrahim, but he will reply: "I am not fit to do this, but go to Moses, for he is Allah's Interlocutor." They will go to Moses, but he will reply: "I am not fit to do this, but you go to Jesus for he is the Spirit of Allah and His World." They will go to Jesus, and he will reply: "I am not fit to do this; you better go to Muhammad." Then they will come to Muhammad, and he will say: "I am in a position to do that." He will appeals to Allah, and his intercession will be granted.

In many *ahadis*, Muhammad tells us that among the apostles he has a special intercessory power, for "no Apostle amongst the Apostles has been testified as I have been testified." If this is true, it gives substance to his claim that among the apostles he "would have the largest following on the Day of resurrection." Thanks to his special role, "seventy thousand persons of [my] *Ummah* would enter Paradise without rendering an account", and Muslims "would constitute half the inhabitants of Paradise." Considering that unbelievers, infidels, and polytheists are strictly kept out, and that they entry of Jews and Christians also is prohibited, one wonders who will be the other half of the population of Paradise.

How did Muhammad acquire this special intercessory power? Muhammad himself answers this question: "There is for every Apostle a prayer which is granted, but every prophet showed haste in his prayer. I have, however, reserved my prayer for the intercession of my *Ummah* on the Day of Resurrection." The translator makes this statement clearer for us. He says: "The Apostles are dear to Allah and their prayers are often granted. But with every Apostle there is one request which may be called decisive with regard to his *Ummah,* and with it is decided their fate; for example, Noah in a state of distress uttered: `My Lord! leave not any one of the disbelievers in the land' *(al-Quran 71.6)*.Muhammad reserved his prayer for the Day of Resurrection and he would use it for the salvation of the believers."

We have no means of knowing about the curse of Noah, but this kind of cursing is quite in Muhammad's line. For example look at this curse against several tribes: "O Allah! trample severely Muzar and cause them a famine ... O Allah! curse Lihyan, Ri'l Zakwan, Usayya, for they disobeyed Allah and His Messenger."

In any case, when the disbelievers are being hurled into the Fire, Muhammad will not intercede even when he knows that no other intercession would avail: "Thou shalt not damn thy enemies, but needst not go out of your way to save them."

The Prophet's Feather and Uncles

We must admit, however, that Muhammad was consistent. He reserved his power for saving his *ummah,* those who believed in Allah to the exclusion of Allat and 'Uzza, and in his own apostleship.

He did not use it to save even his dearest and nearest ones like his father and uncle. Regarding his father, he told a questioner: "Verily, my father and your father are in the Fire." But he was somewhat more kind to his uncle, Abu Talib, who brought him up and protected him but who did not accept his religion. About him, Muhammad tells us: "I found him in the lowest part of the Fire and I brought him to the shallow part." But even this shallowest part must have been roasting the poor uncle. Muhammad assures us that "among the inhabitants of the Fire Abu Talib would have the least suffering, and he would be wearing two shoes of Fire which would boil his brain." Would you call that much of a relief?

Though Muhammad took pride in "establishing ties of relationship," he himself repudiated all ties with the generations of his forefathers and their posterity. "Behold! the posterity of my fathers . . . are not my friends," declares Muhammad. On the Day of Resurrection, their good works will not avail them. `Aisha, the Prophet's young wife, reports : "I said: Messenger of Allah, the son of Jud'an [a relation of hers and one of the leaders of the Quraish] established ties of relationship, fed the poor. Would that be of any avail to him? He said: it would be of no avail to him."

God's mind is made up with regard to the polytheists; therefore, a true believer should not even seek blessing on their behalf. As the Quran says: "It is not meet for the Prophet and for those who believe, that they should beg pardon for the polytheists, even though they were their kith and kin, after it had been known to them that they were the denizens of Hell."

Muhammad's Night Journey to Heaven

Various other matters, such as Muhammad's night journey to Jerusalem, and the coming of Dajjal and Jesus before the Day of Resurrection, are also discussed in the "Book of faith." These are quite important in Islamic lore.

One night, riding on al-Baraq, "an animal white and long, larger than a donkey but smaller than a mule," Muhammad was taken to the Temple in Jerusalem and from there to the different regions, or "circles" (as Dante called them), of heaven, on the way meeting different apostles. Adam he met in the first heaven, Jesus in the second, Moses in the sixth, and Abraham in the seventh. Then he met Allah, who enjoined on the Muslims fifty prayers a day. But on the advice of Moses, Muhammad made a representation to Allah and the number was reduced to five. "Five and at the same time fifty"—one prayer will now count for ten—for "what has been said will not be changed." So nothing was really lost in efficacy, and five will do the work of fifty.

The more mystic-minded explain this journey spiritually, but Muhammad's Companions and later on most Muslim scholars believe that the journey or ascension *(mi'raj)* was physical. Many in his day scoffed at Muhammad and called his journey a dream. But our translator argues that precisely because it was not believed, it was not a dream! For "had it been only a dream, there would have been no occasion for such a reaction about it. Visions like this can flit across the imagination of any man at any time."

Jesus

Muhammad had a belief of a sort in Jesus. In fact, this belief, along with his belief in the apostleship of Moses and Abraham, is often cited as a proof of Muhammad's liberal and catholic outlook.

But if we look at the matter closely, we find it was more a *motivated* belief, meant partly to prove his own apostolic pedigree, and partly to win converts from among the Jews and the Christians. In any case, his opinion of Jesus does not amount to much. He turned Jesus into a *mujahid* (crusader) of his entourage. When Jesus returns in the Second Coming, no more than a pale copy of Muhammad, he will be waging war against the Christians as well as others: "The son of Mary will soon descend among you as a just judge. He will break crosses, kill swine, and abolish *Jizya,"* Muhammad proclaims. How? The translator explains: "Cross is a symbol of Christianity Jesus will break this symbol after the advent of Muhammad. Islam is the *din* (religion) of Allah and no other religion is acceptable to him. Similarly, the flesh of the swine is a favorite dish of the Christians. Jesus will sweep out of existence this dirty and loathsome animal. The whole of the human race would accept Islam and there would be no *zimmis* left, and thus *Jizya* would be automatically abolish." Jesus is regarded as a just judge, but this only means that he will judge according to the *Shari'ah* of Muhammad's. For, as the translator explains, "the *Shari'ah* of all the earlier prophets stands abrogated with the advent of Muhammad's Apostleship. Jesus will, therefore, judge according to the law of Islam."

Purification (Taharah)

The next book is the "Book of Purification." it deals with such matters as ablution, defecation, and abstersion. It relates not to inner purity but to certain acts of cleanliness, physical and ritualistic, that must be performed before reciting the statutory daily prayers. The main topics discussed in Muslim *fiqh* (canon law) under this heading are : (1) *wuzu,* minor ablution of the limbs of the body, prescribed before each of the five daily prayers and omitted only if the worshipper is sure that he has not been polluted in any way since the last ablution; (2) *ghusl,* the major, total ablution of the whole body after the following acts which make a person *junub,* or impure; coitus *(Jima)*, nocturnal pollution *(ihtilam),* menses *(hayz),* and childbirth *(nifas);* (3) *tayammum,* the minor purification with dust in the place of water; (4) *fitra,* literally "nature," but interpreted as customs of the previous prophets, including acts like the use of the *toothpick* miswak), cleansing the nose and mouth with water *istinshaq),* and abstersion *(istinja)* with water or dry earth or a piece of stone after evacuation and urination; (5) *tathir,* the purification of objects which have become ritualistically unclean.

Some broad injunctions on the subject of purification are given in the Quran (e.g., verses 4:43 and 5:6), but they acquire fullness from the practice of the Prophet.

Ablution *(Wuzu)*

Muhammad emphasizes the need for bodily cleanliness. He

tells his followers that "cleanliness is half of faith" and that their prayer will not be accepted in a state of impurity till they "perform ablution." But *impurity* here has a strictly ritualistic meaning.

Muhammad was a Unitarian in his theology but a Trinitarian in his ablution. He performed his ablution like this: "He washed his hands thrice. He then rinsed his mouth and cleaned his nose three times. He then washed his face three times, then washed his right arm up to the elbow three times, then washed his left arm like that, then wiped his head, then washed his right foot up to the ankle three times, then washed his left foot," and so on. Muhammad said that "he who performs ablution like this ablution of mine . . . and offered two *rak'ahs* [sections] of prayer ... all his previous sins are expiated." This became the standard ablution. According to Muslim canon scholars, this is the most complete of the ablutions performed for prayer. There are twenty-one *ahadis* repeating Muhammad's practice and thought on the subject as given above.

Cleansing the Nose

The nose should be properly cleansed. Muhammad says: "When any one of you awakes from sleep... he must clean his nose three times, for the devil spends the night in the interior of one's nose."

Cleaning the Teeth *(Miswak)*

Muhammad loved toothpicks and used them often. "Were it not that I might overburden the beleivers—I would have ordered them to use the toothpick at every time of prayer," he said.

The Five Acts *(Fitra)*

There are nine *ahadis* on five acts natural to man and proper to Islam: circumcision, shaving the pubes, cutting the nails, plucking the hair under the armpits, and clipping the moustache.

About the moustache and the bread, the prophet said: "Act against the polytheists, trim closely the moustache and grow beard." The next *hadis* substitutes the word "fire-worshippers" for "polytheists." The translator provides the rationale for this injunction: "Islam created a new brotherhood on the basis of belief and good conduct... For the identification of faces, the Muslims have been ordered to trim the moustache and wear the beard, so that they may be distinguished from the non-Muslims who grow a moustache and shave beard."

Bodily Functions

Now Muhammad takes us to the toilet. He forbids his followers "to face the *qibla* [i.e., toward the mosque at Mecca] at the time of excretion or urination, or cleansing with right hand or with less than three pebbles."

Cleansing after excretion must be done an "odd number of times," and one must not use "dung or bone" for this purpose. There is a story explaining why the use of bones and dung is forbidden. Muhammad once spent a night with *jinns* (genii) reciting the Quran to them. When they asked him about their provision of food, he told them: "Every bone on which the name of Allah is recited is your provision. The time it will fall in your hand it would be covered with flesh, and the dung of the camels is fodder for your animals. He, therefore, told his followers: "Don't perform *istinja* with these things for these are the food of your brothers."

He also tells his followers: "When anyone amongst you enters the privy, he must not touch the penis with his right hand."

'Aisha tells us that the "Messenger of Allah loved to start from the right-hand side in his every act, i.e., in wearing shoes, in combing, and in performing ablution."

Tathir

Muhammad enjoins that "when the dog licks the utensil, wash it seven times, and rub it with earth the eighth time."

Don't Expose Your Private Parts

Muhammad says that "a man should not see the private part of another man," nor should men lie together "under one covering." In this connection, he also tells us that the Jews used to take their baths naked and looked at each other's private parts, but Moses took his bath alone. Instead of feeling ashamed for not following their leader's example the Jews taunted him. they said he refrained from exposing his private parts because he suffered from scrotal hernia. But God vindicated him. Once, while taking his bath, Moses put his clothes on a rock, but the rock moved away. "Moses ran after it crying: O stone, my clothes: O stone, my clothes." The Jews then had a chance to see Moses' private parts, and said: "By Allah, Moses does not suffer from any ailment."

Soiled Clothes

'Aisha tells us that the "Messenger of Allah washed the semen, and then went out for prayer in that very garment and I saw the mark of washing on it." There is another *hadis* of similar import, but it also narrates some material of Freudian significance. A guest who was staying at 'Aisha's house had a nocturnal seminal emission. Next day he dipped his clothes in water for washing. A maidservant observed this and informed `Aisha. She asked the guest" "What prompted you to act like this with your clothes?" He replied, "I saw in a dream what a sleeper sees." Then `Aisha asked him "Did you find any mark of fluid on your clothes?" He said: "No." She said: "Had you found anything you should have washed it. In case I found that semen on the garment of the Messenger of Allah dried up, I scratched it off with my nails."

Bathing After a Seminal Emission

There are dozen *ahadis* on the subject of bathing after a seminal emission. Once Muhammad called out an *ansar* who was in the midst of sexual intercourse. "He came out and water was trickling down from his head. Muhammad said: perhaps we put you to haste. The man said yes. The prophet said: When you made haste and semen is not emitted, bathing is not obligatory for you, but ablution is binding." In another *hadis,* Muhammad says that when a man leaves his wife in the midst of an intercourse without having experienced organism, "he should wash the secretion of his wife, and then perform ablution and offer prayer." But when there is a seminal emission "bath becomes obligatory."

Once there was a controversy on this point between some *muhajirs* ("Emigrants" or "Refugees") and some *ansars* ("Helpers"). One of them came to 'Aisha for clarification, asking: "What makes a bath obligatory for a person?" She answered: "You have come across one well-informed." Then she reported what Muhammad had said on the subject: "When anyone sits amidst fore parts of the woman, and the circumcised parts touch each other a bath becomes obligatory. And on yet another occasion, a man asked Muhammad whether a bath is obligatory for one who parts from intercourse with his wife without having had an organism. The Prophet, pointing to 'Aisha, who was sitting by him, replied: "I and she do it and then take a bath."

Tayammum

If water is not available, you can take to *tayammum,* i.e., wiping your hands and feet and forehead with earth, and that should be as good as ablution with water. The translator explains why. He says that "the main purpose behind ablution and bathing is a religious one and the hygienic one is a matter of secondary importance ... Allah has directed us to perform *tayammum* in case water is not available ... to retain the spiritual value of ablution as a means of directing us from the mundane activities of life and directing us to the presence of the Lord." There is a verse in the quran and eight *ahadis* on this subject. "And if you be ailing or on a journey or one comes from the privy, or you have touched women, and you find no water, then betake yourself to clean earth and wipe your faces and your hands therewith."

One *hadis* tell us of the words of 'Ammar to 'Umar: "Do you remember, O Commander of the Faithful, when I and you were in a military detachment and we had had a seminal emission and did not find water for taking bath and you did not say prayer, but as for myself I rolled in dust and said prayer, and when it was referred to the Apostle, he said: `It was enough for you to strike the ground with your hands and then blow the dust and then wipe your face and palms.' "

Food and Ablution

Muhammad enjoined that "ablution is obligatory for one who takes anything touched by fire." But later on this command was abrogated. "The Messenger of Allah took meat of goat's shoulder and offered prayer and did not perform ablution."

Ablution is necessary after leaving the privy if you are going to pray but not if you are going to eat. "The Apostle of Allah came out of the privy, and he was presented with some food, and the people reminded him about ablution, but he said: Am I to say prayer that I should perform ablution?"

Menstruation ***(Haiz)***

The third book is on menstruation. The subjects of this book and the previous one overlap, for both have to do with ritualistic purity. Therefore, some cross-reference is inevitable. This chapter too, in fact, does not have very much to say on menstruation as such but a great deal on ritualistic ablution and bathing after sexual intercourse.

On the subject of menstruation, Muhammad's practice appears, in some respects, different from what was enjoined by the revelation in the Quran. The Quran uses rather strong language on the subject: "They ask thee concerning women's courses. Say: They are a hurt and a pollution. So keep away from women in their course, and do not approach them until they are clean."

But perhaps *approach* here means to have sexual intercourse, for except for coitus all other contacts were permitted by the Prophet. Maimuna tells us; "The Messenger of Allah used to lie with me when I menstruated, and there was a cloth between me and him." Umm Salama reports the same. Aisha says: "When anyone amongst us menstruated, the Messenger of Allah asked her to tie a waist-wrapper over her and then embraced her."

Other *ahadis* make the same point, besides throwing interesting sidelights on some of the more intimate habits of the Prophet. 'Aisha reports: "The Messenger of Allah would recline in my lap when I was menstruating, and recite the *Quran.*" Rather an unlikely place for *svadhyaya,* or scriptural studies.

Carrying the same sexual overtones taught by Freud, 'Aisha again reports: "I would drink when I was menstruating, then I would hand over the vessel to the Apostle and he would put his mouth when mine had been, and drink, and I would eat flesh from a bone when I was menstruating, then hand it over to the Apostle and he would put his mouth where mine had been."

The Prophet would also allow 'Aisha to comb his hair when she was menstruation and he was supposed to be observing *Ptikaf* technically segregating oneself and staying in a mosque for a certain number of days, especially during the last ten days of the month of Ramzan. "The Messenger of Allah put out from the mosque his head for me as he was in *Ptikaf* [her room opened on the mosque], and I washed it in the state that I was menstruation, "Aisha reports."

All this was opposed to the Jewish practice, which forbade not only sexual intercourse but also kissing and all other forms of physical contact during menstruation. Some Muslims wanted to go whole hog in their opposition to Jewish practice and suggested to Muhammad that he should permit sexual intercourse too since the Jews forbade it. But Muhammad did not go that far.

Sexual Pollution and Ablution

'Aisha reports: "Whenever the Messenger of Allah had sexual intercourse and intended to eat or sleep, he performed the ablution of prayer." The commentator explain that this was done "so that the soul of man may be transported from the urges of the flesh to its original spiritual domain."

Muhammad enjoined the same on his followers. For example, "Ummar once went to the Prophet and told him that "he became *junbi* [unclean] during the night. The Messenger of Allah said to him: Perform ablution, wash your sexual organ and then go to sleep." The same advice was conveyed to Ali, who as his son-in-law was shy in putting this question to Muhammad directly. His problem was *mazi* (prostatic fluid) and not *mani* (semen). "Ablution is obligatory in such a case," he was told.

Ablution was also necessary if one wanted to repeat the intercourse. In the words of Abu Baker, the narrator of this *hadis*, "between two acts, there should be an ablution."

Bath (*Ghusl*)

For the exercise of prayer, the whole body must be washed to absolve it from uncleanliness after certain acts: menses, puerperium, coitus, and *pollutio nocturna.* This practice is derived from the Quranic verse: "If you are polluted, then purify yourselves."

There are over two dozen *ahadis* on the subject of Muhammad's own custom in this regard. 'Aisha says: "When allah's Messenger bathed because of sexual intercourse, he first washed his hands; he then poured water with his right hand on his left hand and washed his private parts...."

Muhammad's practice was that after the sexual intercourse,"sometimes he took a bath and then slept, and sometimes he performed ablution only," postponing the bath till the end of the night before the morning prayer. When Aisha reported this to the narrator of this *hadis,* his pious reaction was: "Praise be to Allah Who has made things easy" for the believers.

The same obligation lay on women. One Umm Sulaim went to Muhammad and asked him: "Is bathing necessary for a women when she has a sexual dream?" Muhammad replied: "Yes, when she sees the liquid [vaginal secretion]." Muhammad's wives were scandalized when they learned that Umm Sulaim had put a question to the Prophet which suggested that a woman too could have a sexual dream. "You humiliated the women," they told her.

Single Bath for Multiple Coitus

Unlike ablution, the bath need not be repeated after each act of intercourse. Anas reports that "the Messenger of Allah used to have sexual intercourse with his wives with a single bath" , or in the colorful Language of Tirmizi: "with one bath, the Apostle walked over all his women" (vol. I, *hadis* 124). The translator explains: "The holy prophet did not take a bath after every intercourse: the simply performed ablution and took a bath at the end"

Bathing Together

Many *ạhadis* narrate how the Prophet and his wives used to bathe together after sexual intercourse. 'Aisha reports: "The Messenger of Allah took a bath from the vessel [which contained 15 to 16 pounds of water]. And I and he [the Prophet] took a bath from the same vessel." She reports the same idea with more details in another *hadis:* "I and the Messenger of Allah took a bath from one vessel and our hands alternated into it in the state that we had sexual intercourse."

Two other wives of Muhammad, Umm Salama and Maimuna, also report that they and Muhammad took their baths together.

The translator feels that the practice of the Prophet needs defense from the likely attacks of hostile critics. He tells us that this bath was quite a modest act. There were no glaring lights; and though the Prophet and his wives on occasion took a bath from the same vessel, it was not a tub-bath where a couple sit together; moreover, they took their bath in pitch darkness, and thus there was no question of their seeing each other's bodies

Conserving Body Heat

If one lost too much body heat during the bath, it could be regained by lying again in the embrace of one's wife. According to a *hadis* quoted by Tirmizi, 'Aisha reports: "On many occasions it happened that the apostle of Allah came back to me after the bath of purification with the intention of warming up. I 'wrapped' him up round me even though I myself had not taken bath [and was therefore, in a state of impurity]"

Notwithstanding all these rules and regulations, Muhammad was not bound by them. He had his Apostle's privilege, which, in this case, he shared with Ali. According to Abu sa'id, Muhammad told Ali: "O Ali! It is not lawful for anyone except me and thee to go to a mosque in a state of sexual defilement"

Prayer *(Salat)*

The fourth book is the "Book of Prayer" (*Salat*). It is the longest, with 1,398 *ahadis* divided into 203 chapters. But in all these pages, one looks in vain for any reference to such problems as self-exploration and self-knowledge, problems of enduring concern for the spirituality of the Indian tradition. There is not even a remote hint of different men endowed with different natures taking different paths toward a divinity differently figured. As there is one Allah, one guide, one Book, there is also one Prayer, caught and fixed in a single formula.

From the titles of the 203 chapters this book contains, one can see that they all relate to the externals: *azan* (the call to prayer), postures like bowing, prostrating and rising, the number and times of the different prayers, the place of *imam* in the system of prayers, the merits of prayers at different times, the prayer for rain, the prayer for protection against windstorms and other calamities, the prayer relating to the dead, and so on.

Azan

We are told how the institution of *azan* began. In the beginning, the Medina, people forgathered in the mosque without knowing when they were to pray. As a means of calling people to prayer at fixed times, some suggested using a bell, as the Christians did; others a horn, as the Jews did. Some even suggested that a fire should be lighted. All these methods were ruled out. To make the Muslim practice different from that of the Jews, the Christians, and the Fire—worshippers, the system of the human voice was introduced. Bilal, who was very loud-throated, and 'Abdullah b. Umm Maktum, who later became blind, were the first *mu'azzin* (callers).

Azan is very effective. "When Satan hears the call to prayer, he runs away to a distance like that of Rauha," a distance of 36 miles from Medina.

Attacks on Non-Muslims

Azan became a great indicator. Where it was heard, it meant that everything was not *kufr* (infidelity). "The Messenger of Allah used to attack the enemy when it was dawn. He would listen to the *Azan;* so if he heard an *Azan*, he stopped." This the commentator finds greatly virtuous in Muhammad. The greatest contribution made by the Holy Prophet in the sphere of warfare is that he elevated it from the surface of reckless murder or slaughter to the level of humanized struggle for the uprooting of evil in society. The Holy Prophet, therefore, did not allow his Companions to take the enemy unawares under the cover of darkness of night."

Blessings for Muhammad

When men hear the *mu'azzin,* they should repeat what he says and invoke blessings on Muhammad. They should "beg from Allah *al-Wasila* for me, which is a rank in Paradise fitting for only one of Allah's servants. If any one who asks that I be given the *Wasila,* he will be assured of my intercession," says Muhammad.

In a variation on this theme, if a man who hears a caller responds by testifying that he is "satisfied with Allah as my Lord, with Muhammad as Messenger, and with Islam as *din* [religion] his sins would be forgiven."

In seeking blessings for himself, Muhammad does not forget his wives and progeny. "Apostle of Allah, how should we bless you?" Muhammad is asked. He replies: " O Allah! bless Muhammad, and his wives and his offspring.... He who blesses me once, Allah would bless him ten times."

Posture During Prayer

Muslim prayer is not carried on in one tranquil posture, sitting or standing; it is accompanied by many bodily movements. These have been codified on the basis of the practice and precepts of Muhammad. There are many *ahadis* on the subject. One narrator saw Muhammad "raising his hands opposite the shoulders at the time of beginning the prayer and before bowing down and after coming back to the erect position after bowing, but he did not raise them between two prostrations." Another saw his "hands lifted opposite to ears." He also saw that the prophet "then wrapped his hands in his cloth and placed his right hand over his left hand. And when he was about to bow down, he brought out his hands from the cloth, and then lifted them.... And when prostrated, he prostrated between the two palms."

Muhammad was commanded by Allah that "he should prostrate on the seven bones and he was forbidden to fold back the hair and clothing." The seven bones are: "The hands, the knees, and the extremities of the feet and the forehead." But he asked his followers to "observe moderation in prostration" and not to stretch out [their] forearms on the ground like a dog."

Originally the practice had been to put one's hands together, palm to palm, and then to put them between one's thighs. But later on this practice was abrogated and the followers were "commanded to place them [hands] on the knees."

Another precaution: "People should avoid lifting their eyes towards the sky while supplicating in prayer, otherwise their eyes would be snatched away."

The Imam

Muslim prayer is mostly group prayer. It should led by an *imam*. Muhammad enjoins that "when there are three persons, one of them should lead them."

Muhammad exhorts his followers to follow their *imam*. "When he prostrates, you should also prostrate; when-he rises up, you should also rise up," he tells them. He also forbids them to bow and prostrate themselves ahead of the *imam*: "Does the man who lifts his head before the *imam* not fear that Allah may change his face into that of an ass"? Also, those who are being led in prayer are required to keep pace with the *imam* and are forbidden to recite so loudly as to compete with him. When someone once did this, Muhammad told him: "I felt as if [you were] disputing with me...and taking out from my tongue what I was reciting." The *imam* is authorised to appoint anyone as his deputy, when there is a valid reason for doing so, just as Muhammad appointed Abu Bakr during his last illness.

The First Mosque: Facing the Qibla

Somebody asked Muhammad which was the mosque "first set up on the earth." He answered that it was the Ka'ba. The second one was the great mosque in Jerusalem.

In the beginning, when Muhammad was trying to cultivate the Jews he prayed facing their temple in Jerusalem. But later on, the direction (*qibla*) was changed to Mecca. One tradition says: "We prayed with the Messenger of Allah towards *Bait-ul-Maqdis* for sixteen months or seventeen months. Then we were made to change our direction towards the *Ka'ba*". The followers had no difficulty and adjusted to the new change with alacrity. Some people were praying their dawn prayer and had recited one *rak'ah.* Someone told them that the *qibla* had been changed. "They turned towards the new *qibla* in that very state."

The translator assures us that "this was a change of far-reaching importance...It strengthened the loyalty of the Muslims to Islam and the prophet." It must have made a strong appeal to Arab nationalism.

Allah Allows Muhammad Terror and War Booty

While giving his opinion of the first mosques, Muhammad makes some interesting disclosures. He does not deny that the Jews and the Christians also had their prophets but adds: 'I have been given superiority over the other prophets in six respects: I have been given words which are concise but comprehensive in meaning; I have been helped by terror (in the hearts of the enemies); spoils have been made lawful to me.....; I have been sent to all mankind; and the line of prophets is closed with me." The whole earth is also made a "mosque" for him and given to him as a legitimate place of prayer for him and his. This is the idea of the word as a "mandated territory" bestowed on the believers by Allah.

We see here that European imperialism with all its rationalizations and pretensions was anticipated by Islamic imperialism by a thousand years. In Islam we find all the ideological ingredients of imperialism in any age: a divine or moral sanction for the exploitation of the barbarians or heathens or polytheists; their land considered as a *lebensraum* or held as a mandate; they themselves regarded as the wards and special responsibility *(zimma)* of the civilizing masters.

Another *hadis* mentions Muhammad's power of "intercession" on the Day of Judgment, which other prophets lack. Other *ahadis* mention other points. "I have been helped by terror.....and while I was asleep I was brought the keys of the treasures of the earth," says Muhammad. This wealth the followers of the Apostle "are now busy in getting them," adds Abu Huraria, the narrator of this *hadis*.

Women and Mosques

Women can go to the mosque but they "should not apply perfume," a privilege not denied to men who can afford it. They were also told not to precede men in lifting their heads from prostration. The translator explains that this *hadis* relates to a period when the Companions were very poor and could not afford proper clothing. The instruction was meant to give them time to adjust their clothing before the women lifted their heads (*hadis*).

Muhammad commanded the believers to "take out unmarried women and purdah—observing ladies for *'Id* prayers, and he commanded the menstruating women to remain away from the place of worship of the Muslims." But in a footnote explaining the standpoint of the islamic *shari'ah* with regard to women joining men in prayer, the translator says: "The fact is that the Holy prophet deemed it preferable for women to say their prayers within the four walls of their houses or in the nearest mosque."

Dos and Don'ts

There are many dos and dont's. For example, to wear shoes

while praying is permissible, but clothes having designs and markings on them are distracting and should be avoided. The Prophet commanded the believer that while praying "he should not spit in front of him, for Allah is in front of him when he is engaged in prayer." According to another tradition, he "forbade spitting on the right side or in front, but it is permissible to spit on the left side or under the left foot."

To eat onion or garlic is not *haram* (forbidden), but Muhammad found their odors "repugnant" and, therefore, forbade coming to the mosque after eating them, "for the angels are harmed by the same things as men."

Curse on the Jews

It is meritorious to build a mosque, for "he who builds a mosque for Allah, Allah would build for him a house in Paradise." But it is forbidden to build mosques on graves and to decorate them with pictures. 'Aisha reports that when the Prophet "was about to breathe his last...he uncovered his face and said in this very state: "Let there be curse upon the Jews and the Christians that they have taken the graves of their Apostles as places of worship.' "

Dinner Before Prayer

This rule may seem to lack piety but in some ways it is realistic. The believer is told to prefer supper to prayer. "When the supper is brought and prayer begins, one should first take food," says Muhammad. First things first.

Prayer in Time of Danger

According to Muslim jurists, there are different forms of prayer for sixteen specific dangerous situations. For example, during a war, one group prays while the other one fights.

Friday Prayer

Friday is a special day. "On it Adam was created, on it he was made to enter Paradise, on it he was expelled from heaven."

Every *ummah* was given the Book before the Muslims. But though Muslims "are the last," they shall be the first on the Day of Resurrection." While the Jews and the Christians observe Saturday and sunday as their respective days, Muslims were fortunate to have Friday as their day, the day prescribed by Allah Himself for them. "We were guided aright to Friday, but Allah diverted those who were before us from it."

An interesting story is reported in this connection. One Friday, when the Prophet was delivering a sermon, a caravan with merchandise from Syria arrived. People left the Prophet and flocked toward the caravan. Then this verse was revealed: "And when they see merchandise or sport, they break away to it and leave you standing."

Muhammad as a Preacher

Jabir b. 'Abdullah draws for us a pen-portrait of Muhammad delivering a sermon. He reports: "When Allah's Messenger delivered the sermon, his eyes became red, his voice rose, and his anger increased so that he was like one giving a warning against the enemy and saying" 'The enemy has made a morning attack on you and in the evening too.' He would also say: 'The Last Hour and I have been sent like these two,' and he would join his forefinger and middle finger (just as there is no other finger between these two, similarly there will be no new Prophet between Muhammad and the Day of Resurrection) and would further say: 'The best of the speech is embodied in the Book of Allah, and the best of guidance is the guidance given by Muhammad. And the most evil affairs are their innovations; and every innovation is error.' "

There are other eyewitness accounts of Muhammad's sermons. One report says: "Allah's Messenger stood up [to pray] and we heard him say: `I seek refuge in Allah from thee,' Then said: 'I curse thee with Allah's curse three times,' then he stretched out his hand as though he was taking hold of something." When asked to throw light on this unusual behaviour, he replied: "Allah's enemy *Iblis* came with a flame of fire to put it in my face." But even though cursed, he did not retreat. "Thereafter, I meant to seize him. I swear by Allah that had it not been for the supplication of my brother Sulaiman he would have been bound, and made an object of sport for the children of Medina."

Music, Dance, and Sports

'Aisha reports: "The Messenger of Allah came in my appartment while there were two girls with me singing the song of the Battle of Bu'as. He lay down on the bed and turned away his face. Then came Abu bakr and he scolded me and said: Oh! this musical instrument of the devil in the house of the Messenger of Allah. The Messenger of Allah turned towards him and said: Leave them alone. And when he became unattentive I hinted them [the girls] and they went out, and it was the day of *Id*." Muhammad added: "Abu Bakr, every people have a festival and it is our festival [so let them play on]."

This is the only *hadis* that can be construed as an instance of Muhammad's approving of music. In a large measure he was indulging his child-wife 'Aisha, but the sufi schools of Islam, in which music plays an important role, make the most of this *hadis*.

On the same occasion, Muhammad, with 'Aisha's head resting on his shoulder, was watching some Abyssinians engage in a mock armed fight. 'Umar came and wanted to drive them away by throwing pebble at them. But Muhammad told him: "Umar, leave them alone."

Prayers for Different Occasions

There are prayers for rain, prayers for protection against wind-storms or terrible dark clouds, prayers to be recited at the time of a solar eclipse (1966-1972). However, Muhammad had no friendly eye for nature. He regarded clouds and winds with terror. "When there was on any day windstorm or dark cloud its effect could be read on the face of the Messenger of Allah, and lie moved forward and backward in a state of anxiety," 'Aisha tells us. She further says: "I asked him the reason of this anxiety and he said: I was afraid that it might be a calamity that might fall on my *Ummah*."

Muhammad deals with the problem with the help of an incantation. 'Aisha tells us: "Whenever the wind was stormy, the Apostle of Allah used to say: O Allah! I ask Thee for what is good in it, and the good which it contains, and the good of that which it was sent for. I seek refuge with Thee from what is evil in it, what evil it contains, and the evil of that what it was sent for."

Prayers for the Dead

There are also prayers for the dead and the dying. The dying must be treated to a bit of theology. "Exhort to recite, `There is no god but Allah,' to those who are dying," says the Prophet.

When you visit the sick or the dead, supplicate for good, because "angels may say amen to whatever you say." Umm Salama tells us: "When Abu Salama died, I went to the Apostle of Allah and said: Messenger of Allah, Abu Salama has died. He told me to recite: `O Allah! forgive me and him [Abu Salama] and give me a better substitute than he.' So I said this, and Allah gave me in exchange Muhammad, who is better for me than him [Abu Salama]."

Umm Salama was the widow of Abu Salama, to whom she had borne many children. He died at Uhud, and Muhammad married her four months later.

Weeping Over the Dead

Muhammad discouraged weeping over the dead: "The dead is punished because of his family's weeping over it." He also taught haste in the disposal of dead bodies. "If the dead person was good, it is a good state to which you are sending him on: but if he was otherwise it is an evil of which you are ridding yourself."

Muhammad himself wept over the dead of his loyal followers. Weeping over the dying sa'd b. Ubada, he said: "Allah does not punish for the tears that the eye sheds or the grief the heart feels, but He punishes for this [pointing to his tongue], meaning loud lamenting." Muhammad also sobbed aloud, according to certain traditions, over his expiring child, who was only eighteen months old. His followers tried to comfort him by reminding him of his own exhortation not to weep. Muhammad replied: "It is not this that I forbade, but loud wailing and false laudation of the dead."

Muhammad and His Mother

Muhammad tells us: "I sought [Allah's} permission to beg forgiveness for my mother, but He did not grant it to me. I sought permission from Him to visit her grave, and He granted it to me." This was a fine gesture of Muhammad's part after sending his mother to hell in fulfilment of the demand for theological consistency.

The Poor Tax (Zakat)

The fifth book in an *al-zakat* (charity or poor tax). Every society preaches and to some extent practices charity toward its less-fortunate brothers. Muhammad too stresses the importance of charity, or *zakat,* an old Arab practice. But with him it became a tax, an obligatory payment made by the Muslims to the new state that was forming, and to be spent by its representatives. In this form, those who and *zakat* were resentful, and those who spent it actually acquired a new source of power and patronage.

Much of the "Book of *Zakat*" is concerned with the question of power. In the beginning, Muhammad had many followers who were needy, and most of them, being migrants, depended a great deal on the goodwill and charity of the people of Medina. Perhaps the rhetoric on charity emanates largely from this situation. There was as yet no universal fellowship as such for a brother is distress, no sense of a larger human brotherhood. *Zakat* was solely meant for the brothers in faith, and everyone else was excluded on principle. This has been the Muslim practice ever since.

Uses of Zakat Funds

According to the Quran, the *zakat* funds are meant for "the poor and the paupers (*fuqara* and *miskin),* for those in bondage and debt, and for the wayfarers," All these are conventional recipients of charity. The funds are also to be used for the "bureaucracy," those who collect and administer the funds. But two other items are also mentioned which deserve special attention. The funds are to be used in "the service of Allah" *(fisabili' llah)* and for "gaining over (or reconciling, or inclining) the hearts *(muallafa qulubuhum)*" to Islam (quran 9:60).

In the technical vocabulary of Islam, the first phrase, "in the service, or way, of Allah," means religious warfare, or *jihad. zakat* funds are to be spent on buying arms, equipment, and horses. The second phrase, "gaining over, or reconciling, hearts," means "bribes" in unadorned language. The faith of new converts should be strengthened with the help of generous "gifts," and that of adversaries should be subverted by the same means. This was an important limb of the Prophet's religious offensive and diplomacy, and as the Quranic verse shows, it had for the Prophet, as it still has for his followers, a heavenly sanction.

Exemptions and Incentives

There was a lower exemption limit. "No *Sadaqa [zakat]* is payable on five *wasqs* of dates or grain [1 *wasq* = about 425 pounds], on less than five camel heads and on less than five *uqiyas* of silver [1 *uqiya* = about 10 *tolas,* or 1/4 pound]." Also, "No *Sadaqa* is due from a Muslim on his slave or horse." There was no tax on horses meant for use in a *jihad.* "The horse which is used for riding in *jihad* is exempted from the payment of *zakat."*

An Unpopular Tax

There is an interesting *hadis* which shows that the *zakat* tax was unpopular even with the highest. 'Umar was appointed the collector. When he reported that Khalid b. Walid (who later become a famous Muslim general) and even the Prophet's own uncle, 'Abbas, had refused to pay the tax, Muhammad replied: "You are unjust to Khalid, for he reserved the armours and weapons for the sake of Allah; and as for 'Abbas, I shall be responsible . . . 'Umar, bear in mind, the uncle of a person is like his father."

The resentment against *zakat* was general. It was particularly strong among the non-Medinan Arab tribes, who shared the burden of the tax but not its benefits. The Bedouins complained to the Prophet that the "collectors of *Sadaqa* come to us and treat us unjustly. Upon this the Messenger of Allah said: Please your collectors."

But things were rougher and not as easily settled at this *hadis* seems to suggest. After the conquest of Mecca, when the power of Muhammad became supreme, the collection of the tithe became aggressive. In the beginning of the ninth year of the Hijra (Hegira), parties of collectors were sent out in different directions to realize the tax from the Kilab, Ghifar, Aslam, Fazar, and several other tribes. It seems that the opposition of a section of the tribe of Banu Tamim to the collection was somewhat forceful. So Muhammad sent a punitive force consisting of fifty Arab horsemen, who took the tribe by surprise and brought fifty men, women, and children back to Medina as hostages. They had to be ransomed, and after this the tax collection became smoother.

The Quran itself is an eloquent witness to the Arab resentment against the tax. Allah warns Muhammad: "Some of desert Arabs look upon their payments as a fine, and they wait a turn of fortune against you; but against them shall a turn of evil fortune be; for God both hears and knows."

In fact, the resentment was so great that as soon as Muhammad died, the Arab tribes rose in revolt against the infant Muslim state and had to be reconquered. Their opposition ceased only when they became partners in the growing Muslim imperialism and their *zakat* obligation was drowned in the immense gains derived from military conquests and colonization abroad.

Divine Sanctions

The divine punishment for not paying the poor tax is more gruesome than any secular punishment devised by a human agency. "If any owner of gold or silver does not pay what is due on him, when the Day of Resurrection would come, plates of fire would be beaten out for him; these then would be heated in the Fire of Hell and his sides, forehead and his back would be cauterized with them. And when these cool down, the process is repeated during a day the extent of which would be fifty thousand years." And for someone who owns camels and does not pay, "a sandy plain would be set for him, as extensive as possible" and his camels "will trample him with their hoofs and bite him with their mouths during. . . . a day the extent of which would be fifty thousand years." The same fate awaits the tax-defaulting owner of cows and sheep. "They will gore him with their horns and trample him with their hoofs" for the same period.

Charity Should Begin At Home

There was a lot of uncoerced charity in its non-tax version among the Arabs of pre-Muhammad days. For example, the Arabs of that time would take their camels to a pound every six or seven days and there milk them and distribute the milk among the needy.

Muhammad's response to this generosity was positive. But he taught, and in some ways wisely that charity should begin at home. This point is brought out in many *ahadis*. The order in which one should spend his wealth is this: First on one's ownself, then on one's wife and children, then on relatives and friends, and then on other good deeds.

Following a common practice, an Arab once willed that his slave was to be freed after his death. When Muhammad heard this, he called him and asked him if he had any other property. The man replied on. Muhammad then sold the slave for 800 dirhams, gave the money to the owner, and told him: "Start with your own-self and spend it on yourself, and if anything is left, it should be spent on your family, and if anything is left it should be spent on your relatives."

There is another story that makes the same point. A lady set her slave-girl free. When informed about it, Muhammad told her: "Had you given her to your maternal uncle, you would have a greater reward."

So the morality that Muhammad taught on the question was not particularly heroic, but it agrees with the general practice. Nor was it really revolutionary. The emancipation of slaves was not a matter of justice but only of charity. And even then it should not conflict with the well-being of the family of the believer.

Deeper Aspects

Rather unusual for the *Hadis,* charity in its deeper aspect is also mentioned in some *ahadis*. People who cannot pay in money can pay in piety and good acts. "Administering of justice between two men is also a *Sadaqa.* And assisting a man to ride upon his beast, or helping him load his luggage upon it, is a *Sadaqa;* and a good word is a *Sadaqa;* and every step that you take towards prayer is a *Sadaqa,* and removing of harmful things from the pathway is a *Sadaqa."*

There are some other passages of equal beauty and insight. Among those whom God affords protection is one "who gives charity and conceals it so that the right hand does not know what the left hand has given." In the same vein, Muhammad tells us that "if anyone gives as *Sadaqa* the equivalent of one date... the Lord would accept it with His Right hand."

And in another *hadis:* "In every declaration of the glorification of Allah [i.e., saying *Subhan* Allah], there is a *Sadaqa*... and in main's sexual intercourse [with his wife—the omission is supplied by the translator], there is a *Sadaqa."*

Urgings and Pleadings

Muhammad makes an eloquent plea for alms-giving. Everyone should give charity even if it is only half a date. Abu Mas'ud reports: "We were commanded to give charity though we were coolies."

One *hadis* tells us: "There is never a day wherein servants [of God] get up at morn, but are not visited by two angels. One of them says: O Allah, give him more who spends, and the other says: O Allah, bring destruction to one who withholds." Was not the first part enough? Must a blessing always go along with a curse?

The Prophet warns believers to make their *Sadaqa* and be

quick about it, for "there would come a time when a person would roam about with *Sadaqa* of gold but he would find no one to accept it from him." He also adds that "a man would be seen followed by forty women seeking refuge with him on account of the scarcity of males and abundance of females." What does this mean? The translator finds the statement truly prophetic. By citing the male and female population figures for postwar England and showing their disproportion, he proves "the truth of the Prophetic statement."

Theft, Fornication, Paradise

Some of the material included in certain discussions in the various *ahadis* is not in fact relevant to the nominal topic of the discussion. This is true, for instance, of *Ahadis* 2174 and 2175, which both relate to *zakat* but also treat matters that have nothing to do with charity, although in their own way they must be reassuring to believers. For example, Abu Zarr reports that while he and Muhammad were once walking together, Muhammad left him to go some other place, telling him to stay where he was until he returned. After a while Muhammad was out of sight but Abu Zarr heard some sounds. Although he was apprehensive of some possible mishap to the Prophet, he remembered his command and remained where he was. When Muhammad returned, Abu Zarr sought an explanation for the sounds. Muhammad replied: "It was Gabriel, who came to me and said: He who dies among your *Ummah* without associating anything with Allah would enter Paradise. I said: Even if he committed fornication or theft? He said : Even if he committed fornication or theft."

Charity and Discrimination

There is a *hadis* which seems to teach that charity should be indiscriminate. A man gives charity, with praise to Allah, first to an adulteress, then to a rich man, then to a thief. Came the angel to him and said: "Your charity has been accepted." For his charity might become the means whereby the adulteress "Might restrain herself from fornication, the rich man might perhaps learn a lesson and spend from what Allah has given him, and the thief might thereby refrain from committing theft." One may suppose that the man's acts of charity had these wonderful results because they were accompanied by "praise to Allah."

Zakat not for Muhammad's Family

Zakat was meant for the needy of the *ummah,* but it was to be accepted by the family of Muhammad. The family included 'Ali, Ja'far, 'Aqil, 'Abbas, and Haris b. 'Abd al-Muttalib and their posterity. *"Sadaqa* is not permissible for us," said the Prophet. Charity was good enough for others but not for the proud descendants of Muhammad, who in any case needed it less and less as they became heirs to the growing Arab imperialism.

But though *sadaqa* was not permitted, gifts were welcome. Barira, Mohammad's wife's freed slave, presented Muhammad with a piece of meat that his own wife had given her as *saaaqa.* He took it, saying: "That is *Sadaqa* for her and a gift for us."

War Booty

Within a very short period, *zakat* became secondary, and war spoils became the primary source of revenue of the Muslim treasury. In fact, the distinction between the two was soon lost, and thus the "Book of *Zakat*" imperceptibly becomes a book on war spoils.

Khums, the one-fifth portion of the spoils of war which goes to the treasury, has two aspects. On the one hand, it is still war booty; but on the other, it is *zakat.* When it is acquired, it is war booty; when it is distributed among the *ummah,* it is *zakat.*

Muhammad regards war booty as something especially his own. "The spoils of war are for Allah and His Messenger" (Quran 8:1). They are put in his hands by Allah to be spent as he thinks best, whether as *zakat* for the poor, or as gifts for his Companions, or as bribes to incline the polytheists to Islam, or on the "Path of Allah," i.e., on preparations for armed raids and battles against the polytheists.

'Abd al-Muttalib and Fazl b. 'Abbas, two young men belonging to Mahammad's family, wanted to become collectors of *zakat* in order to secure means of marrying. They went to Muhammad with their request, but he replied: "It does not become the family of Muhammad to accept *Sadaqa* for they are the impurities of the people." But he arranged marriages for the two men and told his treasurer: "Pay so much *Mahr* [dowry] on behalf of both of them from the *khums."*

Dissatisfaction

Most of the properties abandoned by the Banu Nazir were appropriated by Muhammad for himself and his family. Other funds at his disposal for distribution were also increasing. This new money was hardly *zakat* money but war booty. Its distribution created a lot of heart-rending among his followers. Many of them thought they deserved more—or at any rate that others deserved less—than they got. Muhammad had to exercise considerable diplomacy, combined with threats, both mundane and celestial.

"Gaining Hearts" by Giving Gifts

The principle of distribution was not always based on need, justice, or merit. Muhammad had other considerations as well. "I give [at times material gifts] to persons who were quite recently in the state of unbelief, so that I may incline them to truth," says Muhammad.

To gain hearts *(mullafa qulubhum)* for Islam with the help of gifts is considered impeccable behaviour, in perfect accord with Quranic teaching. Muhammad made effective use of gifts as a means of winning people over to Islam. He would reward new converts generously but overlook the claims of Muslims of long standing. Sa'd reports that "the Messenger of Allah bestowed gifts upon a group of people . . . He, however, left a person and did not give him anything and he seemed to me the most excellent among them." Sa'd drew the Prophet's attention to this believing Muslim, but Muhammad replied: "He may be a Muslim. I often bestow something on a person, whereas someone else is dearer to me than he because of the fear that he [the former] may fall headlong into the fire," that is, he may give up Islam and go back to his old religion. The translator and commentator makes the point very clear by saying that it was "with a view to bringing him nearer and making him feel at home in the Muslim society that material gifts were conferred upon him by the Holy Prophet."

There are other instances of the same type. 'Abdullah b. Zaid reports that "when the Messenger of Allah conquered Hunain he distributed the booty, and he bestowed upon those whose hearts it was intended to win." He bestowed costly gifts on the Quraish and Bedouin chiefs, many of them his enemies only a few weeks before. Traditions have preserved the names of some of these elite beneficiaries, like Abu Sufyan b. Harb, Safwan b. Umayya, 'Uyaina b. Hisn, Aqra'b. Habis, and 'Alqama b. Ulasa. They received a hundred camels each from the booty.

Muhammad did the same with the booty of some gold sent by 'Ali b. Abu Talib from Yemen. He distributed it among four men: 'Uyaina, Aqra, Zaid al-Khail, "and the fourth one was either 'Alqama b. 'Ulasa or Amir b. Tufail."

Pacification

But this course was not without its problems. It created quite a lot of dissatisfaction among some of his old supporters, and Muhammad had to use all his powers of diplomacy and flattery to pacify them. "Don't you feel delighted that [other] people should go with riches, and you should go back with the Apostle of Allah, he told the *ansars* with great success when, after the conquest of Mecca, they complained about the unjust distribution of the spoils. They had grumbled: "It is strange that our swords are dripping with their blood, whereas our spoils have been given to them [the Quraish]."

Muhammad added other words of flattery and told the *ansars* that they were his "inner garments" (i.e., were closer to him), while the Quraish, who had received the spoils, were merely his "outer garments." to cajolery, he added theology, telling them that they "should show patience till they meet him at *Hauz Kausar,*" a canal in heaven. The *ansars* were happy.

Muhammad Ruffled

According to another tradition, Muhammad gave a hundred camels each to Abu Sufyan, Safwan, 'Uyaina, and Aqra, but less than his share to 'Abbas b. Mirdas. 'Abbas told Muhammad: "I am in no way inferior to anyone of these persons. And he who is let down today would not be elevated." Then Muhammad "Completed one hundred camels for him."

In other cases when similar complaints were made, Muhammad could not always keep his temper. One man complained that "this is a distribution in which the pleasure of Allah has not been sought." On hearing this, Muhammad "was deeply angry . . . and his face became red;" he found comfort in the fact that "Moses was tormented more than this, but he showed patience."

The Khwaru

'Ali sent some gold alloyed with dust from Yemen to Muhammad. In its distribution, Muhammad showed favoritism. When some people complained, Muhammad demanded: "Will you not trust me, whereas I am a trustee of Him Who is in the heaven? The news comes to me from the heaven morning and evening." This silenced the men, but one of them, a man with deep sunken eyes, prominant cheekbones, thick beard, and shaven head, stood up, and said: "Messenger of Allah, fear Allah and do justice." This angered Muhammad, and he replied: "Woe be upon thee, who would do justice if I do not do justice?" 'Umar, who was present, said to Muhammad: "Messenger of Allah, permit me to kill this hypocrite." Though the man was spared, he and his posterity were denounced. Muhammad said: "From this very person's posterity there would arise people who would recite the Quran, but it would not go beyond their throat; they would kill the followers of Islam but would spare the idol-worshippers... If I were to find them I would kill them like 'Ad [a people who were exterminated root and branch]."

These men, who later on were called the *Khwarij,* took some of the slogans of Islam seriously. It was about them, according to 'Ali, that Muhammad said: "When you meet them, kill them, for in their killing you would get a reward with Allah on the Day of Judgment." These were the anarchists and purists of the early days of Islam. The injunction about them was: "Pursue them as they are routed and kill their prisoners and destroy their property."

Fasting and Pilgrimage
(Sawm and Hajj)

The sixth and seventh books relate respectively to fasting *(al-sawm)* and pilgrimage *(al-hajj)*. Both of these practices are accounted among the "pillars" of Islam.

Fasts

There are many kinds of fasts in Islam, but the fast during the month of *Ramzan* (Ramadan) is considered the most important. Enjoined in the Quran, it is compulsory. "When there comes the month of *Ramzan,* the gates of mercy are opened, and the gates of Hell are locked and the devils are chained."

Fasting in the Muslim tradition is rather different from fasting in many other religious traditions. In Islam, there is no uninterrupted fasting *(saum wisal),* because Muhammad forbade this practice "out of mercy" for his Companions. During fasts eating is prohibited in the daytime but permitted at night. This has its disciplinary role, but nonetheless there is an attempt to make things easy. One is advised to eat as late as possible before sunrise, and to break the fast as soon as possible after sunset. "Take meal a little before dawn, for there is a blessing in taking meal at that time" and "the people will continue to prosper as long as they hasten the breaking of the fast."

This approach distinguished the Muslims from the Jews and the Christians, who ate early and broke their fasts late, waiting for the stars to appear. "The difference between our fasting and that of the People of the Book is eating shortly before dawn," says Muhammad. The translator explains the advantages that accrued to the *Ummah* from maintaining this difference. It "distinguishes the *Ummah* of the Islam from other *Ummahs,*" and "hammers" into its consciousness the sense of "its separate entity which is the first step towards prosperity of any nation.". In addition, "taking a meal late in the dawn and breaking fast early at the sunset indicate the fact that one feels the pangs of hunger. . . This feeling inculcates in one a spirit of humility rather than of stoic pride."

Sexual Intercourse Allowed During Ramzan

The Prophet softens the rigor of the fast somewhat by proclaiming that "eating and drinking in forgetfulness does not break the fast." Kissing and embracing too are permissible. 'Aisha, Hafsa, and Salama, Muhammad's wives, all report that the Prophet used to kiss them and embrace them while fasting. 'Aisha narrates: "The Messenger of Allah kissed one of his wives while he was fasting, and then she ['Aisha] smiled."

The translator elucidates: "It is one of the great favours of Allah upon humanity that he has guided us in every sector of our life through his Prophet Muhammad. Prior to Islam, the man observing fast separated himself completely from his wives. Islam did not approve this practice."

Sexual intercourse is also permitted during the night of the fast. It has a divine sanction. "It is made lawful for you to go to your wives on the night of the fast," says the Quran. In fact, even if one gets up in a state of seminal emission and the dawn overtakes him without giving him time for the ordained bath, he should still go on with his fast. The state of *janabah* (in which one is "unclean and cannot perform a religious act or join) in religious assemblies) does not break the fast. 'Aisha and Salama, Muhammad's wives, report: "The Messenger of Allah at times got up in the morning in a state of *Junub* on account of having a sexual intercourse . . . in the month of *Ramzan,* and would observe fast." There are other *ahadis* on the same subject.

This *hadis* was checked and rechecked by Abu Bakr himself. At first Abu Huraira thought differently, but when the matter was clarified by 'Aisha and Salama, he said, "They have better knowledge," and retracted his previous position.

Sexual intercourse during the daytime in the month of *Ramzan* could be atoned for either by freeing a slave or, failing that, by observing a two-month fast or, failing that, by feeding sixty poor men—but during the Prophet's lifetime, a poor man who violated this prohibition got his expiation at no cost to himself. Muhammad gave him a basket of dates and told him: "Go and give it to your family to eat."

Missed fasts could be completed later on at any time of the year. Women do not fast during the days of menses but are required to complete the fast the following year before the commencement of the next *Ramzan* (in the month of Sha'ban).

Fasting not Obligatory Under Certain Circumstances

Under certain circumstances fasting was optional. For example, a fast during a journey could be broken. "Fast if you like and break it if you like," Muhammad told a questioner on the subject.

There is even a reward for not observing the fast if you are engaged in the "Way of Allah," i.e., in the act of *jihad*. "You are going to encounter the enemy in the morning and breaking of the fast would give you strength, so break the fast," Muhammad tells the believers.

Women sometimes abstained from fasts so that they could perform their duties to their husbands unhindered. 'Aisha reports: "I had to complete some of the fasts of *Ramzan*, but I could not do it due to my duties to the Messenger of Allah." 'Aisha reports the same about Muhammad's other wives. "If one amongst us had to break fasts [of *Ramzan* due to natural reasons, i.e., menses] during the life of the Messenger of Allah, she could not find it possible to complete them so long as she had been in the presence of Allah's Messenger till *Sha'ban* [the eighth month] commenced." The translator explains that every wife of Muhammad was "so much devoted to him that she avoided fasting lest it should stand in her way in the performance of her duty as a wife to him."

It was not only from devotion but also because of Muhammad's injunction that the wives did not fast. "No woman should observe fast when her spouse is present [in the house] but with his permission. And she should not admit any *mahram* in his house, while the husband is present, but with his permission." A *mahram* is a near relative with whom it is unlawful to marry. A woman can feel free in his presence and thus need not observe *purdah*.

The translator gives us the rationale for this injunction. "Such is the regard which Islam gives to the natural instinct of man that it enjoins upon women not to observe (voluntary) fasts, and not to admit even those relatives of theirs in their apartments who are *mahram* to them so that they may not stand in the way of the husbands to satisfy their sexual urge."

Other Fasts

Several other fasts are mentioned. One is the *Ashura* fast, observed on the tenth day of Muharram. The *Ashur* day "was one which the Jews respected and they treated it as *'Id'* and in the pre-Islamic days, "Quraish used to fast on this day" but after Muhammad migrated to Medina he made it optional for his followers. Other voluntary fasts are mentioned, but we need not go into them here.

One interesting thing about these fasts is that one could declare one's intention of observing them in the morning but break them without reason in the evening. One day, Muhammad asked 'Aisha for some food, but nothing was available. Thereupon Muhammad said: "I am observing fast." After some time, some food came as gift, and 'Aisha offered it to Muhammad. He asked: "What is it?" 'Aisha said: "It is *hais* [a compound of dates and clarified butter]." He said: "bring that." 'Aisha further narrates: "So I brought it to him and he ate it;" and then he said: "This observing of voluntary fasts is like a person who set apart *Sadaqa* out of his wealth. He may spend it if he likes, or he may retain it if he so likes."

The Merits of Fasting

There are many merits in observing the fasts. "The breath of the observer of fast is sweeter to Allah than the fragrance of musk," Muhammad tells us. On the Day of Resurrection, there will be a gate called *Rayyan* in Paradise, through which only those who have fasted will be allowed to enter—and when the last of them has entered, "it would be closed and no one would enter it."

The recompense of one who combines fasting with *jihad* will be immense. "Every servant of Allah who observes fast for a day in the way of Aliah, Allah would remove, because of this day, his face from the Fire of Hell to the extent of seventy years' distance."

Pilgrimage

The book on *hajj* ("setting out") is full of ceremonial details which have little interest for non-Muslims. Its ninety-two chapters contain minute instructions on the rites and rituals of the pilgrimage, providing useful guidance to a *hajji* (Pilgrim) but of dubious value to a traveler of the Spirit.

An Idolatrous Idea

Considered from the viewpoint of Muslim theology, the whole idea of pilgrimage of Mecca and the Ka'ba is close to being idolatrous. But it has great social and political importance for Islam. Even the very first Muslim pilgrimage to Mecca under the leadership of Muhammad was perhaps more of a political demonstration and a military expedition than a religious congregation.

In the sixth year of the Hijra, Muhammad started out for Mecca to perform the 'umrah ceremony (the lesser pilgrimage), the very first after coming to Medina. He headed a pilgrim force of fifteen hundred men, partially armed. In order to swell the number, he had appealed to the desert Arabs to join him, but their response was lukewarm, for no booty was promised and they thought, as the Quran puts it, that "the Apostle and the believers would never return to their families."

Even so, fifteen hundred was an impressive number, and anyone could see that this was hardly a band of pilgrims. The Meccans had to enter into a treaty with Muhammad, called the Treaty of Hodeibia. Muhammad regarded this as a victory for himself, and a victory it turned out to be. Two years later, by a kind of delayed action, Mecca succumbed. In this year of victory, pilgrimage, or *hajj,* was declared one of the five fundamentals of Islam.

Two years later, in March A.D. 632, Muhammad undertook another pilgrimage; it turned out to be his last and is celebrated in the Muslim annals as the "Farewell Pilgrimage of the Apostle." Great preparations were made for the occasion. It was meant to be more than an assembly of believers. It was to be a demonstration of the power of Muhammad. "Messengers were sent to all parts of Arabia inviting people to join him in this great Pilgrimage."

After the fall of Mecca, Muhammad's power was unrivaled, and the Bedouin tribes understood that this summons was more than an invitation to a pilgrimage of the type they had formerly performed on their own, at their own convenience and for their own gods. It was also, they knew, a call to submission. Thus, unlike the last time, their response on this occasion was great."As the caravan moved on, the number of participants swelled," until according to some of the narrators, it reached more than 130,000 *(Sahih Muslim.* Everyone was in a hurry to jump on the bandwagon.

The State of Ihram

The "Book of Pilgrimage" deals with the pilgrim's attire and with the place where he puts on the garments of a pilgrim, entering into the state of *ihram* ("prohibiting"), in which he is forbidden to do certain things till he has completed his worship at Mecca.

For his dress, he is forbidden to "put on a shirt or a turban, or trouser or cap." The use of perfume is disallowed during the state of *ihram,* but not before and after. "I applied perfume to the Messenger of Allah as he became free from *Ihram* and as he entered upon it," says 'Asiha. "The best of perfume," she adds in another *hadis.*

Hunting

Hunting too is forbidden to a *muhrim* (one in a state of *ihram*). Somebody once presented Muhammad with the flesh of a wild ass, but he declined it, saying: "If we were not in a state of *Ihram,* we would have accepted it from you." But if the animal is killed by a non-*muhrim,* its flesh is acceptable to a *muhrim.* The leg of a wild ass killed by a non-*muhrim* Companion was presented to Muhammad. "The Messenger of Allah took it and ate it."

Though hunting of a sort is forbidden to a *muhrim,* this does not make him a Jain or a *Vaishnava.* "Four are the vicious beasts" he should still kill: "Kite, crow, rat and voracious dog." But "what about a snake?" somebody asks. Muhammad replies: "Let it be killed with disgrace."

Circumambulation and Kissing

After a man has put on the pilgrim's robe, two seamless wrappers, he should not shave or pare his nails. He should now proceed toward Mecca singing the pilgrim's song, *"Talbiyah, Labbaika! Allahumma!"* ("I stand up for thy service, O Allah"). After arriving in Mecca, he performs ablutions in the Masjidu'l Haram and kisses the Black Stone *(al-hajaru' l-aswad),* then makes seven circuits round the Ka'ba *tawaf).* Muhammad himself circumambulated "on the back of his riding camel ... so that people should see him, and he should be conspicuous." For the same reason, he touched the corner (Black stone) with a stick. "I saw Allah's Messenger circumambulating the House, and touching the corner with a stick that he had with him, and then kissing the stick," reports Abu Tufail.

The practice of kissing the Stone is idolatrous. 'Umar Said; "By Allah, I know that you are a stone and if I were not to see Allah's Messenger kissing you, I would not have kissed you." Following the lead of Christian theologians who distinguish between *veneratio* and *adoratio,* Muslim scholars argue that the Ka'ba and the Black Stone are objects of veneration and not of worship.

Another important rite is that the pilgrim runs from the top of Mount as-Safa to the summit of Mount al-Marwah, the two "Signs of Allah," according to the Quran. Muhammad says that "Allah does not complete the *Hajj* of a person or his *'Umra* if he does not observe *Sa'i* [i.e., run between *al-Safa* and *al-Marwa*]."

Each time the pilgrim is on the top of these mounts, he recites the following: "There is no deity but Allah... He hath performed His promise, and hath aided His servant [Muhammad] and hath put to flight the hosts of infidels by Himself alone." Muhammad never relaxes. At every turn, he instills an unrelenting enmity toward the infidels.

Casting the Pebbles

Another important ceremony is *ramyur'r-rijam,* the casting of the pebbles. On the tenth day, also the "Day of Sacrifice," the pilgrim throws seven pebbles at Jamrat al-'Aqaba, also known as Shaitanuu'l Kabir, the Great Devil. While doing this, he chants: "In the name of god, the Almighty, I do this, and in hatred of the Devil and his shame." Allah and Devil are somehow inseparable in certain theologies.

This ceremony celebrates an ancient event when the Devil successively met Adam, Abraham, and Ishmael, and was driven away by the simple method which Gabriel taught them of throwing seven small pebbles. The three pillars at Mina represent the three occasions when this happened; therefore, the pilgrim casts seven stones at each of the three pillars.

There are several *ahadis* on the merits of throwing pebbles, on their size and number, and on the best time for throwing them. The pebbles should be small—"I saw Allah's apostle throwing stones like pelting of small pebbles." The best time for throwing them is after sunrise on the Day of Sacrifice—"Allah's Messenger flung pebbles at Jamra on the Day of *Nahr* after sunrise, and after that—on the 11th, 12th and 13th of *Dhu' l-Hijja*—when the sun had declined." Their number should be add. "Odd number of stones are to be used for cleaning the private parts after answering the call of nature, and the casting of pebbles at the Jamrat is to be done by odd numbers (seven), and the number of circuits around *al-Safa* and *al-Marwa* is also odd (seven), and the number of circuits around the Ka'ba is also odd (seven)," says the Prophet.

Animal Sacrifice

Next comes the sacrifice of the *'diu' l-azha*. The *hajji* (pilgrim) could sacrifice a goat or a sheep, or a cow or a camel, "The Messenger of Allah sacrificed a cow on behalf of 'Aisha."

it is permissible for seven persons to join the sacrifice of a cow or a camel. While sacrificing the camel, the *hajji* should not make his camel "kneel down" but slaughter it in a standing posture and in a fettered condition "According to the *Sunnah* of the Holy Prophet." Its left foreleg should be tied to its hindlegs. Cows and goats should be sacrificed after making them lie down.

One who cannot go for *hajj* can send a sacrificial animal to al-Haram and earn merit thereby. 'Aisha reports: "I wove the garlands for the sacrificial animals of Allah's Messenger with my own hands, and then he marked them, and garlanded them, and then sent them to the House, and stayed at Medina and nothing was forbidden to him which was lawful for him before."

As Muhammad's affluence increased, the scale of his sacrifices also increased. On his *'umrah* pilgrimage in the sixth year, his biographers tell us, he sacrificed seventy camels at Hodeibia. On a similar pilgrimage the next year, he sacrificed sixty camels. On the Farewell Pilgrimage in the tenth year, we are told by Jabir, "the total number of those sacrificial animals brought by 'Ali from Yemen [where he had gone on a campaign against the Bani Nakha] and those brought by the Apostle was one hundred." A little further on in the same *hadis* we are told that Muhammad "then went to the place of sacrifice, and sacrificed sixty-three camels with his own hands. Then he gave the remaining number to 'Ali who sacrificed them ... He then commanded that a piece of flesh from each animal sacrificed should be put in a pot, and when it was cooked, both of them ['Ali and Muhammad] took some meat out of it and drank its soup."

To his followers, Muhammad said: "I have sacrificed the animals here, and the whole of Mina is a place of sacrifice; so sacrifice your animals at your places."

Even Jehovah, the God of the Jews, whose Temple was a veritable slaughterhouse, had declared that He "desired mercy, and not sacrifice" (Hosea 6:6); but Muhammad's Allah expresses no such sentiment. Because Islam is so preponderantly Muhammadism, one of the consequences of the Prophet's offering sacrifices is that sacrificing has become a sacred institution in Islam. Thus, we find in Islam none of that generous movement of the spirit against animal sacrifice that we find in some measure in most cultures.

Drink

Muhammad also drank water from the well of Zamzam as part of the ritual. Coming to the tribe of 'Abd al-Muttalib (also his own tribe), he said: "Draw water, O Bani 'Abd al-Muttalib; were it not that people would usurp this right of supplying water from you, I would have drawn it along with you. So they handed him a basket and he drank from it." Katib al-Waqidi, the Prophet's biographer, gives us one further detail which would be considered unhygienic by the impious. Muhammad took part of the content, then rinsed his mouth in the pitcher and directed that the water remaining in it should be thrown back into the well. That was his way of invoking a blessing on a well—by spitting into it. Many such wells are mentioned in the traditions.

He also did not forgo his favorite beverage, *nabiz,* a soft drink. Though the *nabiz* offered him had been fouled by many hands, he took it, declining the offer of a cleaner and purer one. The orthodox pilgrims of every generation have continued the practice.

Shaving : Muhammad's Hair

After the sacrifice, the ceremony of pilgrimage concludes, and the *hajji* has himself shaved and his nails pared and his pilgrim garment removed. Shaving should begin from the right side. Anas reports that Allah's Messenger "went to *Jamra* and threw pebbles at it, after which he went to his lodging in Mina, and sacrificed the animal. He then called for a barber and, turning his right side to him, let him shave him; after which he turned his left side. he then gave these hairs to the people"; the hairs became important Islamic relics.

Now the pilgrimage is over, but the pilgrim should spend another three days in Mecca to rest after the hectic four days of ceremony. Before leaving Mecca, he should again go round the Ka'ba seven times and throw stones at the satanic pillars at Mina seven times. Before returning home, he should go to Medina to pay his homage at the tomb of Muhammad.

Ka'Ba Closed to Non-Muslims

The Ka'ba, which had been open to all in pre-Islamic times, whether they were worshippers of Al-Lah or Al-Lat, was closed to al except Muslims after Muhammad conquered Mecca. "After this year no polytheist may perform the Pilgrimage," it was declared on his behalf. This was Allah's own command. The Quran says: "O you who believe! those who ascribe partners to God are impure, and so they shall not approach the sacred House of worship from this year onward."

Most religions build houses or temples for their gods out of their own labour, but Islam conquered one for its god, Allah, from others. The difference is striking. A worthy habitation for any worthwhile god is the one built by his devotees with the love of their hearts and the labour of their hands. any other house is a monument of imperialist greed and aggrandizement and is not acceptable to the gods of the purified spirit.

MARRIAGE AND DIVORCE (AL-NIKAH AND AL-TALAQ)

The eighth book is entitled the "Book of Marriage"; one section of it also discusses divorce *(al-talaq)*.

Muhammad forbids celibacy. "Those among you who can support a wife should marry, for it restrains eyes from casting evil glances and preserves one from immorality." One of his Companions wanted to live in celibacy, but Muhammad "forbade him to do so."

In fact, Muhammad discouraged self-denial in general. One of his Companions said, "I will not marry women"; another said, "I will not eat meat"; and yet another said, "I will not lie down in bed." Muhammad asked himself: "What has happened to these people that they say so and so, whereas I observe prayer and sleep too; I observe fast and suspend observing them; I marry women also? And who turns away from my *Sunnah,* he has no relation with me."

A woman is a great safety valve, but if even that fails and a man is aroused by some other woman, he should come home and cohabit with his wife. "Allah's Messenger saw a woman and so he came to his wife, Zainab, as she was tanning a leather and had sexual intercourse with her. He then went to his Companions and told them: The woman advances and returns in the shape of a devil, so when one of you see a woman, he should come to his wife, for that will repel what he feels in his heart." We are all too ready to see the devil in others, but not in our own selves.

Temporary Marriage (*Mut'ah*)

Muhammad allowed temporary marriages. 'Abdullah b. Mas'ud reports: "We were on an expedition with Allah's Messenger and we had no women with us. We said: Should we not have ourselves castrated? The Holy Prophet forbade us to do so. He then granted us permission that we should contract temporary marriage for a stipulated period giving her a garment [for a dowry]." At this 'Abdullah felt happy and remembered the Quranic verse: "The believers do not make unlawful the good things which Allah has made lawful for you, and do not transgress. Allah does not like transgressors."

Jabir reports: "We contracted temporary marriage giving a handful of dates and flour as a dower." He told another group "Yes, we had been benefiting ourselves by the temporary marriage during the lifetime of the Holy Prophet, and during the time of Abu Bakr and 'Umar." Iyas b. Salama reports, on the authority of his father, "that Allah's Messenger gave sanction for contracting temporary marriage for three nights in the year of Autas [after the

Battle of Hunain, A.H. 8] and then forbade it."

Sunni theologians regard this form of marriage as no longer lawful, but the Shias differ and still practice it in Persia. The Shia theologians support this with a Quranic verse: "Forbidden to you also are married women, except those who are your hands as slaves.... And it is allowed you, besides this, to seek out wives by means of your wealth, with modest conduct, and without fornication. And give those with whom you have cohabited their dowry. This is the law. But it shall be no crime in you to make agreements over and above the law. Verily, God is knowing, Wise."

Prohibitions

The law appears to be quite indulgent, but it is not entirely so. There are many restrictions on grounds of number, consanguinity, affinity, religion, rank, etc. For example, a man cannot marry more than four free women at a time (Quran 4:3) — there is no restriction on the number of slave concubines. Also, one cannot marry one's wife's father's sister nor her mother's sister. It is also forbidden to marry the daughter of one's foster brother, or even the sister of one's wife if the wife is alive and not divorced.

It is also forbidden to marry an unbeliever. Later on, this restriction was relaxed, and a male Muslim could then marry a Jew or a Christian (Quran 5:5). Under no circumstances could a female Muslim marry a non-believer.

Marriage is also disallowed when the parties are not equal in rank or status *(kafa'ah)*, though what is rank is differently understood by different people. Generally speaking, an Arab is considered higher than a non-Arab, the Prophet's relatives being the highest. One who had committed a portion of the Quran to memory was considered a qualified match by Muhammad himself. A woman came to him and entrusted herself to him. He "cast a glance at her from head to foot ... but made no decision" about her. Then a Companion who was there stood up and said: "Messenger of Allah, marry her to me if you have no need for her." But the man possessed nothing, not even an iron ring for a dowry. He was turning away in disappointment when Muhammad asked him if he knew any verses of the Quran and could recite them. The man said yes. Then Muhammad decided and said: "Go, I have given her to you in marriage for the part of the Quran which you know."

One should also not outbid one's brother. "A believer is the brother of a believer, so it is not lawful for a believer to outbid his brother, and he should not propose an agreement when his brother has thus proposed until he gives it up."

Shighar marriage is also prohibited. This is the marriage which says: Marry me your daughter or sister, and in exchange I will give you in marriage my daughter or sister.

One should also not marry when one has put on the ritual grab of pilgrimage. "A *Muhrim* should neither marry not make the proposal of marriage," reports Usman b. Affan, quoting the Prophet. But this point is controversial, for Muhammad himself "married Maimuna while he was a *Muhrim.*"

One cannot remarry one's divorced wife unless she subsequently married someone else and the new husband had sexual intercourse with her and then divorced her. A divorcee married but then decided to go back to her old husband. Seeking the Prophet's permission, she told Muhammad that all the new husband possessed was "like the fringe of a garment" (i.e., he was sexually weak). The prophet "laughed" but withheld the permission. "You cannot do that until you have tasted his [the new husband's] sweetness and he has tasted your sweetness," he told her.

The Husband's Rights

A husband has complete sexual rights over his wife. "Your wives are your tilth; go then unto your tilth as you may desire." The same idea is also found in the Quran. Another *hadis* in the same group tells the husband that "if he likes he may have intercourse being on the back or in front of her, but it should be through one hole", which means vagina only, as the commentators tell us.

It is the duty of a wife to be responsive to all of her husband's overtures. "When a woman spends the night away from the bed of her husband, the angels curse her until morning."

Women's Rights

In return, a woman has her rights. She is entitled to a lawful maintenance *(nafaqah)*; if the husband fails to provide it, she can seek a divorce. She is also entitled to a dowry *(mahr)*, or what the Quran in some verses (4:24, 33:50) calls her "hire" *(ujurat)*. She can claim it when divorced.

She is also to be consulted in the choice of her partner. "A woman who has been previously married *(Sayyib)* has more right to her person than her guardian. And a virgin should also be consulted, and her silence implies her consent." Theoretically a Muslim woman is entitled to make the marriage contract herself, but in practice it is her nearest kinsman, the guardian *(wali)*, who does it. The father and the grandfather are even called "compelling *walis*." According to some schools, a minor girl given in marriage by a guardian other than her father or grandfather can seek dissolution of the marriage when she attains her majority.

Al-'Azi

Coitus interruptus is permitted, but it is useless if the object is to prevent conception, for that is in the hand of Allah. Abu Sirma reports: "We went out with Allah's Messenger on the expedition ... and took some excellent Arab women; and we desired them ... but we also desired ransom for them. So we decided to have sexual intercourse with them but by observing *'azl*." They consulted Muhammad, and he advised: "It does not matter if you do not do it, for every soul that is to be born up to the Day of Resurrection will be born."

Captive Women

Adultery and fornication are punished according to Muhammad's law, but not if you commit them with the "women that your right hands possess," that is, those women, whether married or unmarried, who are captured by the Muslims in *Jihad,* or holy war. A Quranic verse fortifies this position: "Also prohibited are women already married except those whom your right hands possess."

Ahadis tell us that this verse descended on the Prophet for the benefit of his Companions. Abu Sa'id reports that "at the Battle of Hunain Allah's Messenger sent an army to Autas. . . . Having overcome them [the enemies] and taken them captives, the Companions of Allah's Messenger seemed to refrain from having intercourse with captive women because of their husbands being polytheists. Then, Allah, Most High, sent down [the above verse]:.

The followers had a feeling of delicacy in the matter, based on an old moral code, but allah now gave a new one.

Cast a Glance At the Woman you Want to Marry

It is permissible to cast a glance at the woman one wants to marry, from "head to foot." A believer came to Muhammad, in forming him that he had contracted a marriage with an *ansar* woman and wanted him to contribute toward the dowry payment. "Did you cast a glance at her, for there is something in the eyes of the *Ansars,"* Muhammad asked. The man replied: "Yes." "For what dower did you marry her," Muhammad inquired. "For four *Uqiyas,"* the man replied. "For four *Uqiyas?* It seems as if you dig out silver from the side of the mountain (that is why you are prepared to pay so much dower). We have nothing which we should give you. There is a possibility that we may send you to an expedition where you may get booty." The man was sent on an expedition marching against the Banu 'Abs.

But this permission actually originated in a different incident. An Arab woman named 'Umra, the daughter of one Jaun, 'was mentioned before Allah's Messenger." By now the Prophet was an important man in Arab politics, so he commanded an official of his named Abu Usaid to send a messenger to the woman. She was brought and she "stayed in the fortresses of Banu Sa'idah." Allah's Messenger went out until he came to her to give "her a proposal of marriage." She was "sitting with her head downcast." They saw each other, and Muhammad talked to her. She told him: "I seek refuge with Allah from you." Meanwhile the Prophet had arrived at his own conclusion. He told her: "I have decided to keep you away from me." Then Muhammad retired with his host and told him: "Sahl, serve us drink."

It is in this *hadis* that one finds it permissible to cast a glance at the woman whom one intends to marry.

Deportment Toward One's Wives

Ticklish problems arise if one has more than one wife and if one marries often. One of the problems, for example, is how many nights one should spend with one's newly wed wife? The answer is seven days if she is a virgin, and three days if she is a widow.

Umm Salama one of the wives of Muhammad, tells us that when Muhammad married her, he spent three nights with her. When he intended to leave, she "caught hold of his garment." But the Prophet told her: "If you wish I can stay with you for a week, but then I shall have to stay for a weak with all my wives."

Though a husband should divide his days equally among all his wives, one wife could make over her day to another. *Ahadis* tell us that when Sauda became old, she made over her day to 'Aisha. So Allah's Messenger "allotted two days to 'Aisha."

But sometimes the Prophet himself would ask a wife to forgo her day. One wife told him: "If I had the option in this I would not have allowed anyone to have precedence over me."

Eventually the rule of rotation was withdrawn altogether by a special dispensation of Allah: "Thou may defer the turn of any of them that thou pleasest, and thou may receive any thou pleasest; and there is no blame in thee if thou invite one whose turn thou hast set aside" (Quran 33:51). Allah is very accommodating. 'Aisha, for whose benefit He really spoke, taunted Muhammad: "It seems to me that your Lord hastens to satisfy your desire."

Night Sessions

We have one important *hadis* which provides another indulgence to the believers and also throws some light on the Prophet's sexual code. In order to be impartial, a believer should visit his wives by turn. But while he is in bed with one of them, he is allowed to have his other wives around. Anas, one of the servants of Muhammad, reports that "all the wives of the Messenger of Allah used to gather every night in the house of one where he [the Apostle] had to come. . . It was the night in the house of 'Aisha, when Zainab came there. He [the Holy Prophet] stretched his hand towards her [Zainab], whereupon she ['Aisha] said: it is Zainab. Allah's Apostle withdrew his hand. There was an altercation between the two until their voices became loud." When the morning prayer was announced, Abu Bakr came to get Muhammad; hearing their voices, he said: "Messenger of Allah, come for prayer, and throw dust in their mouths."

On Marrying a Virgin

In other *ahadis*, the Prophet touches upon the excellence of marrying a virgin. Jabir reports: "The Apostle of Allah said: `Jabir, have you married?' I said: 'with one previously married,' whereupon he said: `Why did you not marry a virgin with whom you could sport?" or "who might amuse you and you might amuse her."

Tastahidda

Muhammad also made effective use of what are known in literary criticism as vulgar expressions. Once the Prophet and his party returned from an expedition rather late, and his Companions wanted to hurry to their homes. But the Prophet told them to wait till "the woman with dishevelled hair may comb it, and the woman whose husband had been away may get herself clean; and when you enter, you have the enjoyment."

The translator tells us that the Arabic word for 'get herself clean" is *tastahidda,* which literally means "to remove the hairs on the private pairs," but it is here used metaphorically in the sense of getting ready for the husband's company.

The Original Sin

"Had it not been for Eve, woman would have never acted unfaithfully towards the husband," the Prophet tells us.

Muhammad's Marriage

Some incidents relating to the Prophet's marriages with Safiyya and Zainab bint Jahsh are mentioned.

Safiyya

Muhammad's wars and raids not only fed his coffers, they also swelled his harem. Safiyya, a beautiful girl of seventeen years, was the wife of the chief of a Jewish clan inhabiting Khaibar. Muhammad's custom was to make surprise attacks. Khaibar was invaded in the same fashion. Anas narrates: "We encountered the people at sunrise when they had come out with their axes, spades and strings driving their cattle along. They shouted in surprise; Muhammad has come along with his force! The Messenger of Allah said: Khaibar shall face destruction." There is even a Quranic verse relating to Muhammad's sudden sweep on the valley and the fate of its people: "But when it descends *[nazala]* into the open space, before them evil will be the morning for those who were warned" (Quran 37:177).

In any case, many people were butchered, and many others were taken prisoners. "We took Khaibar by force, and there were gathered the prisoners of war," according to Anas, Safiyya, the daughter of Huyayy b. Akhtab, the chief of the Quraiza and al-Nazir, was one of them. Her husband, Kinana, was put to a cruel death.

Anas continues: "She first fell to the lot of Dihya in the spoils of war." (Incidentally, Dihya was strikingly handsome. Muhammad used to see Gabriel in his form.) But Anas adds that people "praised her in the presence of Allah's Messenger and said: `We have not seen the like of her among the captives of war'." Muhammad took her away from Dihya, Gabriel or no Gabriel, and even took her to his bed the same night her husband was killed, in violation of his own command, which enjoined the believers to wait until the beginning of the next menstrual cycle in their captive women.

Rihana and Juwairiya

Safiyya was no exception. Many other women, among them Rihana and Juwairiya, were taken in and treated as part of the war booty. Rihana was a Jewish girl of the Banu Quraizah. After her husband was beheaded in cold blood along with eight hundred other male members of her tribe in the genocide at Medina. Muhammad kept her as his concubine. We shall touch upon this massacre again in our discussion of *ihad.*

Juwairiya, another of these unfortunate girls, was the daughter of the chief of the Banu'l Mustaliq. She was captured in the fifth or sixth year of the Hijra along with two hundred other women. "The Messenger of Allah made a raid upon Banu Mastaliq while they were unaware and their cattle were having a drink at the water. He killed those who fought and imprisoned others. On that very day, he captured Juwairiya bint al-Haris."

In the division of the booty, she fell to the lot of Sabit ibn Qays. He set her ransom price at nine ounces of gold, beyond the power of her relatives to pay. 'Aisha's reaction when she saw this beautiful girl being led into the presence of Muhammad is recounted in these words: "As soon as I saw her at the door of my room, I detested her, for I knew that he [Muhammad] would see her as I saw her." And indeed, when Muhammad saw Juwairiya he paid her ransom and took her for his wife. Juwairiya was at that time about twenty, and she became the seventh wife of the Prophet. The whole story is given by Ibn Ishaq, the Prophet's biographer.

There was another girl, named Zainab, again Jewish, who had seen her father, husband, and uncle killed. She poisoned the roasted lamb she was ordered to prepare for Muhammad. Suspecting something wrong, Muhammad spat out the very first morsel. He was saved, and she was immediately put to death, according to some authorities.

Zainab Bint Jahsh

Here we shall mention another Zainab, whose affair was not cruel but scandalous. She was the wife of Muhammad's adopted son, Zaid, and therefore, in the eyes of the Arabs, as good as his own daughter-in-law. Muhammad went to her house when her husband was away, saw her in a state of seminudeness, and was aroused. When Zaid heard about it, he offered to divorce her, but Muhammad, fearing a public scandal, told him to keep his wife for himself. At this point Allah spoke and decided the matter (Quran 33:36—40). He chided Muhammad for telling Zaid, "Retain thou in wedlock thy wife," and for hiding in his heart "that which God was about to make manifest." Allah told Muhammad: "Thou feared the people, but it is more fitting that thou should fear God", and He revealed His plan, present and future, to Muhammad thus: "We joined her in marriage to thee, in order that in future there may be no difficulty to the believers in the matter of marriage with the wives of their adopted sons." He now also addressed Himself to the Muslims of all generations: "It is not fitting for a believer, man or woman when a matter has been decided by God and His Apostle to have any option about their decision. If anyone disobeys God and His Apostle, he is indeed clearly on a wrong path."

Thus reassured, Muhammad made Zaid himself go to his wife with his marriage proposal. "Allah's Messenger said to Zaid to make a mention to her about him." The marriage ordered from above was celebrated with unusual festivity. "Allah's Messenger gave no better wedding fast than the one he did on the occasion of his marriage with Zainab."

Divorce (Talaq)

Talaq literally means "undoing the knot," but in Islamic law, it now means annulment of marriage by the pronouncement of certain words.

The marriage and divorce laws of Islam derive from the prophet's own practice and pronouncements. According to the Shias, the prophet had twenty-two wives, two of whom were bondswomen; but that was a special divine dispensation for him alone. The other believers are allowed only four wives at a time, exclusive of slave concubines, who do not count. The total of four wives at one time cannot be exceeded, but individual wives can be replaced through *talaq*. The procedure is not difficult; once a man says the word *talaq* three times, the divorce becomes operative.

Yet there are certain restrictions. For example, it is forbidden to divorce a woman during her menstrual period. 'Abdullah, the son of 'Umar, the future Khalifa, divorced his wife while she was in a state of menses. When 'Umar mentioned this to Muhammad, the latter ordered: "He ['Abdullah] should take her back, and when she is pure he may divorce her."

Three Pronouncements

The word *talaq* has to be pronounced three times before *talaq* becomes operative. But opinions differ as to whether it has to be pronounced on three separate occasions, after three successive menses, or whether three times at one sitting is enough. According to the translator, "traditions are not lacking in which three pronouncements at one sitting were held as irrevocable divorce even during the time of the prophet."

With such easy conditions of divorce, the limitation of wives to four at a time was not unduly self-denying. Wives were constantly replaced. 'Abdar-Rahman, a senior Companion, adviser, and friend of Muhammad, abu Bakr, and 'Umar, had children by sixteen wives besides those from concubines. Somewhat later, Hasan, the son of 'Ali and grandson of Muhammad married seventy—some say ninety—times. People in his day called him the Divorcer.

It is no wonder that women had no sanctity. Wives could be easily disposed of by gifting or divorce. For example, on emigrating to Medina, 'Abdar-Rahman was adopted by Sa'd, son of Rabi, as a brother in faith-in accordance with the arrangement made by Muhammad to join every Emigrant to an *ansar* in brotherhood. As they sat together at supper, the host said: "Behold my two wives and choose one you like the best." One wife was divorced on the spot and gifted away.

Zihar and Ila

There were two other forms of separation not amounting to

legal divorce prevalent among the Arabs at the time of Muhammad: *zihar* and *ila'*. In *zihar,* the husband vowed that his wife would be unto him as the back (*zahr*) of his mother and then stayed away from her for a specified period. This was a customary vow of abstinence among the Arabs, and according to some traditions, Muslims also took it during the period of fasting. The purpose of the abstinence could be penitential or devotional, or the vow might be taken in a fit of anger. The same formula was also used a s a form of divorce. Muhammad condemned divorce by *zihar* (Quran 58:1-5) and allowed a husband who had taken the vow to go back to his wife. The broken vow could be expiated by making a *kaffarah* (literally, "that which covers a sin"), which in this case is either a fast for two months or the feeding of sixty poor men and women.

There was another form of separation called *ila* ("to swear"). In this form, the husband swore an oath to abstain from sexual intercourse with his wife. In the pre-Islamic period, the Arabs regarded *ila* as a form of divorce, but it did not fully dissolve the marriage. The oath of *ila* was sometimes taken to penalize the wife and extort ransom from her. Muhammad forbade this (Quran 2:226). A man who had taken such a vow was to go back to his wife without any blame to himself; if not, the marriage was ipso facto legally dissolved at the end of four months. The broken vow could be expiated. "When a man declares his wife an unlawful for himself that is an oath which must be atoned...There is in the Messenger of Allah a model pattern for you."

In due course, the two forms of separation died away in Islam.

Muhammad's Separation from His Wives

Ila' is a temporary separation from one's wife. In this sense of the term, the believers are indeed fortunate in having a "model pattern" in an example provided by the Prophet.

Muhammad himself had to undergo separation from his wives for a period which lasted twenty-nine days. The *Sahah Muslim* narrates this incident in several *ahadis;* but before we take them up, let us provide some background information.

In visiting his numerous wives, Muhammad observed a rough-and-ready rule of rotation. In fact, the days in his life were known by the name of the wife he was visiting. One day Muhammad was supposed to be with Hafza, but instead she found him with Mary, the beautiful Coptic concubine. Hafza was furious. "In my room, on my day and in my own bed," she shouted. Muhammad, trying to pacify her, promised never to visit Mary again, but he wanted Hafza to keep the incident a secret.

Hafza, however, told 'Aisha, and very soon everybody knew about it. Muhammad's Quraish wives detested Mary and were jealous of the servile wretch, who had even given Muhammad a son. Soon the harem was filled with gossip, excitement, and jeering. Muhammad was very angry, and he told his wives that he would have nothing to do with them. He separated himself from them, and soon the news was afloat that he was divorcing them all. In fact, in the eyes of the believers this rumor was more newsworthy and significant than the reports that Medina was soon to be attacked by Ghassan (the Arab auxiliaries of Byzantium).

In a long *hadis*, 'Umar b. al-Khattab (Hafza's father) reports: "When Allah's Apostle kept himself away from his wives, I entered the mosque, and found the people striking the ground with pebbles and saying: Allah's Messenger has divorced his wives." 'Umar decided to find out what was actually happening. First he asked 'Aisha if she had "gone to the extent of giving trouble to Allah's Messenger." 'Aisha told him to mind his own business. "I have nothing to do with you. You should look to your own receptacle [Hafza]." 'Umar next sought out Hafza and chided her. "You know that allah's Messenger does not love you, and had I not been your father he would have divorced you," he told her. She wept bitterly.

Then 'Umar sought permission to be admitted into the presence of Muhammad. The request was disregarded, but he insisted. "O Rahab, seek permission for me from Allah's Messenger. I think that Allah's Messenger is under the impression that I have come for the sake of Hafza. By Allah, if Allah's Messenger would command me to strike her neck, I would certainly do that," he told Rahab, Muhammad's doorman. He was admitted.

As 'Umar entered, he saw "the signs of anger on his [Muhammad's] face," so he tried to calm him down. He told him "how we the people of Quraish had domination over women but when we came to Medina we found people whom their women dominated. So our women began to learn from their women."

He also told him: "Messenger of Allah, what trouble do you feel from your wives, and if you had divorced them, verily Allah is with you, His angels, Gabriel, Mika'il, I and Abu Bakr and the believers are with you."

Muhammad relaxed.–"I went on talking to him until the signs of anger disappeared on his face...and he laughed," 'Umar narrates. In this new mood, the famous verses descended on the Prophet, freeing him from his oath respecting Mary, threatening his wives with divorce, and incorporating 'Umar's assurance that all the angels and believers supported him: "O Prophet!" said Allah. "Why do you prohibit thyself what God has made lawful to you, craving to please thy wives?...Allah has already ordained for you the dissolution of your oaths." Allah also told the Prophet's wives in no uncertain terms that "his Lord if he divorces you will give him in exchange wives better than you." Allah warned them, particularly 'Aisha and Hafza, in the following terms: "If ye both turn repentant unto God—for your hearts have swerved!—but if you back each other up against him, verily, Allah, He is the sovereign; and Gabriel, and the righteous of the believers, and the angels after that will back him up." Allah also told them that if they misbehaved, being the Prophet's wives would avail them nothing on the Day of Judgment. "God strikes out a parable to those who misbelieve: the wife of Noah and the wife of Lot; they were under two of our righteous servants, but they betrayed them: and they availed them nothing against God; and it was said, 'Enter the Fire with those who enter.' "

The matter blew over, and they became his wives again. The

Holy Prophet "had taken an oath of remaining away from them [his wives] for a month, and by now only twenty-nine days had passed, [but] he visited them." 'Aisha mischievously reminded the Prophet that it was not yet one month but only twenty-nine days, to which Muhammad replied: "At times, the month consists of twenty-nine days."

Now 'Umar stood at the door of the mosque and called out at the top of his voice: "The Messenger of Allah has not divorced his wives." A verse chiding his followers for so readily believing in rumors also descended on Muhammad: "And if any matter pertaining to peace or alarm comes within their ken, they broadcast it. But if they had only referred it to the Apostle, or to those charged with authority among them, the proper investigators would indeed know it" (Quran 4:83; *hadis* 3507).

Option of Divorce Different from Divorce

It seems there were other occasions of domestic discord, some of them centering round money. These must have occurred in the early days at Medina, when Muhammad lacked funds. Once Abu Bakr and 'Umar went to Muhammad and found him "sitting sad and silent with his wives around him." He told the two fathers: "They [his wives and their daughters] are around me as you see, asking for extra money." Then Abu Bakr "got up, went to 'Aisha and slapped her on the neck; and 'Umar stoop up and slapped Hafza."

On this occasion, the Prophet also gave his wives the option of a goodly departure if they "cared more for this would and its adornments than for Allah and His Apostle and the abode of the Hereafter" (Quran 33:28-29). The wives chose the latter.

The moral of these *ahadis* as drawn by the translator is that "mere giving option to women to divorce does not make the divorce effective, but when it is really intended."

No Maintenance Allowance for a Divorce

Fatima bint Quais was divorced by her husband "when he was

away from home." She was very angry and went to Muhammad, who told her: "There is no lodging and maintenance allowance for a woman who has been given irrevocable divorce." But he mercifully helped her to find another husband. She had two suitors, Abu Jahm and Mu'awiya. Muhammad advised against them both, for the former did "not put down his staff from his shoulder" (i.e., he beat his wives), and the latter was poor. In their place, he proposed the name of Usama b. Zaid, the son of his slave and adopted son, Zaid.

Later on a more generous sentiment prevailed. 'Umar ruled that husbands should provide their divorced wives with a maintenance allowance during the period of *'idda* on the ground that the true purpose of the Prophet's words had been misunderstood by Fatima, a mere woman. "We cannot abandon the Book of Allah and the *Sunnah* of our Apostle for the words of a woman."

'Idda is a period of waiting during which a woman cannot remarry. It normally lasts four months and ten days but ends sooner if the woman gives birth to a child. Once *'idda* has ended, the woman can contract another marriage.

Having to provide an allowance for four months at the most was not very difficult. Thus, since husbands had almost no fear of any future burden, and could get rid of their wives so easily, the threat of divorce hung heavily on Muslim women.

Mourning

A woman whose husband dies must abstain from all adornment during the *'idda* period, but mourning for other relatives should not last for more than three days. Abu Sufyan, the father of Umm Habiba, one of Muhammad's wives, died. She sent for some perfume and rubbed it on her cheeks, observing: "By allah, I need no perfume but for the fact that I heard Allah's Messenger say, "It is not permissible for a woman believing in Allah and the Hereafter to mourn for the dead beyond three days, but in the case of the death of the husband it is permissible for four months and ten days."

Li'an (Invoking Curse)

If a man finds his wife in adultery, he cannot kill the adulterous man, for that is forbidden; nor can he make an accusation against his wife, for unless he has four witnesses, he receives eighty stripes for making a false accusation against the chastity of a woman. But if the witnesses are not always forthcoming, which is most likely in such a case, what should he do? This was the dilemma confronting the believers. An *ansar* posed the problem to Muhammad: "If a person finds his woman along with a man, and if he speaks about it, you would lash him; and if he kills, you will kill him, and if he keeps quiet, he shall have to consume anger." Muhammad supplicated God: "Allah, solve this problem." And a verse descended on him (Quran 24:6) which gives us the practice of *li'an*. The word literally means "oath," but technically it stands for that particular form of oath which brings about separation between husband and wife with the help of four oaths and one curse.. A husband's solitary evidence can be accepted if he bears witness four times with an oath by Allah that he is solemnly telling the truth and then invokes the curse of Allah upon himself if he is lying. Similarly, the wife can solemnly deny the accusation four times and then invoke the wrath of Allah on herself if her accuser is telling the truth. One of them must be lying, but this closes the chapter, and they are wife and husband no more.

Emancipating A Slave

For some unexplained reason, a few chapters at the end of the book dealing with marriage and divorce are on slaves. This may be due to a faulty method of classification, or it may be that emancipating a slave was considered a form of *talaq*, which literally means "freeing" or "undoing the knot"; or it may be that the subject really belongs to the next book, which is on business transactions—a slave, after all, was no more than a chattel.

Modern Muslim writers trying to boost Islam as a humane ideology make much of the sayings of Muhammad on the emancipation (*'itq*) of slaves. But the fact remains that Muhammad, by introducing the concept of religious war and by denying human rights to non-

Muslims, sanctioned slavery on an unprecedented scale. Pre-Islamic Arabs, even in their wildest dreams, never imagined that the institution of slavery could take on such massive proportions. Zubair, a close companion of the Prophet, owned one thousand slaves when he died. The Prophet himself possessed at least fifty-nine slaves at one stage or another, besides thirty-eight servants, both male and female. Mirkhond, the Prophet's fifteenth-century biographer, names them all in his *Rauzat-us-Safa*. The fact is that slavery, tribute, and booty became the main props of the new Arab aristocracy. Slaves continued to suffer under the same old disabilities. They were the property of their master (*saiyid*), who could dispose of them as he liked, selling them, gifting them away, hiring them out, lending the, mortgaging them. slaves had no property rights. Whatever they acquired became the property of their masters. The master had the right to live in concubinage with his female slaves if they confessed Islam or belonged to the "People of the Book." The Quran (*Sura* 4:3, 4:24, 4:25, 23:6) permitted this. Slavery was interwoven with the islamic laws of sale, inheritance, and marriage. And though the slaves fought for their Muslim masters, they were not entitled to the spoils of war according to Muslim religious law.

Emancipation of Slaves

The emancipation of slaves was not unknown in pre-Islamic Arabia. Slaves could gain their freedom in several ways. One way, and a very common one, of course, was that they were ransomed by their relatives. Another was when a master granted his slave a free and unconditional emancipation (*'itq*). There were two other forms of emancipation: *tadbir* and *kitabah*. In the first, the master declared that on his death his slaves would be free. In the second, slaves who were not ransomed by their relatives obtained their master's permission to earn their ransom by work.

We have already seen how Hakim b. Hizam "freed one hundred slaves" even before he became a Muslim. We have also observed that it was an old custom among the Arabs of more pious disposition to will that their slaves would be freed at their death, a practice which was opposed in some cases by Muhammad because he did not want such emancipations to take place at the expense of the heirs and relatives of the masters. On the whole, however, Muhammad's response to the practice was positive, but this did not make him into a Messiah of the slaves. On the other hand, he saw the time when the meek and the lowly would inherit the earth as a portent of the approaching end of the world. "When the slave girl will give birth to her master, when the naked, barefooted would become the chiefs of the people—these are some of the signs of Doom," according to him.

To Muhammad, the freeing of a slave was an act of charity on the part of the master, not a matter of justice. In any case, a slave should not seek his emancipation by running away. "The slave who fled from his master committed an act of infidelity so long as he would not return to him," says Muhammad.

Which slaves Deserve Emancipation?

Only a believing slave deserves freedom. Someone once slapped his maid-slave in anger and then, in contrition, wanted to free her. When Muhammad was consulted, he said: "Bring her to me." She was brought. Muhammad asked her: "Where is Allah?" She replied: "He is in the heaven." Muhammad asked: "Who am I?" "Thou art the Messenger of Allah", she answered. Muhammad gave his verdict: "Grant her freedom, she is a believing woman."

Thus there is merit in freeing a slave. "A Muslim who emancipates a Muslim [slave], Allah will save from Fire every limb of his for every limb of the slave, even his private parts for his."

One could also emancipate a jointly owned slave to the extent of one's share in him. For the rest a fair price for the slave was to be fixed, and the slave "will be required to work to pay for his freedom, but must not be overburdened."

Who Inherits a Slave's Property?

Even if a slave's person was freed, any property he might

have or come to have was inherited by the emancipator. 'Aisha was ready to help a slave-girl, Barira, to purchase her freedom on the condition that "I shall have the right in your inheritance." But the owner, though ready to free her for cash money, wanted to retain the right of inheritance for himself. Muhammad gave his judgment in favor of 'Aisha: "Buy her, and emancipate her, for the right of inheritance vests with one who emancipates." Muhammad then admonished: "What has happened to the people that they lay down conditions which are not found in the Book of Allah."

Other Disabilities

A freed slave is subjected to several other disabilities. He cannot seek any new alliance, nor can be offer himself as an ally without the permission of his former owner. One "who took the freed slave as an ally without the consent of his previous master, there is upon him the curse of Allah and that of His angels and that of the whole mankind."

Slavery Has Its Own Reward

Beyond all that may be said or done, the condition of a slave is no great evil. It has its own reward. "When a slave looks to the welfare of his master and worships Allah well, he has two rewards for him."

Proper Reading for Muhammad's Descendants

We close the "Book of Marriage of Divorce" by quoting one of the very last *ahadis*. It is on a different subject but interesting. 'Ali, the Prophet's son-in-law, says: "He who thinks that we [the members of the prophet's family] read anything else besides the book of Allah and the *Sahifa* [a small book or pamphlet that was tied to the scabbard of his sword] tells a lie. This *Sahifa* contains problems pertaining to the ages of the camels and the recompense of injuries, and it also records the words of the prophet.... He who innovates or gives protection to an innovator, there is a curse of Allah and that of his angels and that of the whole humanity upon him."

BUSINESS TRANSACTIONS, INHERITANCES, GIFTS, BEQUESTS, VOWS AND OATHS

The ninth book is the "Book of Business Transaction" (*al-Buyu'*). Let us remind ourselves that Muhammad in his pre-prophetic days was a merchant, so his views on the subject should be of interest.

Speculation Forbidden

Muhammad forbids speculation. "He who buys food grains should not sell it until he has taken possession of it." During Muhammad's own lifetime, as the control of Arabia passed into his hands, his injunctions became state policy. Salim b. 'Abdullah reports: "I saw people being beaten during the lifetime of Allah's Messenger in case they bought the food grain in bulk and then sold them at that spot before taking it to their places."

Because of their speculative nature, Muhammad also disallowed "futures" transactions. He forbade "selling ahead for years and selling of fruits before they become ripe." Transactions with the help of documents (probably the *hundi* or bill of exchange system), were also made unlawful. The injunction was implemented with the help of the police. "I saw the sentinels snatching these documents from the people," reports Sulaiman.

Outbidding

Muhammad also forbade outbidding. "A person should not enter into a transaction when his brother is already making a transaction and he should not make a proposal of marriage when brother has already made a proposal except when he gives permission." He also forbade brokerage, "the selling of goods by a townsman on behalf of a man of the desert."

Contracts

Muhammad recognized the contract system. Unless otherwise laid down in the contract, "he who buys a tree after it has been fecunded, its fruits belongs to one who sells it....and he who buys a slave, his property belongs to one who sells him."

Tenancy

Muhammad also forbade the leasing of land. "He who has land should cultivate it, but if he does not find it possible, he should lend it to his Muslim brother, but he should not accept rent from him."

The Prophet as a Landlord

Several *ahadis* show that Muhammad's own business practices could be sharp. 'Abdullah, the son of 'Umar, reports that "when Khaibar had been conquered, it came under the sway of Allah, that of his Messenger and that of the Muslims." Muhammad made an agreement with the Jews of Khaibar that they could retain the date-palms and the land on the condition that they worked them with their own wealth (seeds, implements) and gave "half of the yield to Allah's Messenger." Out of this half, "Allah's Apostle got the fifth part," and the rest was "distributed." This lends credence to the common observation that those who control the funds, whether in the name of Allah or the state or the poor, are apt to spend them first on themselves.

These acquisitions enabled Muhammad to give each of his wives 100 *wasqs* (1 *wasq* = about 425 English pounds), 80 *wasqs* of dates, and 20 *wasqs* of barley per year. When 'Umar became the Khalifa he distributed the land and gave the wives of Allah's Apostle the option of taking the land or the yearly *wasqs*. Their reactions to this offer differed. 'Aisha and Hafza, two wives of the Prophet, "opted for land and water."

Improper Earnings

Muhammad also "forbade the charging of price of the dog, and earnings of a prostitute and sweets offered to a *Kahin* [soothsayer]." He said that "the worst earning is the earning of a prostitute, the price of a dog and the earning of a cupper."

Muhammad had a great dislike for dogs. He said: "It is your duty to kill the jet-black [dog] having two spots [on the eyes], for it is a devil." 'Abdullah, 'Umar's son, tells us that the Prophet "ordered to kill dogs, and he sent men to the corners of Medina that they should be killed....and we did not spare any dog that we did not kill." Later on, on representation, an exception was made in the case of dogs meant for hunting and for protecting the herds. With the exception of these dogs, anyone who kept a dog "lost two *qirat* [the name of a measure] of reward every day."

Muhammad also forbade the sale of wine, carcasses, swine, and idols. "May Allah the Exalted and Majestic destroy the Jews; when Allah forbade the use of fat of the carcass for them, they melted it, and then sold it and made use of its price."

Barter Disapproved

In some matters, the Prophet was modern. He disapproved of the barter system and in its place stood for money-exchange. The collector of the revenues from Khaibar once brought Muhammad some fine dates. Muhammad asked whether all the dates of Khaibar were of such fine quality. The collector said: "No. We got one *sa* [of fine dates] for two *sas* [of inferior dates]." Muhammad disapprovingly replied: "Don't do that; rather sell the inferior quality of dates for *dirhams* [money], and then buy the superior quality with the help of *dirhams."*

Riba

Muhammad also forbade *riba,* which includes both usury and interest. He "cursed the accepter of interest and its prayer, and one who records it, and the two witnesses"; and he said: "They are all equal."

Though he forbade interest, Muhammad himself sent Abu Bakr to the Qainuqa tribe of Medina with a message bidding them to "lend to God at good interest," using the very words of the Quran, "to lend to God a goodly loan." When they rebuffed him, their fate was sealed, and they were driven away from their homes.

Inheritances, Gifts, and Bequests

The next three books are the "Book of Inheritances" *(al-fara'id)* the "Book of Gifts" *(al-hibat),* and the "Book of Bequests" *(al-wasiyya).* In some ways, they are interrelated. The laws deriving from them are complicated, and we need not go beyond mentioning them here.

Gifts

Anything given as a gift or charity should not be taken back. 'Umar had donated a horse in the Path of Allah (i.e., for *jihad).* He found that the horse was languishing in the hands of the recipient, who was very poor, and considered buying it back. "Don't buy it back... for he who gets back the charity is like a dog which swallows its vomit," Muhammad told him.

Waqf

Muhammad favored *waaf,* i.e., the dedication of the corpus of a property of Allah. 'Umar told Muhammad: "I have acquired land in Khaibar [the land of the defeated Jews, which had now been conferred on the Companions]. I have never acquired property more valuable for me than this, so what do you command me to do with it? Thereupon, Allah's Apostle said: If you like, you may keep the corpus intact and give its produce as *sadaqa...* 'Umar devoted it to the poor, to the nearest kin, and to the emancipation of slaves, and in the *way of Allah* and guests."

Two Thirds for Legal Heirs

The estate of a deceased person can be distributed after certain obligations, such as funeral expenses and debts incurred by the deceased, have been met. A person who professes a religion other than Islam cannot inherit anything from a Muslim, and vice versa. Another principle of inheritance is that "the male is equal of the portion of two females."

Muhammad says that one can will only one-third of one's property; the remaining two-thirds must go to the legal heirs. Muhammad visited Sa'd b. Abi Waqqas, on his deathbed. Sa'd had only one daughter. He wanted to know whether he could will two-thirds or half of his property in *sadaqa* (charity). The Prophet replied: "Give one third, and that is quite enough. To leave your heirs rich is better than to leave them poor, begging from people."

Debts

Muhammad was scrupulous about the debts of the deceased. That was the first charge on the property of a deceased person after the funeral expenses. In cases where the property was not sufficient to meet the debt obligations, money was raised through contributions. But when Muhammad became rich through conquest, he himself met these changes. "When Allah opened the gateways of victory for him, he said: 'I am nearer to the believers than themselves, so if anyone dies leaving a debt, its payment is my responsibility, and if anyone leaves a property it goes to his heirs.'"

Muhammad's Last Will

On a certain Thursday when his illness took a serious turn, Muhammad said: "I make a will about three things: Turn out the polytheists from the territory of Arabia; show hospitality to the foreign delegations as I used to do." The third the narrator forgot.

Muhammad also wanted to write a will in his last moments. "Come, I may write for you a document; you would not go astray after that," he said, asking for writing materials. But 'Umar, who was present, said that the people already had the Quran. "The Book of Allah is sufficient for us," he asserted, and thus it was unnecessary to tax Muhammad in his critical state. When those who were gathered around his bed then began to argue among themselves, Muhammad told them to "get up and go away."

'Umar might have been moved by genuine concern for the dying man, but the supporters of 'Ali later claimed that Muhammad in his last will had wanted to appoint 'Ali as his successor, and that 'Umar, in league with Abu Bakr, had prevented him from doing so by a dirty trick.

Vows and Oaths

The twelfth and thirteenth books, on vows *(al-nazar)* and oaths *(al-aiman)*, respectively, can be treated together. Muhammad discourages taking vows, for a vow "neither hastens anything nor defers anything." Allah has no need of a man's vows. A man once took a vow to walk on foot to the Ka'ba, but Muhammad said that

"Allah is indifferent to his inflicting upon himself chastisement," and "commanded him to ride."

Muhammad also forbids believers to swear by Lat or 'Uzza or by their fathers. "Do not swear by idols, nor by your father," says Muhammad. But he allows you to swear by God, something which Jesus forbade. "He who has to take an oath, he must take it by Allah or keep quiet," Muhammad says.

Abrogation of An Oath

Allah Himself allowed abrogation of oaths if need be. "God has already ordained for you the dissolution of your oaths" (Quran 66:2).

A vow which is in disobedience to Allah or which is taken for un-Islamic ends is not to be fulfilled. Muslim jurists differ as to whether a vow taken during the days of ignorance (i.e., before one embraces Islam) is binding or not. Some hold that such a vow should be fulfilled if it is not against the teachings of Islam.

An oath can be broken, particularly if the oath-taker finds something better to do. "He who took an oath, but he found something else better than that, should do that which is better and break his oath," says Muhammad. Some people once asked Muhammad to provide them with mounts. Muhammad swore: "By Allah, I cannot provide you a mount." But immediately after they were gone, he called them back and offered them camels to ride. Muhammad explained: "So far as I am concerned, by Allah, if he so wills, I would not swear, but if later on, I would see better than it, I would break the vow and expiate it and do that which is better."

The "God Willing" Clause

If one includes the proviso "God willing" *(Insha Allah)* when taking an oath, the vow must be fulfilled. Sulaiman (Solomon) had sixty wives. One day he said, "I will certainly have intercourse with them during the night and everyone will give birth to a male child who will all be horsemen and fight in the *cause of Allah."*

But only one of them became pregnant, and she gave birth to a premature child. "But if he had said *Insha' Allah* he would have not failed," observes Muhammad. In other *ahadis* about the same story, the number of wives increases from sixty to seventy and then to ninety.

6

Islam and Modernization

Modernity, like many other concepts, is a social phenomenon, an analytical instrument to describe and analyse social reality, and also a norm and an ideology by which, reality as such as valued and judged, Modernity is, therefore, treated here at three different levels of its validity: modernity as an analytical instrument, as a social fact, and as an ideology.

Modernity as an analytical instrument is one of such concepts as are used to organize knowledge about society. It is an effective tool to distinguish one class of phenomena from another. It is employed however more in the field of social change. Modernity minus the concept of that social dynamique is an empty word. The theoretical validity of the modern as an analytical instrument largely rests upon its efficacy to organize and deepen our knowledge of social change. Let us remember that, in this context, modernity is not looked upon as an ideology but merely as a concept, as an intellectual tool to generalize and bring order to our awareness of change in society.

What then is the connotation of the concept of modernity as an analytical instrument? What does it imply when it is conceived without any of its ideological associations? It is based on certain facts of social change. The facts of change as such are of two different but inter-related orders. The first order of facts of change consists of highly general and basic condition: speed (an increasing degree of mobility of men, objects, information, knowledge, interests), convergence (global interdependence in economy, politics, and war; international co-operation, tension, and conflict; cross-cultural, inter-epoch, and interpersonal contact, association, and dynamique of interaction), and involvement (co-operation for peace and engagement for war; involvement of the individual man in the total and the plural culture of man). The second order of facts of change refers to the type and the mode of organization through science and technology. The latter, among other things, brings about concentrated masses of mankind, and alienated communities and individuals.

Modernity as an analytical instrument implies thereby five major kinds of phenomena: speed, convergence, involvement, collectivization, and alienation. Modernity from the point of view of this analysis, is a totality of these facts. It is at this level that the two spheres of the validity of the concept of the modern, namely, modernity as an analytical instrument and as a social fact, converge and support one another. This satisfies the scientific postulate that the analytical instrument should be an abstraction and a generalization of the facts it is called upon to analyse.

If modernity is made to imply something different from the facts of social change, it will turn into an ideology, and after this it will cease to operate as an analytical tool. It is not uncommon that a purely intellectual tool turns into an ideology, and a school of thought, a system and a dogma. This has been the fate of certain well-known intellectual tools : the sceptical and the rational, the materialistic and the idealistic, the metaphysical and the positive. The scholastic and the idealistic, the metaphysical and the positive, the scholastic and the empirical, the speculative and the scientific, and the secular and the sacred, which have been just the intellectual tools and conceptual points of departure, ultimately turned into dogmatically held systems and ideologies. The same fate is, probably, in store for the concept of modernity; it too is becoming an ideology and a system. Let us turn to the analysis of this phase of the concept.

How does it come about that a purely intellectual tool turns into an ideology and a dogma? In other words, how does an instrument of work become an object of worship? The situation is perhaps similar to the primitive practice of totemizing the objects to which the tribe owes its survival and continuity. In the sphere of the natural sciences, one rarely comes across any such situation. With the natural scientist, concepts remain concepts, theories always remain theories. But the situation is exactly reverse with the philosopher and the social scientist. They either consciously or unconsciously settle down to regard a purely conceptual tool as an object of ideological and sentimental devotion. This is perhaps due to the dubious character of the philosophic and the sociological terminology, or it owes its origin to the concern on the part of the social philosopher more for explaining than understanding social reality. Sometimes, the existential significance of each conceptual point of view or the ontological implications involved in the use of the concepts in the field of culture and civilization turn intellectual tools into ideological objects. Apart from the terminological, the valuational, the existential, and the ontological factors that turn a concept into an ideology, there is another factor, which, in case of modernity, is far more pronounced. This additional factor is the predominant cultural form that is obtainable at a given stage in the history of society. The predominant cultural form is one which possesses the following characters : (1) it is irreversible in some of its components (say the technological culture based upon the manipulation of power of the steam, the petroleum, the electricity, and the atomic energy cannot be wheeled back); (2) it tends to affect all areas of civilization, its arts, its politics, economy and culture; (3) it turns all other cultural forms into defensive and apologetic positions; (4) it idolizes its agents and spear-heads, and creates its own myth and legend; and (5) it makes the age intellectually blind to the possibility and the validity of any other cultural form.

Modernity in its ideological content is one such predominant cultural form of our contemporary times. What does then modernity as an ideological value imply? We answer this question in three different ways: ideological, institutional, and utilitarian.

The purely ideological content of modernity consists of certain broad metaphysical and sociological interpretations of reality. They are materialism, positivism, empiricism, sciencism, secularism, pragmaticism, sociologism, humanism, individualism and existentialism.

The institutional content of modernity lies in secular polity, social justice, democracy, liberal education, and freedom, of thought and expression.

The utilitarian concept of modernity is something which is altogether different from the foregoing contents, namely, the ideological and the institutional. It was in fact Wilfred Cantwell Smith who first gave this kind of interpretation of the concept of modernity. Mr. Smith considers modernity as such form of behaviour and action as correspond to, and fall in line with, the existing body of the human knowledge. Modernity, in short, lies in utilization. To elaborate, Mr. Smith's thesis does not lie only in using this knowledge to control and transform the physical and the material environment but also to redesign and reorganize social institutions, and also to reconstruct the human outlook in correspondence with the existing knowledge as such. Mr. Smith's definition is one of the least ideological definitions of modernity. It does not inject into the definition any of the systems or the ideologies that accompany the concept in the contemporary mind. It is, therefore, indifferent to the type and the kind of knowledge as obtainable at a given moment of history. He is interested only in bringing about correspondence between knowledge and behaviour. But the definition, in spite of its objective character, is not free from certain ambiguities. These ambiguities lie around the concept of knowledge. Let us describe what these ambiguities are.

Let us first take into account the technological knowledge, the knowledge of inventing, making, reproducing, and improving upon the mechanized instruments. It is so because it does not say anything beyond itself. It is silent upon the issues of the meaning and the purpose, the value and the destiny of man and of humanity at large. In one word, technology is ideological. Technology, in itself, is neutral to the motivations of its use: it can be used with equal efficacy to bring about to sustain a theological social order or a secular dictatorship, a democracy or a totalitarian state. Even the physical technologies. They leave no choice with men. Modernity, in this most reactionary forces in society which are supposedly considered as anti-change, do not obstruct technology but see in it an opportunity to mobilize opinion, and accelerate the growth of their power. Moreover, there is an inevitability and an irreversibility about the context, has an inevitable and irreversible character. Modern technology, for that matter, is not a question of nay decisions. It is already and environment for the contemporary man. It is not something external and exclusive to which behaviour should conform. It is already an integral part of the contemporary behaviour.

What is more important than the technological knowledge is the other set of the forms of human knowledge, e.g. science, philosophy, and sociology. If Mr. Smith thinks that modernity consists of behaviour in correspondence with what science, philosophy and sociology say at a given moment of history, he is demanding something which is best with myriad confusions.

The physical sciences not only discover the real nature of the physical universe but, by implication, say something potentially important about makes being and purpose of his existence In one word, science does make certain metaphysical statements. It does not make these statements overtly. But it does symbolise an outlook and an attitude. According to Mr. Smith's point of view, modernity will consist of behaving in correspondence with what science thus covertly says about the reality of man. This is the exact point at which Mr. Smith's definition of the concept of modernity suffers from ambiguity. Let us illustrate. To repeat, we are not concerned here with what science does; we are more concerned with what it says, and that too covertly. If science says that the only world is the world of matter or of phenomena, and that the methods it employs are the only right methods to have knowledge, and that everything else is either superstition or perverted imagination, and if the psychological and the sociological science, following suit, raise their mansions of research and theorization upon such an uncompromising materialism and such a dogmatic sciencism as the sum total of the available knowledge to which the human behaviour should conform in order to have the title to modernity. Everything else that enlarges the universe by adding to it a non-material dimension, and adds to the methods of science such instruments of knowledge as the artist and the poet, the philosopher and the prophet, have at their disposal, will turn out to be not at all modern, and, in the light of Mr. Smith's definition, will be wrong, backward and conservative. Hence, the definition or modernity as utilization of the existing knowledge to organize behaviour is not as objective as it seems at the surface.

In an exactly similar manner, the human sciences not only describe the human reality, the psycho-special complex, but also imply, at times, too overtly a particular philosophy of life and man. It is usually materialistic, positivistic, evolutionistic, sociologistic, psychologistic, and relativistic. The modern sciences of man have a definitely set attitude and outlook on fundamental questions : they regard the material as final, write off metaphysics from the realm of knowledge, and consider the human as an outcome of the interplay of the blind forces of the physical and biological environment; they present culture and civilization as group determinant stressing the category of the group as the source of all being and becoming, account for man's personality only in terms of certain psychological forces within him denying him thereby any spiritual selfhood, and ultimately limit and narrow down the whole being of man. Thus, the human sciences of today refuse to grant man the validity of universal being, of universal meaning and purpose. If we follow postulate of modernity as behaviour in accordance with the knowledge of our times, we consequently reach the dead-end at which the very being of man is denied and overthrown. Modernity as an ideology rests therefore on a very dubious and a limited concept of man.

The reason why Wilfred Cantwell Smith lays so much stress upon the category of the contemporary knowledge as a criterion of modernity is perhaps his commitment to the Western concept of knowledge. Mr. Smith's approach to modernity is organically inseparable from the concept of knowledge as held by the contemporary Western mind. This is the crux of the whole question.

We were so far occupied with analysis of the entire position of modernity on its own merits. We had accepted the category of the contemporary knowledge, and were all the time concerned with how it works out in ultimate analysis. We have already discovered that it finally ends in the very denial of man. But the key to the entire question lay somewhere else. It was with the very concept of the Western knowledge. We shall briefly refer to this here, as we shall take it into account again in more detail when we shall contrast it with the Islamic concept of knowledge under Section 2 of this chapter.

For the Western mind knowledge is a dynamic category: it grows it changes, it is progressive, it is reorganized from time to time. Knowledge is cumulative. For each new discovery in a given discipline the entire knowledge in that discipline has to serve as a background and a basis. There is a history of the Western knowledge. Its history is bound with the history of the development of the technical aids, the symbolic tools, the operative models, and institutional facilities that a given society evolves progressively. This cumulative and the historical nature of the Western knowledge is of great consequence in matters of culture. It places man in a negative relationship with his cultural heritage. Past civilizations, prophets and seers, religion and literature are rejected as based on ignorance, superstition, and fantasy. Evolutionism which is more a method to describe the relationship between the biological forms and their environement is sweepingly applied to all fields of culture and civilization, philosophy, arts, morals and religion. Marxism which is organically related to the Western civilization goes one step further and tends to describe everything under the sun in terms of mono-causal factors like class struggle. The Western concept of knowledge is thereby a negation of the cultural heritage. It tends to operate in a cultural and a moral vacuum. Modernity, in terms of such a concept of knowledge, compels one to take certain impossible positions. It ultimately ends in nihilism.

Before, we turn to Islam and consider how it is related to modernity as conceived in the foregoing statements, let us sum up what has been stated hitherto.

This chapter proposes not to regard modernity as a simple and a monolithic concept but as a complex and multi-dimensional category. We have, therefore, treated modernity at two chief stages of its validity: modernity as an analytical instrument, and modernity as an ideology. As an anlytical instrument it is based on certain facts of social change. They are speed convergence involvement, collectivization, and alienation. Modernity, at it analytical level is a totality of these facts of change, and as such is a challenge of very vast proportions. Man is called upon to answer this challenge with the entirety of his being. Secondly, modernity as an ideology is composed of that following factors and points of view:

(a) The basic ideological content: materialism, positivism, sciencism, secularism, pragmaticism, sociologism, relativism, humanism, individualism, impressionism, and existentialism;
(b) The institutional content; secular polity, social justice, social welfare, democracy, liberal education, and freedom of thought and expression;
(c) Wilfred Cantwell Smith's concept of modernity as behaviour based on correspondence with, and utilization of, the existing knowledge;
(d) The Western Concept of knowledge as cumulative and historical.

Modernity as an ideology can be considered as the predominant cultural form of our age, and its relationship with any other ideology, e.g. Islam, is relative in terms of whether they converge or diverge in meeting the challenge of the facts of social change.

Islam, like any other religion, can be studied from three points of view: metaphysical, institutional, and historical. The metaphysical involves its conception of truth, its outlook upon the universe and its definition of man's being and his ultimate destiny. The institutional content involves the modes of organization of the conduct of the believer and of the community of believers by creation of appropriate forms of prayer, ceremony, ritual, law, morals, and authority. The historical refers to the changes the aforesaid contents of religion undergo. The historical is always a challenge to the metaphysical and the institutional content of religion.

Religion, or any ideology for that matter, meets the challenge of history in one of the following models: confrontation, transcendence, withdrawal, apology, and chauvinism. History, on its part, encounters religion in one or all of the following modes: politicization, philosophization, fragmentation, communalization, secularization, and ethnicism. History as a political agent affects religion by shifting its preoccupation with eternal truth to concern for organization and distribution of the temporal and the worldly power. History, as a fragmention agent, destroys the unity of faith and the community of a given religion by installing political and theological controversies ultimately solidifying in sects and castes. History as a philosophizing agent, submits the divine and the revealed, the given and the complete truth as espoused by religions to the authority of the human and the empirical religion thus turning the articles of faith into philosophical propositions. History, as a communalizing agent, turns the universal message of religions into exclusive and isolated points of view posed by one community or another. History, as a culturalizing agent, affects religions much more deeply: each religion starting with a categorically a cultural outlook upon man (converned only with the most general and basic conditions of being) ultimately becomes, in the hands of history, a neat and rounded packet of customs and traditions, memories and legends, symbols and rituals. History, capitalizing over man involvement in his immediate material environment, secularizes his outlook either by limiting the role of religion in his life or totally overthrowing it altogether. All these process are accelerated by the operation of the ethnic and the racial, the linguistic and the tribal, forces that corrode a given religious community from within. All religions of today, thus politicized and fragmented, meet the challenge of the facts of social change either through apology or chauvinism. They perhaps lack the adequate potentiality either to confront the modern challenge or transcend it. Islam, in the hands of its present-day adherents, is no exception to this.

Let us examine the position of Islam in relation to this challenge.

Islam And Science

Science, as already stated, says two different things at one and the same time: it offers an objective account of Nature, and also suggests a particular metaphysical outlook. The former, we call the factual content of science, and the latter, the ideological content. Islam has no quarrel with the factual content of science. Neither Islamic metaphysics nor its theology is bound up with any particular description of the physical universe. Islam is unlike the medieval Christianity that had persecuted people like Copernicus and Galileo who had offered a totally different account of the solar system, different from the official conception of the Church. Islam never had any such official conceptions about the behaviour of the physical forces and bodies. Islam in no way obstructs the development of knowledge. *Quran* clearly invites man to ponder over the mysteries of Nature, and declares that the world has been subjugated to man for which he should be grateful. *Quran* thus liberates man from his ancient slavery to the physical environment and paves the way for the development of science. But Islam does not achieve this freedom of man through philosophic instruments or by creating ideal social institutions as it was the case with the ancient Greek civilization of Aristotle and Plato. Islam obtains human freedom by fostering a new relationship, the relationship of submission to one God who is the Creator of the heavens and of the earth, of man and of races of men, who is the Disperser and the Gatherer and nations, and who is the Guardian of not one clan or tribe or race of region but of all mankind. This was freedom from bondage of man to man, of man to his ancestors, and of men to a particular clan or race. It was freedom from fear of the physical forces which the primitive and the ancient cultures had idolized in their religious beliefs. It was freedom from fear of kings and armies, of all forms of temporal and worldly power. It was freedom from fear and superstition which Islam regards as the heritage of the days of ignorance. A system incorporation such a tremendous amount of freedom cannot possibly prevent man from exploring the world. But let us remember that the only limit Islam sets to this immense freedom of man is his submission to God. If science, by its ideological content, pushes man to trespass this very limit, Islam is totally and categorically opposed to science. Science, if it remains within its proper epistemological limits, will avoid any ideological commitments and will go to the extent of just suggesting an agnostic attitude towards the questions of religion. But if science proceeds beyond this limit and suggests overtly or covertly that the world as it is given is the only world and there is nothing beyond or besides, it will be making a highly unwarranted statement. For Islam it will amount to *Kufr* (denial of God, or ungratefulness to God).

As far as the scientific method is concerned, Islam has the same attitude it has got towards science in general. Islam appreciates the scientific method when it is made to operate in its field proper, namely, the study of the phenomenal world. But if it is applied to all levels of reality with a conviction that it alone is the right method, Islam is totally opposed to this; for Islam rests on a completely different instrument of knowledge, namely, the divine revelation. The confusion is confounded when the apologetic advocated of religion borrow the methodology of science to validate their stands, and thus bring about their own defeat: they start to reinstate religion in terms of science, and ultimately surrender the former in favour of the scientific standpoints and conceptual categories. They are ignorant that to accept the scientific method, in the field of religion, is to submit to the Western concept of knowledge to which Islam is categorically opposed. We shall return to this later.

Islam and Social Science

Social sciences, as already stated under part one, not only give an account of man in relation to society but also have a particular philosophic outlook which is based on an arbitrary combination of materialism. evolutionism, positivism, sociologism, and psychologism. We have already noted that such a philosophy refuses to grant man the validity of a universal being, of a universal meaning and purpose. Islam, by virtue of its own concept of man and life, cannot possibly assimilate social science as far as its ideological bases are concerned.

But Islam is more concerned with the modern philosophy of history. Islam within the framework of its system, has its own outlook on the rise and the fall of civilizations. *Quran* pictures the ruins of the bygone civilization and asks us to remember what fate was meted out to people who had falsified their being and had committed the fatal error of regarding the world, its pleasures and possessions, as final and as everlasting. It was Maulana Azad who was the first scholar to bring together archeology, social history, and philosophy of history and *Quran* ; when he substantiated the Quranic passages pertaining the past civilizations in his illustrious *Tarjumanu' l-Qur' an*. Azad retains the sharpness of the Islamic pointer that civilizations decline and die out not because the conditions of their physical and social survival were drastically altered for them but because they had wrought a false relationship with the world as such, and brought unto themselves thereby incalculable harm and final destruction. Islam has the same note of warning for the contemporary civilization as well.

Islam and Modern Technology

In the light of the foregoing analysis, Islam has no quarrel with the factual knowledge of science, and hence Islam should not have any quarrel with modern technology for the latter is after all only an application and an utilization of the factual knowledge. But the matter is not so simple. Modern technology is not a particular and an exclusive instrument of action or communication. It is an environment for the contemporary man, continuous and coefficient with his life and personality.

This chapter refuses to accept as valid the usual approach, in such matters, of contrasting Islam with each of the modern technological devices, say, the radio, the television, or the movies. What perhaps is missed in such approaches is that technology is a total and an indivisible condition. The real question is what relation Islam could have with such an all-inclusive condition as modern technology is.

Islam and Technology as Environment

We are accstomed to regard technology as an exclusive system, an external instrumentality, separate from our being and person. We have not yet become fully aware that technology, in the electric and the atomic age, has become all-inclusive, has turned into an internal relation, and is an organic part of our being. The dichotomy of the means and the ends has just disappeared. The duality of the medium and the content is just wiped out. The means is the end. The medium is the message. This is enormously true of the modern modes of communication and transport. As it is impossible to conceive our bodily aids and instruments of information and communication ; e.g. the eye and the ear ; separate from our physical and psychic self, similarly, and even more so, it is impossible now to draw a line between the modern man and his technology of communication. There is no such thing now as medium and content. The medium itself creates its own content. Meaning is not something external to the medium in which it is communicated. Take the radio. It is insignificant what it says. What is more important is that the radio creates a new environment. Its environment is its message. It demolishes the spatial walls, and turns the immediate surroundings as unreal and fantastic. It creates a new audience, the invisible crowd. It turns the ordinary sounds into a world of fetishes. A highly charged environment of sound is brought to bear upon one's being and self. This was very well exploited by Adolf Hitler. For him the microphone and the radio were the instruments of power. Modern empires exist in the technology of communication. The nineteenth century was a century of the fruition of the culture of the press, of the written word. The twentieth century is a century of the spoken word, of jazz, of bangs around the earth. It strangely resembles the ancient times: the spoken work is reborn and with it the story-telling, the myth-making, the primitivism and the savagery. It was for this reason that Macluhan would call the radio a tribal drum. Add to all this the factor of speed of instantaneity, of immediacy. Pure circulation of men, objects, and information comes about. Man turns a machine, victim of his own media. He loses awareness.

The challenge of the new environment is of such proportions that all our philosophic and ideological tools that were designed in the warehouses to the eighteenth and the nineteenth centuries; rationalism, pragmatism, marxism etc., prove totally inadequate. The reason is quite obvious : these tools rest on the assumptions that the means are different from the ends, the media are separate from the content, and man and his environment are two distinct realities. But the modern technology has totally affected these distinctions. Modernity in its ideological content, is no match for the facts of social change, for the new technology of man. Can Islam take up the challenge?

The question requires to state the difference between the secular and the religious ideologies in their techniques of meeting a given challenge. The secular ideologies meet the social challenge by reorganizing social institutions. They operate within the social environment. They never transcend it. The case is totally different with the religious technique of meeting a similar challenge: it liberates man from his environment, and helps him transcend it. Islam never allows man to be totally subdued by his environment. Islam proposes to transcend the environment, and by transcending one can become conscious of it. To become conscious is to regain self-control and be free. The new technological environment takes away this very consciousness, and thus brings about a new form of slavery and bondage of which man remains unaware. Only a potentially valid ideology which can restore freedom and consciousness can meet the challenge of the modern times. Islam is one of such ideologies. It continues to exist in history as a critique of history, of man, of his environment. Only it is this function of Islam that brings to it a validity and a relevance that it does not possess, in such a degree, on any other score. Islam as a creed of a given population of the world, as a state religion of one country or another, as a community or a political function, has no relevance, and no future in the modern world. Its validity lies in being a critique and a transvaluation. It judges its own community in the same manner as it judges other civilizations. If the Muslims falsify their true being, the same fate will be meted out to them as was the case with other people in the bygone days. *Quran* repeatedly admonishes: travel in the land, and see what fate was meted out to people who lied.

Before we conclude this paper let us touch upon the Western concept of knowledge that has remained vague so far. The basic form of knowledge which the West embraces, is not shared by islam. It is not only the matter of the West and Islam. It is the confrontation of the Orient with the Occidental. The West takes knowledge as progressively related to history: it is only through trial and error, through the cumulative advance, that knowledge is had. But for Islam knowledge is already there, it is not cumulative. It has been given to every nation and civilization from time to time. What happens is that man either accepts on or rejects this knowledge and thereby chooses for himself or another ultimate fate. But the Western knowledge has no such consequences for the being of man. It will have consequences for society and state, culture and civilization but not for the individual person. Knowledge for Islam is realization of one's true being, of God and of the fact that the world as given is not final and conclusive. We cannot at length the Islamic concept of knowledge for it requires a separate altogether. But what we are concerned with at the moment is that Islam with its concept of truth is totally opposed to modernity as far as the latter shares the Western conception of knowledge. The latter fragmentation and denies the true being of man. Islam attempts at its restoration. The future of Islam lies in achieving this validity for the human self.

Modernism and Traditionalism in the sense of basic life attitudes are universal concepts. Every religion in every age has its modernists and traditionalists. In this paper, however, I propose (a) to elucidate the contemporary western meaning of modernity and traditionalism in the sphere of religion and then show how far this conception of religious modernity applies to Islamic modernism and traditonalism; (b) in the place of the 2-dimensional modernist-traditionalist framework suggest a multi-dimensional framework for accommodating the different religious approaches found in contemporary Islam; (c) elucidate the relationship between traditionalism and modernism in general with special reference to Islam.

The word 'modernism' was first used to describe certain

tendencies in late 19th Century Protestant Christianity. Ever since then considerable progress has been made in the philosophy, sociology and semantics of religion. Thus, modernity in religion now signifies something more than modernism in the original Christian sense, namely : (a) emphasis on rationalism and the scientific method, (b) abjuration of dogma and supernaturalism, (c) higher criticism of the Bible. Religious modernity in the contemporary sense is a development of the above line of thinking.

The Essential Features of Religious Modernity

The following points constitute its essential features:

(1) Stress on the fully integrated human personality as distinguished from a fragmented or compartmentalized one. This integration takes into account all the dimensions of human experience like reason, feeling, morality, etc. without suppressing any basic existential or personality need.

(2) Distinction between religious experience and its conceptual interpretation.

(3) Distinction between the essential core and the concrete gestalt of a religion.

(4) Distinction between salvation in the sense of continuous spiritual growth and in the sense of the 'saving' of souls in life after death.

(5) Distinction between intrinsic and instrumental values.

(6) Stress on the cultivation of basic spirituality rather than any one of its diverse forms as represented by particular religions.

(7) Emphasis on spiritual autonomy and the reconciliation of any possible conflict with religious authority.

(8) Emphasis on ceaseless creativity of values and extra dimensional progress as distinguished from the conservation of values and intra-dimensional progress. In other words, the stress is on creative fidelity rather than mechanical conformity to the past.

The above-mentioned eight points sum up the essential features of religious modernity in the West and are more or less self-explanatory. I shall however, comment on the first three points which are foundational:

(1) The concept of the dimensional integration of personality is a much more inclusive and richer concept than of rationalism. Full integration includes the cultivation of reason but is not reducible to it. The hall-mark of 19th century religious modernity in the West was rationalism, which was a legacy of the previous age of reason and enlightenment in Europe. But this mono-dimensional approach has given way to a multi-dimensional approach.

(2) The second basic feature of religious modernity, is the distinction between religious experience and its conceptual interpretation. This distinction applies to all forms of human experience and not merely the religious. Religious modernity emphasises the significance and role of both experience and interpretation in the religious sphere. But it insists that the two should not be confused as is actually the case with most popular conceptions of different religions. Religious experience is *sui-generis* and cannot be reduced without remainder to other forms of experience like the aesthetic, the moral and the logical etc. Hence, religious modernity is not synonymous with pure ethecism or humanism, which are attempts to reduce religion to the purely ethical dimensions of human experience. Religious modernity does not accept humanism or ethical religion as full adequate, because of their reductionist approach to the purely religious dimension of human experience. Man's growth remains incomplete without the flowering of his potential spirituality or spiritual sense as distinguished from his moral potentiality or moral sense. The distinction between the spiritual and the moral sense is analogous to the distinction between the moral and the aesthetic sense. The quest for the existential interpretation of man's experience is a deeply engrained human personality need. Like religious experience, this quest is also *sui-generis* and different from the quest of scientific explanation.

Mere descriptive knowledge and scientific explanation do not fully satisfy man's yearning for an existential interpretation or significance of the human situation within the total cosmic context. This interpretation, however, is a distinct activity from the original and primary religious experience of man as such. Most religious persons do not make any distinction between religious experience and its interpretation. Consequently, they suppose that the denial of their particular interpretation amounts to a denial of the experience as such. Moreover, they are not aware of the essential relativity of all interpretation to socio-cultural space-time. In other words the popular traditionalist believers of different religions remain unaware of : (a) the distinction between experience and interpretation, (b) the organic connection of the interpretation with the socio-cultural conditions and the inherited conceptual framework of the society in which a particular religion grows.

The systematic conceptual interpretation of religious experience is essential and indispensable. The supposed self-sufficiency of mere morality or even religious experience is a romantic illusion born of difficulties or rather man's despair at arriving at a final and universally acceptable conceptual interpretation of the human situation.

Sober religious modernists in the West like Whitehead, Bergson, Hocking Tillich, Niebuhr, Marcel and Buber etc. thus do not reject a metaphysical or philosophical theology, as superfluous, but attempt to reconstruct the basic religious concepts of the Christian or Jewish tradition.

(3) The third foundational feature of religious modernity concerns the distinction between the essential core and the concrete gestalt of a religion. This distinction has been suggested and developed as a result of the growth of sociology of religion on the one hand, and the phenomenology of religion on the other. The sociology of religion shows that all religious traditions have socio-economic determinants as well as dimensions. The phenomenology of religion, on the other hand, draws our attention to the nature of the essential

core of the total religious gestalt. This core consists of a thought-cum-value system in organic interaction with the general conceptual framework prevalent in the parent society in which the religion originates. This thought system is the same as the conceptual interpretation mentioned above.

The value system underlies concrete rules, regulations and precepts of a particular religion and should not be equated with these concrete rules etc. The thought system and the value system jointly entail the precept system of a particular religion and give meaning to its symbolic life. The concrete gestalt of a religion, on the other hand, is influenced by the concrete conceptual and social soil in which the religion grows. The concrete personality or gestalt of different religions, however, includes a system of institutions over and above the thought-cum-value system, even as a living organism has secondary qualities distinct from its essential attributes.

The practical significance of this apparently academic distinction is crucial. Once this distinction is conceptually registered, we are at once liberated, as it were, from an emotional fixation upon a particular cultural gestalt whether Islamic, Christian or Hindu. The confusion between the pure essence and the accidents of its concrete exemplification in social space time is removed. The 'Idea of Islam' in the Platonic sense generates both conceptual space and an inner freedom of movement without thereby repudiating Islam. The possibility of conflict between loyalty to the past and aspirations for the future is reconciled. As a member of the kingdom of ceaseless growth, man is liberated from enslavement to the past as distinguished from a creative fidelity to his religious tradition.

The foregoing analysis of Western religious modernity should also throw into relief the profile of its contrary, i.e., religious traditionalism. But the difference between the two is a matter of degrees, rather than of kind, at least as far as Protestant Christianity is concerned. Consequently, the concepts of religious modernity are not total absent from the traditionalist frame of reference, but are only much less emphasised.

Some Features of Islamic Modernism

Let us see to what extent the foregoing account of religious modernity applies to Islam. For obvious reasons I shall concentrate on the Indian scene.

All Islamic modernists accept in varying degrees the first three foundational points of Western religious modernity. But in general they are much more cautious and conservative than their Western counterparts, whatever the reason may be.

All Islamic modernists have put a question mark against the traditional or popular Islamic thought system. Sir Syed's Quranic exegesis and commentary represents his attempted reconstruction in the religious thought of Islam, under the impact of Western science and rationalism. Iqbal and Azad also reconstruct the thought-cum-value system in the light of modern conditions.

The approaches of Sir Syed, Iqbal and Azad in this matter show significant differences. Sir Syed assumes, on the one hand, that the *Quran* as the word of God, could not contain any error and, on the other, he also holds the scientific propositions of his time as indisputable. Consequently, he tried to reconcile any apparent conflict between the two as best as he could. Iqbal and Azad, on the other hand, were never bothered by any such problem, since they held the *Quran* to be primarily an inspirational document rather than a text book of physics or geography. The portions of the *Quran* dealing with facts of nature deliberately presupposed the scientific frame of reference prevalent in the age of revelation. Any deviation from that framework would have baffled and mystified the people concerned, instead of helping them in their religious quest. The spheres of revelation and of scientific knowledge being different, no clash arises between the two. The *Quran* is the infallible source of value judgments and the fount of wisdom, while the scientific method is the source of all factual judgments and the laws of nature. the later modernists like Sindhi and others accept Azad's standpoint.

Valuable and ambitious as these reconstructions are, they nevertheless fall short of the depth and range of the reconstructive essays of a Whitehead or a Tillich etc. Perhaps one of the reasons for this general shortcoming of Islamic modernism is the lack of pure and professional practitioners among the Islamic modernists. The modernist reconstruction of this concept at the hands of Sir Syed, Azad and even Iqbal fails to overcome the conflict or incompatibility between the claims of revelation and man's spiritual autonomy which is the basis of democracy and the sovereignty of the people. Possibly only Sindhi comes to grips with this very delicate problem. May be Waliyu'llah in the 18th century had also done so. But unfortunately my very meagre study of Waliyu'llah prevents me from being positive about it. However, the thought system of classical Muslim philosophers like Ibn Sina, Ibn Rushd etc. embraced this delicate theme of revelation. The concepts of Nous, Agent Intellect, First Intellect etc. and the grades of emanation and illumination etc. were nothing but their bold and honest attempts to construct a critical theory of revelation and its relationship with reason. In this respect these medieval Muslim thinkers are much more modernist than Islamic modernists like 'Abduh, Sir Syed, Iqbal, etc.

The main tasks that Islamic modernists have set for themselves are concerned more with a critique of the status of *Hadith* on the one hand, and on the other, with the implications of the distinction between the core and gestalt of Islam. Here their approach and achievements are creditable. Let us consider these two points separately.

All modernists concede that while *Hadith* is very important for living the good life, it is not binding in the sense in which the *Quran* is. All Islamic modernists would perhaps vacillate in their attitude, should any part of the *Quran* may contradict plain commonsense, clear observation, or one's conscience. But they would not hesitate to reject any *Hadith* that may come in this category even if it satisfied all the canons of authenticity prescribed by the science of *Hadith*.

Theoretically, the status of the word of the prophet has always been lower than that of the word of God. It is significant that for the first almost two hundred years no attention was paid to the collection and arrangement of *Hadith.* In this period Islamic jurisprudence (*Fiqh*) was the only discipline that supplemented the *Quran.* It is also significant that the school of the greatest Muslim jurist Imam Abu Hanifa (d. 767) was known as the school of reasoned opinion (*Ahlu'r-Ra'y*). But later on when the other schools of jurisprudence emerged and differences of opinion arose, the attention of scholars and theologians was naturally drawn to the possibility of using *Hadith* as a criterion of validity. It was in the period after Bukhari (d. 870) that the concept of revelation or *Wahy* was developed. This led to the distinction (in my humble opinion extremely uncalled for and invalid) between the 'open' and 'implicit' revelation (*Wahy-i-Khafi* and *Wahy-i-Jali*). Be this as it may, the logic of these theological developments is quite clear. The interpretation of *Hadith* as an implicit revelation certainly raises the status of the word of the prophet, making it barely distinguishable from the word of God. If the *Quran* was openly revealed, while the *Hadith* was implicitly revealed, then for all practical purposes, the *Quran* and the *Sunna* become the joint final authority. In other words, *Quran* and *Hadith* become the ultimate court of appeal and the infallible criterion of validity.

Bukhari and other traditionalists certainly held that in the case of an irresolvable conflict between the word of the prophet and the word of God, the latter was to prevail. But since the *Quran* confines itself to general principles, broad precepts and value judgments, numerous concrete details of *Hadith* could not possibly be judged according to the above criterion. Consequently, they tended to acquire practically the same status as the word of God. It was at this time that the doors of reinterpretation or *Ijtihad* were closed. One of the essential features of Islamic modernism is, therefore, a vigorous protest against this closure, as well as against the practical nullification of the distinction between the word of God and the word of the prophet. Different modernists may differ in their assessment of the status of *Hadith*; but they certainly agree that it cannot be accepted as infallible in the sense in which the *Quran* is infallible.

Let us now turn to the distinction between the essence and total gestalt of Islam. All Islamic modernists have attempted the task of the distillation of the pure essence of Islam.

The medieval version of Islam had a considerably strong puritanical flavour, resulting in either the prohibition or the discouragement of music, dancing, sculpture, most forms of painting etc. Islamic modernists protest against this puritanism, and opt for aesthetic liberalism. They stand for the harmonious growth of the human personality without suppressing the aesthetic impulse in man. It is significant that this approach of aesthetic liberalism is not something foreign to the *Quran.* Rather the contrary approach was foreign to the spirit of the *Quran.*

Sir syed was quite clear that dress, food and living habits, marriage customs etc. of the prophet were the accidents of time and place. Certainly, Sir Syed would not have gone to the extent of questioning the validity of social laws expressly found in the *Quran.* But he insisted that contemporary conditions be taken into account while applying Quranic laws. Sir Syed, thus, would have distinguished between eternal Islam and temporal Mohammadanism. Following this distinction, one could say that the followers of Abraham or Jesus were Muslims without being Mohammadans.

For all his liberalism, however, Sir Syed was acutely class conscious and biased in favour of the upper and middle classes. Evens the prospect of adult franchise and equality of opportunity was too heavy a democratic dose for his way of thinking.

Similarly, Iqbal criticised democracy based on the counting rather than the weighing of heads. In spite of his intellectual attainments, Iqbal's approach to social problems, particularly the position and status of women was out of tune with his dynamic approach in other spheres of life. He shrank back from the full reconstruction of the value system and institutional system of

Islam. There was some inexplicable resistance in his mind on this score. To say that his approach to the question of the status of women and other related matters, was influenced by Nietzsche, can be no justification of his stand.

Azad on the other hand, had a more liberal outlook on social matters. Perhaps this was due in large measure to his political affiliations after the first world war. But since he did not write much on such matters during the last twenty-five years of his life, it is difficult to assess the exact degree of his religious modernity.

The names of 'Ubaydu'llah Sindhi, Niyaz Fatehpuri (d. 1965) Akbarabadi, K.G. Saiyidain, Ajmal Khan, A.A.A. Fyzee, Khalifa Hakim (d. 1959) and Gulam Ahmad Parvez of Pakistan must be mentioned in this context. All the above have a very modernist approach specially Sindhi, who deserves the utmost attention.

The Limitations of Islamic Traditionalism

In view of what has already been said about Islamic Modernism, only some brief comments will be made on Islamic Traditionalism.

Contemporary Islamic traditionalists like Abu'l Hasan 'Ali an-Nadwi, Maulana Tayyib, Mawdudi and others are certainly aware of some of the distinctions and concepts that constitute the core of religious modernity. But they do not concern themselves with the implications of these concepts. The traditionalists often chide Muslims for verbally professing beliefs without understanding their implications or acting in accordance with them. It appears to me that the traditionalists are guilty of the same charge, though the concepts or beliefs may differ in the two instances. Mawdudi, for example, does make a distinction between intrinsic and instrumental values, and also between essence and gestalt, even though his conception of essence may be rather crude. Yet he totally fails to deduce their implications, or to apply them to the human situation. This is due to his views about *Hadith* and *Sunna*. He may allow a few superficial changes or modifications here and there but he is essentially fixated upon the concrete gestalt of medieval Islam. Hence the revivalistic strand in his thought, as distinguished from the traces of conservatism, found in certain aspects of Sir Syed's or Iqbal's outlook. It is a pity that in the estimation of his followers and admirers, Mawdudi, stands for dynamic Islam. Unfortunately the word dynamic is a prize or prestige word like democracy, justice, humanism, equality, etc. and hence used very loosely.

The basic limitation of all Muslim traditionalist is their rather uncritical and crude conceptual framework for dealing with religious experience, and relating it with other dimensions of human experience. Their phenomenology and sociology of religion and the conceptual tools which they habitually employ for the interpretation of religious experience, *i.e.*, their conceptions of God, revelation, creation, etc. fail to remove the intellectual difficulties or dissonances that flow from these concepts. To begin with, the traditionalists are not even aware of all the difficulties. But even when they do register these difficulties, and attempt to overcome them through the reconstruction of these concepts, their attempts lead to patch work structures and half way houses. Due to their lack of consistency and organic unity, they fail in evoking an integrated conceptual response to the mystery of man in the universe. The traditionalists are too involved with the conceptual models of the past to be able to look at them with a measure of critical detachment. Moreover, they presuppose that the slightest change in those models must inevitably destroy or weaken the value structure of Islam. Consequently, in spite of making the distinction between the core and the gestalt of Islam, they fail to see that the core itself is not static or inert like Democritus' or Dalton's atom. The core is rather like the Rutherford's atomic nucleus consisting of a charge of electricity. The implication is that no conceptual model employed by man for the interpretation of his experience can be accepted as final. But the traditionalists sit conceptually idle. Even our modernists, barring one or two are not sufficiently aware of the depth and range of modifications necessary in the tradition, in order to effect a real break-through in Muslim society. Even the basic values of Islam, like brotherhood, equality, etc. as understood in the ancient and medieval period of Islam require a thorough revision to become alive again for contemporary man exposed to the thought of Marx, Freud and

Rostov, etc. Unless this is done, many new socio-political and economic patterns are liable to be rejected straightaway by Islamic societies, even though they may be for more effective promoters of the basic intrinsic values of Islam, than the traditional patterns hallowed by time. It is, therefore, a matter of deep regret that reputed traditionalists like Abu'l-Hasan 'Al-an-Nadwi, Tayyib and others should continue to declare that it is not Islam, but the individual Muslim that stand in need of reformation or reconstruction.

Patterns of Religious Response in Islam

The two dimensional modernist-traditionalist framework though valid in its own way, fails to draw our attention to the different responses or approaches to Islam or any other religion. I have suggested an 8-dimensional framework for this purpose. This scheme can be applied to different religions at every stage of their history. But it applies primarily to the later stage of a religion, when sufficient growth has already taken place. In a sense, there is tension between modernity and traditionalism at every stage of human history. But the early period of every religion is taken up by the articulation and crystallisation of the different facets and strands of the tradition, rather than by the tension between modernity and traditionalism. The reason is that traditionalism presupposes an antecedent tradition which takes time to grow. The tension between modernity and traditionalism does not result in a simple unilinear movement either towards or away from a given tradition. There are separate cycles or spirals of modernity-traditionalism, each cycle consisting of the following stages :

(1) Felt disvalues of given tradition t_1.
(2) Articulation of protest.
(3) Growth of momentum of protest.
(4) Crystallization of new values.
(5) Inception of a new tradition t_2.
(6) Growth of the new tradition t_2.
(7) Felt disvalues of given tradition t_2.

In one sense, the process of crystallization or the formative period of Islam ended in 632 A.D. In another sense, it ended with al-Ghazzali's magnum opus. *Ihya'ul-'Ulum* (near 1100 A.D.) which attempted to combine the three major strands or impulses in Islam, after their prolonged crystallisation over a period of about 400 years. These are the impulses of rationalism, mysticism and legalism. Each of these impulses took about 150 years for its full unfolding. In yet another sense the formative period of Islam will, or at least, should last for ever. There is a very striking analogy between the above three sense of development on the one hand, and the three or four stages of human development on the other. In one sense man is complete at the moment of birth, in another sense he is complete only after the attainment of puberty, while in another and the most important sense, man is never complete, but always continues to grow.

It is, thus, about 1100 A.D. that the process of articulation of the Islamic genius was completed. At this stage the 8-point scheme becomes fully applicable. The situation remains the same ever since then with the exception of one major or rather crucial development, namely the scientific revolution of the West. The impact of science on Islam is however beyond the scope of this paper.

The following are the patterns of religious response in Islam:

1. Selective Reduction.
2. Pietist Conservation.
3. Activist Conservation.
4. Piecemeal Adjustment.
5. Transformation.
6. Substitution.
7. Agnosticism—Nihilism.
8. Cultural Emergence.

I will make extremely brief explanatory comments on the above types of religious attitudes.

(1) Selective reductionism means that the individual reduces the tradition to a few selected features of the tradition without

creating or adding any new features. In other words, he prunes the tradition. An example is 'Abdu'l-Wahhab in the 17th century.

(2) Pietist conservatism: The individual tries to conserve the tradition as it exists in his age and believes in simple piety and the sincere practice of faith without much ado about socio-political improvements in the environment. Examples are the members of the *Tablighi Jama at* in present day India.

(3) Activist Conservatism: The individual believes in not only conservation of the tradition and simple piety etc., but maintains that an active participation in socio-political movements calculated to reform society is a part of their religious duty. Examples are the members of the *Jama 'at-i-Islami.*

(4) Piecemeal adjustment: The individual is dissatisfied with some feature or features of the tradition, but hesitates to undertake any systematic and sustained thinking with a view to come to a definite conclusion. Under-pressure of circumstances however he just makes piecemeal adjustments to remove his difficulties, *e.g.,* the average Indian muslim today.

(5) Transformationism: The individual is not only highly dissatisfied with the tradition but is also skilful and gifted enough to think independently. In the process, he completely transforms the tradition. Examples are the members of the Bahai faith.

(6) Substitutionism: The individual is so much attracted by another tradition that he substitutes it entirely, in place of his original religious tradition. Examples are those Muslims who are converted to some other secular or religious faith like Christianity, Communism, etc.

(7) Agnosticism—Nihilism: The individual is utterly perplexed. Nihilism is only the ultimate stage of despair. The individual has no faith left in any system of values. Examples are the Muslim Beatniks, etc.

(8) Emergentism: The individual appreciates the elements of

value in the tradition but is dissatisfied with the elements of disvalue. But instead of merely pruning the tradition, he also believes in its creative growth. Cultural emergents combine continuity with change and thus represent the fusion of conservation and creativity. Examples are Sir Syed, Iqbal, 'Ubaydu'llah Sindhi, etc.

The Relationship Between Modernity and Traditionalism

The creation of new values and the conservation of the old that have stood the test of time are both equally necessary. In fact they depend upon each other. The creation of new values pre-supposes a valuational base or support. Similarly, the effective maintenance of this base demands awareness of the subtle changes in the nuances and rhythms of human experience. Eternal and intelligent vigilance is the price of keeping old values alive in the condition of dynamic inter-action with the environment rather than as show pieces in the museum of man's heritage.

Creativity ever spurs man to go ahead in the realm of values and to yearn for the better rather than be content with the good. The function of tradition on the other hand, is to strike a note of caution, lest the pace of change increase to the point of giving diminishing returns. The function of tradition is not the stoppage of growth but only the regulation of the speed of growth. The conservative approach thus, has its own function in the economy of human progress, provided it does not over-reach itself.

Creativity and conservation should therefore devetail into and supplement each other. Without creativity conservation leads to fossilization, while without conservation, creativity lead to irresponsible experimentation. While such adventures in the realm of art and literature may not be injurious, they could prove catastrophic in the realm of moral and social relationships. The new sex morality of Western Europe and America, according to which the game of sex may be played between any two willing parties without any mutual obligation arising therefrom, has played havoc with the spiritual growth of the contemporary western man. It appears to me that the west is gradually realizing its fallacy and that a more balanced interpretation of sex is in the process of crystallization. Similarly the limitations of different movements like nationalism, capitalism, socialism, scientism, etc. are being acknowledged. Humanity would have been spared countless tears, had the human judgment been more balanced and well informed. But man is neither a mathematician nor a fly in the fly bottle, or a rat in a maze. He is an honest evaluator who commits errors of evaluation. He blunders and pays the penalty in the course of time and gradually forges ahead.

It is precisely man's constant blundering that grips the imagination of the champions of the traditional interpretation of Divine Revelation. They constantly reiterate man's in capacity to regulate his own affairs and point out that the only way open to man is the complete submission to the word of God and the example of His Prophet. These persons are, however, not aware of the different meanings of submission to God. They accept only on conceptual model or meaning, namely the model of the dutiful son or subject submitting himself completely to the will of the authoritarian father or king who acts through his agent.

Similarly, the traditionalists do not realise that their concept of revelation is based on the conceptual model of human communication through the spoken language. This model generates its own conceptual difficulties which the traditionalists tend to ignore in the interest of preserving the integrity of their faith. This evasion of conceptual difficulties has, however, very harmful consequences, though apparently it may serve to keep the faith alive. This type of conceptual pain killing, as it were, leaves man with no intellectual motivation to explore other possible conceptual models for the interpretation of the Prophet's religious or mystical experience of which the *Quran* is the concrete product. Thus, the traditionalist Islamic approach remains unconvincing to the mind alive to the complexities of the human situation. Those individuals whose conceptual framework has kept pace with the continual developments in the natural and social sciences of the modern west have outgrown the conceptual clothes or models which appealed to medieval man whether Muslim, Hindu or Christian. These are the people who yearn for a new language and idiom for the articulation of their own authentic religious experience. It appears to me however, that the Islamic tradition is not a monolithic mausoleum but a garden where a hundred flowers have bloomed, and may still bloom. While getting depressed at the arid deserts of extreme orthodoxy and conservatism that we have to cross in the 1400 year old journey of Islam, we must not loose sight of the magnificient mountains and deep rivers that also greet and cheer the traveller. I refer to such liberal intellectuals as al-Farabi, Ibn Sina, al-Ghazali, Ibn-Rushd, Ibn Khaldun, Rumi, Ibnu'l-'Arabi, Khayyam, al-Biruni, etc. Islamic modernists or those who may reject the Islamic tradition outright, unnecessarily deprive themselves of the resources that ought to have been judiciously harnessed for cultural growth, instead of being indiscriminately spurned.

Every age must look afresh and reinterpret its heritage of concepts and values. The task of revaluation and reconstruction of the Islamic thought-cum-value system will even remain incomplete as long as man continues to grow and exercise the privilege and the duty of the ceaseless creativity of values.

In the context of Indian Islam such a fresh look by Indian Muslim intellectuals is absolutely essential for giving enlightenment and guidance to the common Muslim who stands totally baffled and perplexed by the antagonistic pulls of theocracy and democracy, clericalism and secularism, traditionalism and modernity. The average Indian Muslim is more or less a split personality and must be helped to integrate himself. There can be no doubt that the integration promises to be oriented towards modernity rather than traditionalism. Like it or not, the human family as a whole is steadily moving in this direction. The angularities and imbalances that are inevitably generated in different societies are also in the process of being corrected, although this process is bound to take a fairly long time to be completed. Different religions are at different stages of modernization, and within the same religion, different groups are likewise at different stages. Even within these groups individual differences obviously exist. But the push of science and the pull of theology are definitely working to the advantage of modernization.

The need of the age is an authentic dialogue between Islamic modernists and traditionalists. The spirit of polemics only generates mutual resistance in both the quarters helping neither the cause of modernity nor the cause of traditionalism. Unfortunately, many Muslim modernists and traditionalists have a genius for giving offence to each other through various devices. The traditionalist is prone to lament over the opportunism and disloyalty on the part of the modernist. The modernist, on the other hand, is irritated at the fixation or rather fossilization of the conservative or traditionalist mind. The way out of this unfortunate predicament lies in greater tolerance and an authentic dialogue between modernity and traditionalism. The outcome of such a dialogue, to my mind, should be the reconciliation between the two through the liberating concept of 'cultural emergents' that combine continuity with change. The effective promotion of this approach is much more difficult than the downright denunciation of modernism or traditionalism, just as, in a very important sense, living the good life is much more difficult than rejecting life through suicide.

The study of the history of other religions is very useful for a deeper insight into our own religion. It is always easier to detect the psychological defence mechanisms and motives of self-interest, etc. in the case of others than in one's own. The same applies to groups. The limitations of other religions are much more easily grasped than those of one's own. Consequently a critical sociological survey of other religions helps us in a better understanding of the stages and laws of growth of our own culture or religion, its strength and its limitations. This comparative sociology of religions tends to dissolve our natural ethnocentricity and group self-conceit. Self-conceit prompts us to treat our own religion as a class by itself, and hence exempt from sociological laws that apply only to religions other than our own. Having outgrown this natural ethnocentricity and 'group snobbery', if I may call it, we are in a much better position to appreciate the points of excellence of our own religion and its unique contribution in the economy of the human family at large. Moreover, the realization of the variegated changes wrought by time in the fabric of the religious tradition, sets our creative imagination at work. Fresh visions are stirred that make us forward-looking, and growth-oriented as distinguished from backward-looking and tradition-oriented.

Creative growth, however, implies the conservation of the values of the past. Cultural borrowing from others is one of the means of such growth. Early Islam was conspicuous for its spirit of assimilation of Greek, Iranian and Indian cultures. The cross-fertilization of intercultural concepts and values is an ever recurring world process, though it usually operates at the unconscious level. Its conscious practice, however, does not render it any the least objectionable.

Cultural assimilation need not be confused with immitation or a patch work synthesis. At its best, cultural assimilation is neither imitative nor synthetic but creative. It pre-supposes a critical evaluation of the culture of others no less than one's own. It is precisely this creative fusion that leads to 'cultural emergents.'

The basic ingredients of the different world religions are essentially the same, namely a thought-cum-value system, a precept system and an institutional system that is certainly an organic part of the total cultural gestalt but not included in the religious core. provided the genius of a particular religion has been grasped, its basic nuclear content can be preserved and cherished in the midst of a conscious assimilation of other concepts and values without impairing the basic integrity and personality of that religion.

The concepts and values, which to my mind, need to be consciously integrated into a dynamic Islam are the basic concepts and values of Western modernity, and one or two concepts or values of Indian culture. The concepts and values of Western modernity have been described by me in a paper: What is modernity? I shall, therefore, not repeat them here. But the value of 'authenticity' as it has emerged in Western Europen under the stimulus of existentialist thought, was not included in that paper. Hence, a brief elucidation of this value would not be out of place here, in view of the crucial need for the cultivation of this value irrespective of one's religious denomination.

The contemporary age is the age of spiritual crisis and nihilism. A simple faith, whether in religious or secular values, has become more or less impossible for the sensitive and informed person, unless he first goes through a period of intense self-searching. One is, therefore, sorely tempted to cut short this arduous and long journey in the dark night of the soul in order to reach quickly the haven of faith and certitude. Man is eager to end the painfulness, nay the torture and agony involved in the loss of faith and a naked exposure to a total nihilism. The value of authenticity is an appeal to man not to fall a prey to intellectual dishonesty, self-alienation, and the compartmentalization of his personality, in order to escape doubts or the awareness of conflict between his different attitudes and beliefs.

Conclusion

There is no unbridgeable chasm between modernism and traditionalism. The ideal is to be a growth-oriented person rather than be a traditionalist or modernist in the chronological sense. The growth-oriented approach implies that no one vision, whether of a ghazali, a Waliyu'llah, or Sir Syed or an Iqbal, or for that matter, Gandhi, Tagore, Russel, Marx or Mao, can be accepted as final. Ghazali's great synthesis in the 11th century between the strands of rationalism, mysticism and legalism was an achievement even as the *Summa* of St. Thomas was in later Christendom. Similarly, Ibn Sina, Ibn Rushd, Ibn Taymiya, Ibn Khaldun and Waliyu'llah each in his own way has left us with a synoptic vision. But no vision or interpretation can be allowed to become static.

The conceptual interpretation of the totality of human experience is a collective and progressive enterprise that should transcend the barriers of region and time, language and religion. The task of interpretation can never be completed. Human experience grows, yielding fresh factual data. This, in its turn, reacts or should react upon the conceptual interpretation in the lap of which the data first confronted man. This dialogue between experience and interpretation (leading at times to the discovery of fresh facts and at others to the formulation of fresh interpretations) is a part of the unending human adventure or men's quest of value. To give only one example of this dialogue, the conquest of poverty and disease and the control of human population are profoundly modifying, in the Christian framework of ideas, the conception of a Personal God, and, by implication, of revelation. On the other hand, it was the concept of a Supreme and Just Creator that had centuries earlier helped in the emergence of the concepts of cosmos and science. The important thing to note is the organic character of the interpretative framework which attracts data from every dimension of human experience. This interaction between science and religion is rather marginal in Islam, since the impact of science and technology has just begun. The moment it gains momentum, similar changes are most likely to follow in Islam.

The reconstruction in the meaning of traditional symbols and images takes time. There may said to be a 'conceptual lag', just as there is a cultural lag: The concept of conceptual lag makes us tolerant towards the tradition-oriented person. In this respect, the methodological approach of some Western philosophers is also relevant. These philosophers avoid philosophical disputes, holding that different philosophical theories are merely varying formulations of the same set of facts. They differ because they select different facts for emphasis: Hence the important thing is not the verbal formulation but rather the full awareness of the complexity of the situation concerned. Provided this complexity is grasped, any formulation may be retained. This principle may aptly be called the 'principle of formulational tolerance.' This principle together with the concept of conceptual lag should help our modernists in carrying out an authentic and fruitful dialogue with the traditionalists, as recommended above.

The principle of formulational tolerance is not an innovation in the cultural tradition of either Islam or Hinduism. The well-known story of Moses and the Shepherd, in the *Mathnawi* of

Maulana Rumi (d. 1273), is perhaps the most striking and pregnant recommendation for the acceptance of this principle. Indeed, Rumi goes on to say that the violation of this principle leads one to 'conceptual idolatory,' i.e., the worship of one's conception of God, rather than God Himself. similarly, Waliyu'llah's concept of *'Tatbiq'* is very fruitful.

Earlier still, both Ghazali and Ibn Rushd had posited the principle of 'formulational dualism'. According to this principle, truth must be communicated to suit the mental level of the hearer. This dualism must lead us to what I call 'formulational pluralism'. This concept releases us from the monopolistic grip of traditional formulations on the one hand, and the formulations or jargon of our own pet interpretative systems, whether Marxism, Positivism, Idealism, Theism, Vedantism or what not, on the other.

Every interpretative or value system no matter who the individual or which the historical tradition has limitations which must be acknowledged and overcome. These limitations are due to the spatio-temporal traces which cling to very individual in spite of this creative dynamism. This applies to every historical individual and epoch including the Prophet and the *Khilafat-i-Rashida.*

The quest of growth must not, however, blind us to the power of the symbols and images of a tradition. These symbols must be retained and at the same time they must be reconstructed. If the symbols are discarded, the new ideas and values have no legs to stand upon, or no vessels to be poured into. If on the other hand, the symbols are retained, it becomes very difficult to make them first absorb or assimilate and then convey the new ideas and values in question. The symbols cast their shadows and tend to obscure and distort the fresh strings of the human soul. Moreover, even if this difficulty be overcome, there is another dilemma. If the symbols are retained in their traditional sense, the reformer is heard and understood by the group, but the group does not move forward or towards the vision of the leader. If the symbols are nominally or formally retained but their meaning or significance radically altered, he is liable to be charged with hypocrisy by these members of the group who rightly or wrongly have no reason to feel dissatisfied with the traditional meanings of the symbols in question. Every creative individual, therefore, has to solve this predicament. The fear of the charge of hypocrisy should not deprive him of the advantages of his membership of living church or tradition. Provided he feels an emotional involvement with the tradition and genuinely finds many elements of value in the historical personalities and events of that tradition, he should go ahead in the task of the reconstruction of the tradition in question. The charge of hypocrisy cannot after all be treated as more discouraging or demoralizing than the charge of *Kufr* or apostasy that was the order of the day in medieval times nay, right up to our own.

the charge of hypocrisy will be valid only if the individual distorts his authentic meanings in order to get an audience. But, if the recommended changes in the meanings of the traditional symbols are not concealed but fully and frankly acknowledged, then their employment for facilitating the genuine and creative growth of the community, can never be regarded as hypocrisy. Indeed this is the only way to further the cause of cultural revolution or emergence. Socrates, Buddha, Christ, Muhammad and Gandhi, and in an important sense even Marx, all have followed the same principle.

Proof of the pudding is in the catching.

Islam is the culmination of that Prophetic movement in the Middle East which had emerged in that region when the non-prophetic systems of beliefs could not resolve and internal crisis with the heightening of religious consciousness and reflective thinking. The proposition that with Islam the prophetic movement comes to a close is not a mere expression of faith, it is a brute historical fact. The theological language of Islam describes it as the cessation of Divine revelation to man and the *Quran* calls it as the 'completion of the Faith (*ad-Din*). In the personality of Muhammad history finds the last builder of a religion who claimed to have spoken the 'Divine Word.' The phenomenology of religions reveals that each religion has its own central concept. Buddism stresses the centrality of Dhamma, Judaism makes Law its central notion, Christianity regards the Divile Person's its fundamental idea, Islam gives to the Book central importance for the religious life of the community. It is not incorrect to say that Muhammad was the first Prophet who introduced the idea of a religion based on Book. If Jesus was considered the uncreated Divine Logos by Christian theologians, *Quran* was regarded as uncreated Divine Word by the early Muslim theologians. One of the fiercest theological battles was fought on this issue in the early period of Islamic History. The Book claims that 'In it is guidance sure, without doubt, to those who fear God' (II, 2). Theoretically the Book enjoins upon the believers to accept the previous Books but theologically it means an unconditional acceptance of the 'Book', as it is alone the infallible Word of God. Next to the Book is the personality of Muhammad, the seal of the Prophets, and according to the passionate believers the best and the highest among them. The Book itself declared that

> "Say: If ye do love God,
> Follow me: God will love you
> And forgive you your sins:
> For God is Oft-forgiving,
> Most Merciful" (III, 31)

The Prophet was not only the last among the prophets who in the most authentic manner communicated the 'Word of God' but also practised it for the benefit of mankind and therefore, *Quran* declares:

> Ye have indeed
> In the Apostle of God
> A beautiful pattern (of conduct)
> For anyone whose hope is
> In God and the Final Day,
> And who engages much
> In the praise of God, (XXXIII, 20)

Methodologically it mans that there are two sources of infallible truth; the Book and the practice of the Prophet. The Prophet did not only teach the word of God, he also founded the 'Best Community' (*Khayra Ummatin*), the 'model community for mankind', one which was destined to be a 'witness for the whole of humanity' (*Shuhada 'ala'n-Nas*). The 'community' became the preserver of the faith (*ad-Din*), the translator of the Divine Will on Earth. Again, according to the majority of the believers the community remained infallible during the reign of the guided Khulafa.' Thus there are three infallible principles; the Book, the Prophet, the Community, and they are complementary to each other. The Book infallibly reveals the Will of God, the Prophet practised it unerringly, and the Community preserved it historically. A popular *hadith* gives to the community almost a divine status by declaring that 'My community will never agree on error.'

From another angle, the Book communicates the system of beliefs and the law, the Prophet presents a living example, and the Community the 'Way of Life.' Thus the book is Islam as a system of beliefs and law, the Prophet is Islam as a person, and the Community is Islam as a way of life. Islam is an impersonal faith, Islam is a personal religion, and Islam is a way of life, at the same time. It is in this sense that tradition is not an accretion in islam; it developed as an integral part of it. The three principles of the Book, the Prophetic traditions (*sunna*), and the concensus of the community (*ijma*), are implied in the early Faith itself. These principles are the ideational foundations of the Islamic tradition. Theology and legal practice added the fourth principle *qiyas,* which, however, does not have any clear basis in the Book. The idea of 'finality', which was very soon going to transform itself into the 'illusion of finality', is intimately related with these principles. Islam is the final message, *Quran* is the final Book, Muhammad is the last among the prophets, and the Community (*umma*) is the final Umma, and it is through them that the Divine ideal became actual. It is not an uncommon belief that with the utterance of the 'final word' the purpose of the Divine Creation itself was fulfilled. It was not a far-fetched idea for some sensitive souls that the next significant event could be the end of time alone. It gives rise to a tension between the polar concepts of history and eschatology and some of the best creative minds among the historians and the Sufis tried to resolve this tension. As a result of this tension some unforeseen creative possibilities of Islam also emerged in islamic literature. The esoteric and the exoteric aspects of Islam derive their inspiration from these fundamental principles. The Sufis explored the hidden meaning of the book, and the aspect of *hikmat,* so much emphasised in the *Quran*, becomes their dominant concern. The principle of the Prophet becomes for them the 'eternal teacher' whose 'memory' is recurrently reenacted in the minds of the Sufis. The principle of the Community gives rise to the Sufi brotherhoods, the devoted seekers of the truth and passionate searchers of the final vision. The theologians tried to systematize the 'dogma' from the 'scattered' verses of the *Quran* and seek concrete guidance from the sayings of the Prophet. The principle of the Community inspired the idea of the university, the centres of learning, and in the course of time '*ulama* claimed to be the 'heirs' of the Prophet of God. The legists painstakingly developed one of the best legal systems of the old world out of the principles of the book, the Sunna, and the consensus of the Community. The different challenges that the Community was to face were resolved by a creative synthesis of these principles. It was by their aid that different elements of culture, theology, law, politics philosophy, and sufism were unified into an organic whole and the Community could keep up its image in the moments of expansion and decay both. The qualitative difference of these two moments was, however, going to make crucial difference for the subsequent generations. In the moments of expansion, the joy of expansion itself was creative source for further expansion and the stresses and strains created by expansion and contact with different cultures provided occasions for further creativity in the field of thought and action; but the moment when the internal schisms and external challenges, both political and ideological, grew in intensity the fundamental principles of cohesion-in-expansion degenerated into forces of conservatism and stagnation. The idea of finality concurrently degenerated into the illusion of finality and islam split up into many closed systems. The point of contact between theology, law, philosophy and sufism was lost and in the course of time the subdivisions of these aspects themselves assumed a rigidity that each one of them claimed 'finality' for itself. The intimate relation of politics and religion in early Islam not only provided a creative occasion for the development of law into legal schools but it also conferred upon the legists a privileged position which was practically denied to the other creative minds. This tendency in the early and medieval Islam made the transformation of religion into jurisprudence easier and theology itself became a subservient part of the jurisprudence. The consolidation of the four rival legal schools in the Sunni Islam and abandonment of the principle of *ijtihad* synchronized with the emergence of the *Ash'ari* theology and the final defeat of the free speculative thought. The emergence of al-Ghazzali and the death of philosophical enquiry were, in a sense, symptomatic of the intellectual decay of Islamic community. The *Ash'ari* compromise, a part of which was al-Ghazzali's reconciliation of theology and sufism, was the final triumph of 'unreason', in the history of Islamic thought. *Quran* claimed that it had completed the revelation and had given the final guidance. Now the actual completion of the faith in all its ramifications was done by the theologians and the legists. The divisions of Islam into Sunnis and Shi'is and of the former into four legal schools having Ash'arism as their ideological basis was 'final'. It became the inarticulate assumption of the community that the 'Truth' has been completely 'revealed'.

Methodologically the concept of revelation had, by this time, assumed an entirely different meaning. From the epistemological point of view there could be only one source of knowledge and that is 'completed tradition'. It further meant that there could not be any meaningful addition to knowledge, and if any such attempt was made it was a deviation from the right path, or a heresy. It implied that knowledge is not an advancement from the known to the unknown but is a mere application of the known and the completed laws to the seemingly new situations. Ontologically it meant that the universe and the human situation are closed systems and that nothing really novel can occur. The concept of change does not only lose its ontological status, it also loses its axiological significance. It was felt that change could only be from bad to worse and it was the duty of all right-minded persons to resist change. The identification of novelty with heresy seems to be a natural result of the illusion of finality. The approximation of knowledge with the 'knowledge of the sciences of religion' meant the banishment of reason and experience from the world of man. Historically the final triumph of theology coincides with the final defeat of scientific and philosophic reason. The acceptance of al-Ghazzali's theory of knowledge and *Ash'ari* metaphysic of occasionalism meant the victory of not of the prophetic tradition but of traditionalism in the World of Islam. In fact, the tendency to revive the prophetic tradition, whichh was to occupy the intellectual resources of some of the best minds in the Islamic world, was essentially a movement away from traditionalism. Ibn Taymiya, the crusader against all trends of 'innovation' and an enemy of the division of Islam into four legal sects and an opponent of the inward intuitive experience of the Sufi, represented the swing to the other side, away from the *ijma* of the theologians and the legists. In the thrilling voice of Ibn Taymiya is concealed his desperate attempt to revive the 'original' tradition of the Prophet. Traditionalism of the orthodox was at least accommodative of the folk-religion. It had, no doubt, closed the doors of *ijtihad* in Islam but was not unprepared to accommodate the gradual *ijma* of the community, only if it was not repugnant to the broad spirt of Islam. The 'fundamentalist' movement of Ibn Taymiya was, in a sense, completely anti-historical in its attitude to communal life. This movement was going to introduce one more principle of 'division' in the collective life of Islam. The zahiris of Ibn Hazm type were in certain respects intellectually akin to the 'fundamentalists'. Their distrust of philosophy mysticism and reason was mutual.

With the emergence of these schools, the Islamic world was divided into orthodox, (of the Sunni and Shi'a types), and the fundamentalists who were not prepared to accept anything unless it was sanctioned by the Book and the practice of the Prophet. Methodologically it meant that the knowledge and action should conform to two criteria, the Preserved Book and the Tradition which was not absolutely preserved. It further implied an equality of status between the two. It is a noteworthy fact of history of Islamic thought that no serious theological school of Islam was satisfied with the principle that the *Quran* alone is the infallible guide. The Shi'as supplement it with *Imama,* the Sunni orthodoxy of the traditionalist type with *sunna* and *ijma'* of the Community and the Sunni orthodoxy of the Fundamentalist type with *sunna.*

The traditionalism of the orthodox had many things which could not by any stretch of imagination, be justified by a strict adherence to the principles of the book and *sunna.* The traditionalist Islam was gradually moving towards an unconscious acceptance of the principle of folk-religion as distinct from the religion of the elite. Besides, it was also inclined to accept the validity of an existential difference between the temporal and the religious aspects of human life. The religious thought of Ghazzali had the seeds of an ethical theory which could claim autonomy from the strict legist interpretation of the religious injunctions. The Sufi always looked beyond the 'legally permissible' to the ethically justifiable. Islamic civilization lacked much and its further intellectual expansion suffered much on account of the approximation of 'law' with morality. The dominance of the legal categories in a civilization tends to retard the development of an autonomous ethical conscience.

The insistence of the fundamentalist on the outward form and the pre-occupation of the zahiris with the 'letter' were only two aspects of the same attitude. Both these movements implied the 'shrinking' of the intellectual horizon of the community and the impoverishment of its spiritual life. These movements did not ultimately overcome the traditionalist Islam but left a deep impact on the community.

There was, now, one more ideal before the community in times of spirutual distress and weakness in political power. The fundamentalist movement gave a terrible blow to the gradual emergence of the principle of *ijma* as a guide for the secular life of the community. This movement implied that the highest ends of the individual and the highest ends of the community must coincide with each other and that the highest end of the latter is to enforce law in its most overt form. It revived the lure of power which was slowly dying out from the upper consciousness of the folk on account of the sufi teaching for a higher spiritual life. A more humble attitude was developing in the heart of the traditionalist believer and that was to seek refuge in the infinite grace of God in times of distress and to seek spiritual strength in the face of calamities. The decline of the central authority and the corruption of politics had made a powerful impact on the religious-minded person that higher religion can survive the loss of political power. Ibn Taymiya, on the contrary, declared it a duty to consider the exercise of power a form of religion, as one of the acts by which man is drawn nearer to God. The idea was implicit that the true believer must strive for the establishment of a society and state in which the duality of power and religious life is finally overcome.

There was nothing wrong in the fundamentalists ideal that political activity must strive for the realization of higher values but their insistence that higher values, embodied in a religion, have been finally institutionalised was far from their higher ideal. The same methodological error is revealed in the outlook of the modern followers of Ibn Taymiya. Their guiding principle that Islam does not believe in the formal division of the secular and the religious is not theoretically untenable but what is missed is a more fundamental point that the unity of the secular and the religious can never become a completed act. Further, what Islam had meant was to emphasise the ontological unity of all existence. This sort of unity does not preclude the possibility of an existential difference between the different levels of life and a further possibility of evolving plural standards for them which are ultimately united on a higher level of unity. The ideal unity of the secular and religious can hardly mean that political power is to be used for the instantaneous establishment of religious law. It will eventually result in the stagnation of political theory and secondly the religious ideal will become secondary to the political power in its actual status. The Roman Catholic Church's control of secular power before Reformation was an attempt at such unification. The Hindu states of ancient India were yet another manifestation of the same attitude. The absence of the priestly class in Islam is besides the point because in the Islamic states the '*ulama*' and the legists had assumed practical authority to interpret the 'law'. The only difference was the mechanism of interpretation and the actual sources of law. One more serious loss was the fact that a proper theory of human rights could not develop in Islamic political thought, the seeds of which were present in the *Quran* and the sayings of the Prophet. The Christian world had to wait till the actual separation of the Church and state for the flowering of a theory of human rights which was greatly inspired by the early Christianity. The decline in the Muslim world, a serious problem for the fundamentalists, was explained as caused by the time-distnace of the Community with the Golden Age of the Prophet and the Khulafa-i-Rashidin. The purpose was to make the idea of the 'golden age' an articulate aspiration of the Community in its political life. The idea of a 'golden age' is an essential ingredient of religious life but the fundamentalists picked up the political as the highest moment of the Prophetic life. This gave rise to a cognitive and affective attitude which longs for and aims at the revival of the 'original pasts', and looks at the present as a fall or return to the pre-guidance age. The spiritual longing of the Sufi—traditionalist theologian to approximate his life of belief and action to the exemplary life of the Prophet is given a secular orientation. Ibn Taymiya could neither reverse the historical process of political decline in his own age ńor her could dethrone traditionalism of his contemporary Islam. History had to wait for a few more centuries to witness the possibilities which his violent ideology had contained. He became an Imam of the revivalists and there is hardly any reviver who is not at least partially influenced by him. There were, now, two thought-patterns before the community: one of al-Ghazzali and the other of Ibn Taymiya. Their mental attitudes are mutually exclusive but the community developed an admiration for both types.

The tension between the polar concept of 'piety'—the ideal of the traditionalist Sufi—and power—the ideal of the fundamentalist—created an unhappy consciousness in the Community. The Community could never unhesitatingly look beyond the political power as an essential element of religious life. This is true about the medieval Islam and is more true about the post-medieval Islam. The latter is in reality the revival of ideology preached by Ibn Taymiya. The epistemological assumptions of the post-medieval Islam and its world-outlook are not different from those of the medieval Islam. The post-medieval Islam is governed by the belief that tradition covers the whole of human life. It will be more accurate to state that the post-medieval Islam is more pre-occupied with this idea than the traditionalist Islam. The assumption of most of the recent Islamic movements is the idea that the ills of the present-day Muslim society are due to the loss of political power and that it was caused by the Community drifting from the original sources of the Book and the *sunna*. Even a cursory study of the ideas of Shah Waliyu'llah, 'Abdu'l-Wahhab of Najd, the later Waliyu'llahi writers, the young Azad, and the *'ulama'* of Deoband indicates their preoccupation with the medieval epistemology, the medieval world outlook and the medieval political thought. It still remains a challenging task to question the validity of the proposition that tradition covers the entire human life. The point which is common to the Nadva School and the *Jama at-i-Islami* is that no aspect of human life is outside the purview of Islamic Law. It contains infallible laws for the entire life of man, whether referring to his metaphysical needs or moral aspirations or relating to secular aspects of life or the greater details of state administration.

There seems to be a fatal semantic confusion between 'infallible guidance (*hidaya*) which the *Quran* claims to possess and actual laws which these revivers try to find in the tradition. The proposition that a book or a religious tradition offers guidance in multiple spheres of life-apart from its being true or false—is semantically different from the proposition that they contain infallible, immutable laws involving absolute permanence for all occasions. The former proposition does not altogether deny the possibility of the emergence of novel situations in the life of the individual or community, whereas the second proposition makes all change meaningless. It makes the different periods of historical time ontologically identical with each other and obliterates the difference between the human world and the physical universe. It is a simple mechanism expressed in religious language which forgets to admit that there is a qualitative difference between an earthquake and a war. It means that the present itself has no ontological status and that every event is only an occasion to vindicate tradition. It is tentamount to deny that there is any genuine history. It suggests that knowledge is not the discovery of new propositions but is a mere reinterpretation of the older theories and it fails to prove why another religious tradition is not equally infallible. The whole attitude behind this proposition is essentially authoritarian, the indisputable quality of the medieval mind. It has, on this account, been suggested that most of the contemporary Islamic movements are continuation of the medieval attitude. Almost all the authors of these movements, emphasise the need of reinterpreting the tradition in accordance with the needs of modern times, without, however, suggesting a new world outlook and new epistemology which has taken into account the progress in the field of sciences, natural as well as social, psychology and even religious phenomenology. Iqbal is, perhaps, the only exception who made a serious attempt to examine the world outlook of medieval Islam.

The different revivalist movements differ on the scope and range of reinterpretation. Some of them, like the Hanbalis of Saudi Arabia and the neo-Hanbalis, like the leaders of *Jama 'at-i-Islami* believe that the need for reinterpretation is marginal. The fundamental task of the Islamic movements according to them is to wage a relentless war against the modern age as it is a reversal to *Jahiliya.* The others, like the early *Salafiya,* feel that there is a wider scope of interpretation. But the philosophical method of these schools, with their varied aims, is still medieval and scholastic as they feel that the task of the present-day thinker is to construct a reformed *kalam* or a modified *fiqh* which is still governed by the pre-scientific theory of knowledge. Some of the more liberal among them are keen to open the doors of *ijtihad* by taking into account the modern needs. In the field of dogma, they would like to give a few concessions to modern knowledge by giving new meanings to words and phrases. Such attemps often leave the Community bewildered and sometimes creates quite an opposite effect on their minds that there is nothing new in the modern world which was not anticipated in the tradition.

The medievalists among the moderns, like Abu'l Hasan 'Ali an-Nadvi and the advocates of *Jama' ai-i-Islami* share the belief that Islamic Community is the Prophetic Community and that the world is ill because of their inactivity. The assumption that the world is fast moving to destruction is an *a priori* of their thought. A parallelism found in the movement of Sri Aurobindo in recent Indian Philosophy which also believes that the world is ill and that India, i.e. Hindu India, has a divine mission to fulfil. The world view of these medievalists is theocentric, their social thought is theocratic, and their view of history is providential. They have not yet made an attempt to make a distinction between knowledge of the world and the cognition of values. The recent advance in the theory of knowledge has not made any effect on their mode of thinking. Scientific theories are still examined in the light of the 'word of God' and they are often summarily rejected. The theoretical basis of this attitude of examining the scientific theories is a questionable proposition that religion, and in their case Islam, reveals all truths, and Islam being the final religion, has spoken the 'final truth'. There seems to be a small confusion here, the simple claim of the *Quran* is, that God has completed the religion or *din*. There is a vast semantic difference between completion of *din* and completion of all truth. The finality of revelation and the completion of *din* have certain restricted meanings beyond which they lose their relevance. It simply means that Islam is the last and the final religion of revelation and the *Quran* is the last revealed Book. In the restricted religious sphere, it gives authenticity to the revelation and also makes the religious group an authentic one. It also provides to the believer, as Iqbal has pointed out, an authentic religious criterion and gives to religious life a definite character. The idea does not, however, entail that all truth has been spoken, neither it gives a valid criterion of truth outside the restricted field of religious knowledge. It gives something different which may even be called higher from the point of view of values. It gives to the process of truth-finding an axiological basis. But it does not involve a rejection of any proposition belonging to the field of sciences, natural and social, only because it appears contrary to the revealed word, neither it means a hasty attempt to adjust revelation to the contemporary theories; it only means a patient and untiring search for truth, leaving the question of absolute truth outside the process of truth seeking.

In the case of Islam, it is soul-consuming task. Islam has a metaphysical and a social approach at the same time and both are parts of revelation. The religious thinker has to remember one important fact that religions get their distinctness on account of their metaphysical vision and it is the vision which opens further possibilities for metaphysical speculation. The history of Islamic thought in its period of intellectual expansion provides us with many examples which prove this proposition. The term 'innovation' or 'heresy' can be hardly applied to any philosophical sepeculation based on the revealed vision. The history of philosophy itself shows that all philosophies have one or the other vision as their presupposition. The history of Western philosophy presupposes the vision of Christianity but the variety of the ways in which this vision leads to different philosophical solutions enriches the religious consciousness of the West itself. So far as metaphysical speculation is concerned Islamic societies have been very liberal and there are very few instances when a particular metaphysical discussion had been violently resisted. Similarly, in the field of empirical sciences, Islam in its days of intellectual expansion very infrequently suppressed a scientific school.

The real difficulty lies in the human world, where there is a greater need for free discussion. It is in this field that the traditional Islamic world had shown signs of intolerance and rigidity of outlook. It needs to be remembered that many questions of tradition belong to the world of man. It looks really paradoxical that the total number of verses in the *Quran* dealing with the organisation of human society are not more than one tenth of the *Quran,* and the amount of traditions developed upon it has no proportion with the size of the Quranic verses. It was no account of the smallness of number of such legislative verses that the need was felt to supplement it with *sunna, ijma,* and *qiyas*. The compulsions of political power gave to this department of human knowledge an importance greater than it could have in any scheme of religious knowledge. The logic of political power demands that the problem of human organisation is given the highest importance and the same thing happened in Islam. It is again the logic of political power that the state and its structure is kept intact. It is on this account that there is an element of conservatism in political activity. The early Islamic state was no exception. The forces of political conservatism very soon appeared and the whole fabric was given a religious sanction. The state being an ideological state—this will be a less controversial term than theocratic—also took upon itself the duty of preserving the system of beliefs, so far as it could be within the comprehension of the political authority. It is not surprising that the legal schools in the Sunni world, could not exceed four, whereas the number of purely dogmatic schools far exceeds the imagination of an average believer. Many terms in Islamic scholastic literature really belong to the realm of law and politics. Even the most respected term *sunna* has hardly any relevance in a purely metaphysical discussion. The famous *hadith* of Mu‘adh itself, which is the source of *sunna* and *qiyas* in legist literature, properly belongs to the sphere of legal decisions. The linguistic analysis of that *hadith* does not confirm the view that it was meant to be binding on all generations to come. The outcome of such a view is the commonly accepted notion, much emphasied by the contemporary fundamentalists, that there can be no legislative activity in nan Islamic state and that such a state has to enforce the laws already legislated by the Book or the *sunna*. Similarly, the view that all ‘sovereignty’ belongs to God is derived from such traditions and a misreading of the *Quran*. The semantic confusion is again clear that no political writer used the term sovereignty in the sense in which it can be used about God and no theist can deny that the ultimate authority belongs to God. The fundamentalist is committing the same methodlogical error of trying to confer finality on medieval political terminology because it appears to be religious. A detailed and dispassionate study of the Islamic legal and political tradition confirms the hypothesis that there is a considerable gap between the Quranic vision of man and its transition in legal terms and historical institutions.

The Quranic approach to the human problems is based on the Quranic vision of man as a free and morally responsible being, who is a value by himself. The ultimate fact in the human world, according to the *Quran,* is the individual who strives for perfection, suffers for it and endures this suffering with the final hope that he will have the final vision (*liqa' u-Rabbihi*). Some of the best passages of the *Quran* are those which deal with the human situation and describe the ultimate dignity of man, as the vicegerent of God. The life of the Prophet itself consists in a series of actions which were the concrete translation of this vision in the historical time in which he was situated. In this historical situation he was sometimes guided by the ‘revelation’ and more often he had to depend on his own Judgment, the motive being in both the cases, a passionate desire to elevate human status. The mechanical interpretation of the *sunna*—the words and the deeds of the prophet—ignores the historcal situation and thus is unable to imagine the unlimited possibilities which are implied in the Quranic vision. The creative energies of some of the best Islamic thinkers were devoted to comprehend this vision as it was translated in the finite historical time, mostly in the form of law. The historical reason for giving to the *sunna* and *ijma* an almost equal place with the Book was a natural tendency to preserve the form that was given to human society by the Prophet, so far as it was possible in the turbulent days that followed that death of the Prophet. *It is, perhaps, peculiar to Islam that the 'purely contingent' was confused with the essentially religious. If the contingent is raised to the level of necessary the result is the philosophic error of the negation of change, an error to which attention has been drawn earlier*. From this philosophical confusion arises the anti-scientific and anti-philosophical attitude of the conformist and particularly the neo-Hanbalis. This confusion is the real source of their resistance to the normal growth of the scientific and philosophical values which are the bases of modern civilization. Modernism is a convenient term to express the unity of these values, which themselves presuppose a pluralistic view of human life, at least at its existential level. It is not a chronological term; it is mental attitude which governs the explorative behaviour of the modern man in his attempt to conquer the forces of nature to ameliorate the human situation. This attitude is not inconsistent with Quranic vision of man. One can hardly agree with von Grunebaum that "...it would be difficult to claim that the revelation tends to render man truly human and encourages him to use the forces of the physical universe as instruments of self-liberation (a term which I prefer to the more static conception of 'liberty') even though such a tendency has been found by some Muslim modernists in the sacred text". It is not the mental ingenuity of the modernist that the humanist tendency has been discovered in the *Quran*; on the contrary, Quranic vision of man in its totality encourages him to use the forces of the physical universe as an instrument of not only self-liberation but also self-realization. The Quranic account of the coming of Adam on earth itself is a revaluation of man in the history of the sacred religious texts. *Quran* marks it an imperative to conquer and subjugate the forces of nature. It is true that this tendency of the *Quran* was not given its proper importance by the medieval sufi and the theologian of the inward type who were moved more by verse which emphasized the transitory character of the wordly existence which was only one of the moments of the *Quran*. Religion, like art, has a symbolic aspect on account of which each culture interprets it according to its own cultural horizon. The medieval treminology in which Islam is still clothed, could not grasp this very important moment of Book. It is one of the greatest achievements of Iqbal, as has been pointed out by Dr. (Miss) Schimmel, that he made a revaluation of man, much neglected in Islamic literature. It is quite plain that religious humanism whether Quranic or Christian cannot be humanism without God; God being the 'beginning' and the 'end' of all religions. It will be restricting the meaning and scope of humanism if it is limited to the atheistic type or to a particular religious type, as is unfortunately done by von Grunebaum.

The example of Iqbal proves one important point to which attention has been drawn earlier that without a new philosophic approach which takes into account the contemporary frontiers of knowledge, Islamic thought and institutions cannot meet the demands of modern times. One can hardly expect any attempt to reinterpret Islam to succeed if the basis is still medieval. Modernism as a philosophical tendency implies the view that neither the universe nor the human world is static; change has an ontological as well as an axiological status. The traditionalist and the neo-Hanbalis deny this when they widen the significance of the tradition. The recent changes in the human situation demand a more humble view of infallibility. In their enthusiasm to stress the infallibility and finality of the tradition, the neo-Hanbalis actually claim infallibility for themselves and for their own knowledge of the Word and Prophetic tradition. The paradox that arises out of the apparent incompatibility of the revealed word and the modern knowledge, derived from humanly reliable sources of reason and experience, is not easily resolvable by an *ad hoc* interpretation. It is not a mere religious question; it is also an epistemological question. It cannot be resolved either by abandoning the scientific result or by throwing away the revealed word. The second approach would imply that the idea of infallibility is transferred to science which is not its intent. The more humble course would be to limit the relevance of the respective fields of enquiry. So far, religious men, and for the purpose of the present enquiry the Muslims, were seeking guidance from religion even in matters which could be easily guided by human reason and experience. One of the assumptions behind this attitude was that there must be one source of knowledge which could inform us about all our questions. Religious revelation is not the only valid source of knowledge, it is simply a source of knowledge especially suited for regions which do not usually come under the grip of dialectical reason or experience. The guidance, which revelation offers in matter suited for rational enquiry, is more of an ethical nature than legal character. It is after all man, the believer, who has to fix the meanings of the language of revelation. It suits the nature of revelation more if meanings of a more universal character are given to the revealed word. Quranic revelation uses ethical as well as legal language and the tendency of theologio-legal mind had been to subordinate the ethical to the legal and to ignore the meaningful distinction between the violation of the legal norm and of a moral law, not because of any lack of moral insight but because he had to study the problem from a political angle. Now when the nature of the modern state has changed the requirements of law have also changed. Divine law was a logical presupposition of 'divine state.' This change in our attitude towards state is part of the total change which has come in our human situation. The lure for power in religious group is inconsistent with the changed outlook of the present day humanity. This lure for politics undermines the democratic foundations of the modern society, if it seizes a religious group. There seems to be a direct conflict between the consensus of a large number of humanity and the consensus of a limited number of *'ulama'* on the question of the ultimate ideal and working a modern state. This conflict cannot be resolved by a mere mechanical adherence to a solution which was offered by a limited number of specialized scholars who lived in entirely different times when theocratic state was the generally accepted norm of political activity. It only shows that religious opinion, even when guided by the best intentions, can become archaic in a field which is not properly religious. We do not find the same situation when the religious judgments about the ultimate problems of existence are examined.

Modernisation, in the true sense of the term, is not possible unless this sort of totalitarian attitude towards life is not finally given up. Change in mere external forms of life, without corresponding changes in intellectual attitudes, may result in a greater disaster and that is modern technological society with an extreme totalitarian attitude. This is the general problem which Muslims all over the world face today. The situation in India is, however, different. the Indian problem is the modernisation of the majority of the Hindus who will ultimately determine whether India is going to be a modern state or a state governed by the medieval Hindu values. The Indian Muslims can accelerate the process of modernisation, if only they accept the suggestion that the values of secular demorcary are more in tune with a higher ethical ideal than futile attempts to recapture the past politico-legal traditions which are neither in tune with modern times nor can be shared by their contemporaries belonging to faiths different from theirs. Indian Society can only be modernised on the basis of a value-system which can be shared by all its members and such a value-system can emanate from the humanistic tradition of the contemporary world alone.

Turkey is a modern country and the Turks are Muslims. This familiar fact encompasses the history of Turkish transformation and the consequent change in the status of Islam in Turkish

Society. The Turks had to pass through various stages of political and social development to establish the entity of Turkey as a modern country. This development synchronised with a change in the religious attitudes of the Turks. The history of political development of Turkey and the changing attitudes of the Turks towards Islam provide a chain of revolutions and counter-revolutions, progress and reaction.

The origins of the Turkish transformation, in all its salient features, can be traced back to the early 18th century. The sporadic attempts at reform and the realization of the desirability of change in the existing systems by some educated individuals and enlightened monarchs characterise the early phase of the transformation. The *Tulip* era, the *Nizam-i-Cedid* of Selim III (1788-1807) and the reforms of Mahmud II (1808-1839) are some of the landmarks in the history of Turkey's orientation towards a modern country. The *Tanzimat* era was a step forward in this direction. It provided new incentives in political, social and cultural fields and confirmed the belief of the reformers that some changes in the structure of the Ottoman administration were inevitable. The initiatives taken by the Tanzimatists in the field of education, inspite of their anomalous character, produced an intelligentsia with an enlightened outlook. The ideas of liberty and progress became the nucleus of the first Constitutional movement in Turkey led by the young Ottomans. The short-lived First Constitution was followed by the absolutist government of 'Abdu'l-Hamid II (1876-1909) which opened an era of suppression and tyranny in Turkish history. With the restoration of the Constitution in 1908, the Second Constitutional period began. This period provides the immediate background to the Republican Turkey. The intellectual foundations of modern Turkey were laid in this period.

The most striking feature of the early phases of Turkish transformation which bears relevance to our present discussion is the dominance of religion. The sole criterion of the admissibility of a reform or an innovation was the sanction of religion or more truly of the religious class whose interpretation of religion was unquestionable. The reformist attempts, during this period, were opoosed by the 'clergy' who, as time passed, became increasingly vehement and rigid in their attitudes--this notwithstanding the fact that the history of modernization in Turkey presents, in the main, an attempt towards adjustment with Islamic tradition.

A phase of direct and active participation of the Turks to establish a new order began with the Kemalist regime following the collapse of the Ottoman empire in the First World War. Mustafa Kemal (later Ataturk) was clear in his objectives and knew what he was striving for. National reconstruction and the establishment of a new Turkey were his aims. The Kemalist regime was the first experiment in a republican form of government in the world of Islam. Besides external forces, one of the major factors conditioning the development of the Republic was the struggle of the new leaders against the conservatives. The opposition of the orthodox elements made Kemal alive to the dangers inherent in establishing a new order.

The formal separation of State from religion was effected through the revolutionary reforms of Mustafa Kemal. The abolition of the Caliphate, in 1924, was the most radical step that Kemal took in this regard. It was followed by the dissolution in 1925 of the religious orders and closure of cloisters (*tekkes*)—the age old sanctuaries of popular religious devotion. In 1926 the *Sharia* (Seriat) was replaced by the Civil Code which accelerated the pace of Turkish transformation. Its most significant effect was the change in the legal status of women the impact of which was also felt in the social and economic life of the people. In 1928, the constitutional provision declaring Islam as the religion of the State was deleted, followed in 1937 by the inclusion of secularism as one of the principles of the Constitution.

A period of acclimatization followed the formal completion of the Turkish revolution. The course of the process of identification of the people with the revolution was not smooth. It was marked by many attempts to counteract and even to reverse the flow of the revolution. These attempts were characterised by religious enthusiasm and were made in the name of religion. But the revolution had succeeded in creating a group of ardent followers led by certain intellectuals who devoted their efforts to the popularisation of Kemalist reforms and the new ideological bases of Turkey through public platform as well as through the press.

The Kemalist revolution, symbolized in the reforms of Ataturk, gave a new direction to the development of secularism in Turkey. The secularization of the State deprived religion of its institutional support—Islam as a polity gave way to new institutions. The question was how the emergence of the idea of secularism could be reconciled to Islam which had been both a faith and a way of life throughout turkish history. Ataturk believed in religion as a source of enlightenment and rationality. He emphasised that Islam was a worthy creed—natural and rational. Though appreciative of the role of religion in public life, he was convinced of the ingnorance of the interpreters of Islam. Islam was misused, he thought, by the corrupt men of religion to promote their own interests. This conviction found expression in his attempt to free religion from the domination of the religious class.

The development of Turkish nationalism, first as a cultural and literary movement and then as a political ideology, has been a significant factor in the advancement of Turkey towards modernism. Secular nationalism is an idea of comparatively recent growth in Turkey. Turkish nationalism had to pass through patriotism, religious nationalism and pan-turkish to arrive at its present form. During the early period of Turkish Republic, nationalism remained associated with religion which continued to be regarded as one of the component parts of Turkish nationalism. However, things changed with the emergence of nationalism as a secular idea and the development of secularism as an ideology. The Turkish intellectuals now found themselves free to elaborate the concept of nationalism without emphasizing its religious affiliations.

A very intimate aspect of turkish transformation is reflected in Turkish language and literature. Turkish literature has gone through a radical change in respect of both form and content. Turkish language has become the symbol of Turkish revolution. Recent developments in turkish literature, particularly after the Second World War, have invested it with a law and popular basis. Turkish writer now derives his themes from the life of the common man, sharing his aspirations, frustrations and hopes. Literature has become the critique of Turkish Society and the Turkish writer has successfully attempted to establish that there was a social basis to the problems of the people the solution of which had to be worked out socially and not through religious prescriptions.

However, the challenge of religion to Turkish society has not completely abated. The introduction of a multi-party system in 1946 created a more free and liberal atmosphere in the country. The newly-formed Democratic Party made religious freedom a plank of its programme and advocated that secularism did not mean opposition to religion. Likewise, Peoples Republican Party, taking stock of the new developments, took steps to restore religious freedom. The opening of the *Imam-Hatip* schools, the Faculty of Theology at Ankara and the introduction of religious instructions in public schools were received with enthusiasm among the people. The coming to power of the Democratic Party in 1950 was heralded as the victory of the orthodox over the 'atheistic' Peoples Party. One of the first steps that the new government took was to restore the call to prayer in Arabic which had been replaced by Turkish since 1933.

The restoration of some formal aspects of Islam encouraged the orthodox elements in Turkish society to assert themselves. Religious sentiments manifested themselves in such outbursts as the giving of *'adhan (ezan)* in Arabic by certain members of the Tijani (ticani) Sect in the National Assembly in 1949 when it was in session. The same sect started a campaign to demolish the statues of Ataturk. But the activities of the sect were controlled by the passage of a law for the protection of Ataturk's memory. The sect had to suspend its open activities after the prosecution of its leader Kemal Pilavoglu. The attempt to murder the famous journalist Ahmet Emin Yalman, in November 1952, for his liberal and secular views, was another expression of religious fanaticism. A Democrat member of Parliament went so far as to question the indebtedness of the Turkish nation to Ataturk's revolution.

Religious upsurge was expressed more significantly in the Nurite (*Nurcu*). Movement whose leader Said-i-Nursi (1867-1960) had played an important role in the 31st March incident of 1909 during the second constitutional period of Turkey. The main objective of this movement has been to establish an Islamic State based on the *Sharia* (Seriat). The opposition of the Nurites to Turkish revolution embodying the concept ofsecularism as well as Turkish nationalsm, emanates from their belief in Islam as a way of life. In their opinions, Islam should be the religion of Turkish State and *Quran* its law. They oppose the idea of reform in Islam as contrary to the *Sharia* (Seriat), criticize the changes taking place in society under the impact of new ideas and preach a return to Islam in its pristine purity. They regard the changes in the dress of men and women as social evils while favouring strict observance of veil among women. They even go so far as to advocate the restoration of polygamy in Turkey.

This sudden upsurge of religious fanaticism, however, does not mean that the foundations of Turkish secularism are shaky or the Turkish intellectuals are but an isolated class having no roots in society. Rather, it betokens a stage in Turkish transformation in which the people in general, whatever the nature of their role may be, are participating. The activities of the Tijanis (Ticanis) and Nurites were condemned by the Turkish press, and there was resentment among a considerable section of the educated classes. One of the charges levelled against the Menderes Government which contributed to its fall on 27th May 1960, was that it was encouraging religious revivalism for political purposes.

Opinions, about the Turks as Muslims, differ inside and outside Turkey. The dominant view outside Turkey is that the Turks have renounced Islam. But this view would seem absurd and distasteful to the Turks. They would claim that they were Muslims-enlightened and modern as Islam commands them to be—and all they had done was to free Islam from its traditional garb and domination by the degenerate 'clergy'. They would further claim that religion was a matter of private life, a thing of conscience. The Turkish case regarding religion can also be studied as a development within Islam, its position *vis-a-vis* the turkish transformation and its various manifestations: modernism, nationalism and secularism. In the early phase of Kemalist revolution, Islam, i.e., traditional Islam, assumed a posture of hostility against the Turkish transformation. But gradually, a period of compromise ensued. Of course, this emergence was facilitated by the weakening of Islamic institutions. Thus, we cannot fail to note a remarkable adjustment of Islam with Turkish transformation, despite the fact that the former has lost its dominant status. Islam seems to have started assimilating the Turkish revolution. The causes and nature of this adjustment require separate treatment.

7

Islamic Modernization in India

Modernity as used here may be defined as the process by which historically evolved institutions adapt themselves to change in outlook, reflecting explosive increase in knowledge. Such change may legitimately be described as revolutionary, as in its relevance and context it represents a total or partial break in attitudes and norms of thinking from the past. For the debate before us modernity in Islam is to be taken as a process of change from established norms under the impact of extension of knowledge over the centuries.

The significance of such transformations can be fully appreciated in the context of the course of world history. Consider, for instance, the earliest transformation which marks the emergence of human beings about a million years ago, after thousands of years of evolution from primate life. The capabilities of even the most primitive humans were of an entirely different character from those of the primates, although the latter were not lacking in organising abilities and sense of communal living. The primitive man was able to make tools, shelter, weapons, and means of transportation; he could communicate his reactions through the medium of speech and written signs. Instead of being dependent on Nature for subsistence and survival he emancipated himself from dependence on her caprices.

The second transformation to modernity takes place 7,000 years ago in the valley of the Tigris and Euphrates as set down in Hebrew (v. 2-4), the eleventh chapter of the Book of Genesis thus :

"And it came to pass, as they journeyed from the east, that they found a plain in the land of Shinar; and they dwelt there. And they said one to another, Go to let us make brick, and burn them throughly. And they had brick for stone, slime had they for morter. And they said, Go to, let us build us a city and a tower whose top may reach unto heaven; and let us make us a name, lest we be scattered abroad upon the face of the whole earth."

This, in a few sentences, is an account of the origin of the earliest, the oldest, the first civilisation created—the civilisation of the land of Shinar, the land of Sumer. This change marks the second transformation, the transformation from the primitive to a civilised society. Much larger and more complex than the primitive, this society invented a system of writing as a means of communication. More important than all this, these civilised societies came to have sophisticated conceptions expressed in religious beliefs, of the identity of man, of his relationship to his environment. They employed symbols of varying abstraction to express their perception of eternal truths dwelling in the world known to them at the time.

But the most epoch-making of such transformations in human affairs, and of the same order of magnitude as that from prehuman to human life, and from primitive to civilised societies, was the twelfth century awakening in Western Europe heralding the fourteenth-fifteenth century Renaissance and the seventeenth century Scientific Revolution. Describing the period Friedrich Heer Says :

"Everywhere in Western Europe during the twelfth century, in France, Germany England, Italy and Spain, men's hearts and minds were working to a new appreciation of the world, its colour, its vastness, its perils and its beauty. There was curiosity about the world in all its aspects, the world of men, the world of the spirit, the world of the cosmos and the world of Nature. This was a germinal time pregnant with a thousand possibilities and the material and themes treated by the men and women of this age retained a compelling attraction for poets and speculative thinkers right through the Renaissance and Baroque periods and down into the eighteenth century."

The century may truly be described as the beginning of the era when the human intellect was quickened and strove for the understanding of nature by the use of reason instead of reference to authority—the Pope or Aristotle. It was an open age, that is, men came to have confidence in the power of reason, to give decisive answers to the puzzles of the universe. For the first time systematic use of reason in the discovery of truth came to be openly advocated. The Cathedral school at Chartres is described as perhaps "the most luminous symbol of the intellectual movement of the twelfth century in all its pristine youthfulness and egregious audacity". God, the cosmos, nature, and mankind can be examined, reasoned about, comprehended and measured. "To theologise means to philosophise" was a common saying. A sustained effort was under way to understand the cosmos in its mathematical structure and at establishing theology as the mother of all the sciences, as something to be established rationally, an art governed by strict logic. One of the students introduced the logical concept of the axiom into theology, and tried to rethink theology as a logical system. The aim was to construct a pellucid, rational theology, "light, and clear like the Gothic cathedrals, in which the number, light, music and architecture of the cosmos—all based on numerical relationships--*showed forth* the nature of the Godhead itself". The small group of teachers at Chartres said and taught all these unorthodox things without inviting the attention of the Church as, it is said, they were all past masters in the art of *Nicodemism* that is to say, the art of clothing in symbolical and allegorical forms and putting into the mouths of classical poets, dangerous thoughts, dangerous allusions to topical ecclesiastical affairs, and, above all, to ideas hard or impossible to reconcile with the dogma of the Church or the maxims of the prevailing theology. "And Chartres", says von Heer, "was very much influenced by Islam", and that "men were interested in the Kuran and in Islam generally". J. Ribena Y. Tarrago, a Spanish scholar, has maintained that the medieval university owed much to the educational system of the Arabs.

Perhaps here I owe my listeners an explanation why I have devoted, more than the attention I bestowed on the first two instances of transformations in human history, to modernity in our own era, in the twelfth century. My explanation derives from the twin-faced fact of history that the intellectual efflorescence witnessed in Western Europe in the 14-15th century Renaissance, followed by the emergence of Humanism, the Protestant Reformation, the Scientific Revolution and the Age of Enlightenment, all had their seeds planted in the twelfth century and, secondly that the intellectual ferment in Chartres referred to above, derived in its turn, stimulus from the cultural consummation which the Muslims had brought about between the eighth and early twelfth century in an area stretching from the easternmost districts of Iran to the heart of Spain. In the words of late Professor Alfred Guillaume:

"Had the Arabs been barbarians like the Mongols, who stamped out the fire of learning in the East so effectually that it never recovered, and possibly never will recover, from the loss of its libraries and its literary tradition, the Renaissance in Europe might well have been delayed more than one century."

Having said this, however, let me hasten to add a note of caution against the mistaken nation often used by apologists for Islam that "Islam is the parent that begot and nourished European civilsation", or that "the birth of modern science owes it to the concept of the unity of God as preached by the founder of Islam", as against some of the Western authors' declaration that the Muslim culture was a mere hotch-potch of the remnants of the Sassanid and Byzantine civilisations both at a state of exhaustion and decomposition when the Arab Muslims overran Iran, Syria, Egypt and North Africa. The truth that emerges from these extreme views is now proven fact that the West benefitted to a considerable degree from translations of Greek thought, and original philosophical works, by the Arabs, which were transmitted to Europe by Jewish scholars from Muslim Spain in the twelfth century.

Be that as it may, the conclusion one is led to draw is, that the intellectual modernity of our era owes a measure of debt to the Muslim civilisation in the Middle Ages. In the words of Professor Hitti: "They (The Muslims) laid the basis of that canon of knowledge which lay at the bottom of the modern European renaissance." Here it may be instructive to provide, as a background, as outline of the faith the Muslims professed and within whose framework trends of modernity appeared.

The youngest of the three Semitic religions, Islam was born "in the broad daylight of history" in the early part of the seventh century of the Christian era. In line with the other two, it claims a book—the *Quran,* which is regarded as a literal transcript of the word of God revealed to Muhammad—"the last in the lipe of prophets"—messenger of God's will to mankind, and as such not subject to change in form or content. But unlike the Torah or the Bible, the *Quran* is held to be a complete code of conduct for man in life in all its spheres of activity—social, political, economic, and ethical, in addition to being a scripture like the other two. To it were added the sayings and precepts of Muhammad, heard by or known to his companions, and transmitted from generation to generation. Together, the *Quran* and the Prophet's sayings called the Traditions or *Hadith,* evolved in course of time a comprehensive system of ideal morality, a moral classification of human acts called *Sharia* or the way "by which men could walk pleasingly in the sight of God and hope to reach Paradise".

If and when the Islamic community faces a problem whose solution is not available either in the *Quran* or in the Prophet's sayings, a way is provided to determine the *vox populi*, the expressed will of the community as demonstrated by the slowly accumlating pressure of opinion over a long period of time. This principle, called *ijma'* or consensus, was however, rejected by the stricter theologians from the third century onward of Islam, for fear that, invoked for what is not explicity authorised by the *Quran* or a Tradition, it may sanction "innovation" or "heresy".

The counterpart of *ijma'* is *ijtihad,* which literally means "exerting oneself", and not, Iqbal's "principle of movement" nor, as some apologists intepret it "freedom of judgement". It simply means "striving to discover the true application of the teachings of the *Quran* and Tradition to a particular situation, and it may not go against the plain sense of these teachings". Proceeding, the same authority says: "The orthodox theologians, fearing that, to recognise the legitimacy of *ijtihad* might open the door to individual reinterpretation and schism, have always done their best to limit its scope. According to classical doctrine, the range of *ijtihad* was progressively narrowed down, as successive generations, supported by "consensus", filled up the gaps in the doctrinal and legal systems. Finally, no more gaps remained to be filled, or only very insignificant ones, and thereupon 'the gate of *ijtihad* was closed, never again to be reopened'. Islam henceforth became a closed system.

That in sum is the religious structure of Islamic thought as it developed in early Islam in the context of the historical situation obtaining in Arabia at the time. It served the spiritual needs of the unsophisticated Arab of the seventh century Arabia and provided him with a unifying principle in life. Unquestioning conformity to the word of Allah satisfied the Arab's moral cravings.

The Founder of Islam died in 632 and by 732 the Muslims had established an empire stretching from the "confines of China to the shores of the Mediterranean, and from the Atlantic ocean to the Indian". "Looking back at its complete record one may say that this empire reflected the light of the Hellenic sun, when its day had fled, and that it shone like a moon illuminating the darkest night of medieval Europe". It was not only an empire the Muslims founded, but here, in this empire, "between the middle of the eighth and the early part of the twelfth century, the Arabic speaking people held their intellectual supremacy throughout the civilised world."

The truth of the matter is that a unique and complex civilisation emerged in the Muslim empire in the Middle ages which may actually be described as an offspring and continuation of Classical civilisation. It was unique in the sense that its architects were multi-racial-Arabs, Syrians, Jews, Persians, Turks, Egyptians, Berbers, and Spaniards. Its chief ingredients were: Greek science and philosophy; Persia has been described as 'the principal channel irrigating the somewhat arid field of Islam with the rich alluvial flood of ancient culture'; Sufism was its gift; Islam's greatest theologian al-Ghazzali was Persian. Among its famous men belonging to Persia were: Razi (Rhazes), the great physician who first distinguished smallpox from measles; Tabari, our chief source on early Muslim history; Ibn Sina (*Avicenna*), the finest scientific thinker of Islam whose medical writings instructed the world for centuries; Biruni, a many-sided genius; 'Umar Khayyam, better known in the East for his mathematical achievements than for his poetry; Nasiru'ddin al-Tusi, a distinguished astronomer, and Rashidu'ddin Fadlu'llah, author of the first world history, worthy of that name. Add to these luminaries in the firmament of science and scholarship, the poets—Firdawsi, Sa'di, Runa whose shone lustre on their country's literature, and the picture becomes brighter. Finally, its unique character derives from the fact that it was not specifically Muslim—Islam provided it with a frame-work and a universal language.

In the words of Renan as reproduced by Albert Hourani:

"Renan admitted the existence of Arabic philosophy and science, but according to him these were Arabic in nothing but language, and Greco-Sassanain in content. They were entirely the work of non-Muslims in inner revolt against their own religion; by theologians and rulers alike they had been opposed, and so had been unable to influence the institutions of Islam. This opposition had been held in check so long as the Arabs and

Persians had been in control of Islam, but it reigned supreme when the barbarians - Turks in the East, Berbers in the West, took over the direction of the Umma. The Turks had a total lack of the philosophic and scientific spirit, and human reason and progress had been stifled by that enemy of progress, the State based on revelation."

In support of the latter statement I shall but refer to a declaration I heard not many weeks ago by an eminent Muslim theologian who sarcastically said, while delivering a sermon ;" I feel amused to hear people cite contributions to philosophy, science, and art by Muslims in the Middle Ages as examples of Islamic civilisation ; on the contrary, all this was un-Islamic. To acquaint yourselves with real islamic civilisation you should study the lives of early Imams."

While the theologian, unwittingly to be.sure, has drawn his audience's attention to a fact of history and Renan's observations on the civilisation which in J.J Saunder's words was "one of the most brilliant civilisation in the history of humanity" are too sweeping to be considered accurate, the impulse behind what both stress in their awareness of a departure in medieval Islam from its earlier world-view. Hidden behind both observations in other words is the fact of the emergence of modernity in Islamic thought.

Stated briefly the civilisation which emerged in the lands which the Muslims overran in the 7th-8th centuries reflected, in its essence, adaptation by Muslims to changes in norms and attitudes resulting from accumulation of knowledge through contacts with peoples of different ancient cultural traditions. These contacts confronted them with the problem of reinterpreting the teachings of the Quran in the light of the new knowledge they came to acquire and the problem was of reconciling the will of God expressed through the Quran for all time about how men should live in society and the implication of the irreversible movement of the civilisation they had created which by its very nature was compelling them to live and think in a certain other way. In other words, Islam, like Christianity, felt the need of an intellectual interpretation of its tenets in order to correct the literal interpretation of the *Quran* upheld by the fundamentalists of the day. Its early contacts with Greek philosophy gave rise to a philosophico-religious speculation which was represented by the Mu'tazilites who stressed the need of resorting to reason in the interpretation of revelation. They insisted on the justiçe of the divine will and refused to admit that good and evil were only such because God had willed them to be either good or evil. Last but not least, they fought against all anthropomorphic representations of God.

The Caliph al-Ma'mun (813-33), the founder of the *Baytu'l-Hikma* accorded royal patronage to the Mu'tazilite doctrine. In his enthusiasm for the rationalist views of these seceders from the Orthodox, the Caliph imposed on theologians the rationalist doctrine that the *Quran* was created and not eternal.

But the Mu'tazilites were succeeded by an officially-supported orthodox reactionary group of theologians who upheld the *Quran* and the *Sunna* as the only valid source of knowledge and rejected all the findings of exact science, and philosophical speculation as leading to heresy, unbelief and, atheism. A compromise was attempted in the tenth century using logical argument in the demonstration of theological truth. The attempt satisfied neither the philosophers nor those who rejected any process of thought or argument which was not expressly authorised by the scriptures. In his inimitable manner Professor H. A. R. Gibb opines on the consequence of the attempt.

"The earliest theologians in Islam were scholars who had been suddenly introduced to Greek philosophy and, under its fascination, set out to systematise the teachings of the *Quran* in agreement with the doctrines of Aristotle and the Neo-Platonists. It was a perfectly ligitimate object. That is what theology is for; to state the truths of religion (which are, so far, only intuitively known) in terms of the highest intellectual concepts of the time. But one thing the theologian may not do. He may not, on the pretext of accommodating religion and philosophy, question the truths he has set out to defend. At this point theology stops short. But these early Muslims went on, with the result that the great body of believers was outraged. The orthodox theologians evolved, in their turn, a dialectic weapon; to the cutting edge of Greek logic they fitted, in place of the universals of Greek speculative thought, the positive doctrines of the *Quran* and with this they ultimately drove the Hellenizers from the field. It was not any intrinsic superiority in their logic but the intuitive clinging of the masses of the community to the truths of the Quran that really defeated the Hellenizers. That the *Quran* is anticlassical in spirit seems to me undeniable; to that extent the popular and the scholastic reactions were in harmony." On the same issue Iqbal's observation is revealing:

"They (the early Muslims) read the *Quran* in the light of Greek thought. It took them 200 years to perceive—though not quite clearly-that the spirit of *Quran* was anti-classical, and the result of this perception was a kind of intellectual revolt etc."

This repudiation of Greek philosophy, which was paving the way for modernity in Islamic thought, by orthodox theologians resulted in some Muslim thinkers pursuing philosophy for its own sake. Thus men like al-Kindi, al-Farabi, Ibn Sina and Ibn Rushd were philosophers not theologians. This fact had for its consequence a complete reversal of the process of change in harmony with growing knowledge in the Islamic world. The movement to divide learning into subjects that were indigenous to Islam such as, on the one hand, jurisprudence, traditional lore, grammar, lexicography, history, the study of literature, poetry and metrics and on the other, science, philosophy and mathematics which were regarded alien and a danger to Islamic orthodoxy, gradually set a seal on the movement onward in the intellectual adventure of Muslims in the Middle Ages. Scholars and religious philosophers had to work under the watchful and suspecting eyes of the champion of orthodoxy and of a people jealous of the purity of their faith. Many of them were accused of heresy and persecuted—and their works were burned. Some were condemned to exile and some even murdered. A curious but significant development takes place as a consequence of the theologians separating themselves from Greek learning and denouncing thinkers pursuing it. In contrast, in the West, Christian theologians were making the greatest contribution to philosophy under the insppiration of the writings of Muslim philosophers.

In the words of Christopher Dawson : "The development of Western theological speculation was decisively influenced by the discovery of Arabian philosophy and of the philosophy of Aristotle. St. Thomas Aquinas in the 13th century was greatly influenced by Aristotelianism as conveyed to Europe through Latin translations from Arabic in effecting an understanding between Christianity and the new knowledge. Ibn Rushd's Influence was no less significant. A spirit of enquiry and passion for knowledge was stirring in the West. Toledo, the cosmopolitan centre, with its mixed population of Jews, Muslims and Christians attracted the new intelligentsia of the West in quest of knowledge in the 12th century-more so because of the school of translators founded by Archbishop Raymond I. The entire Aristotelian corpus was translated from Arabic into Latin and this was followed by translations of the chief works of the great Islamic and Jewish philosophers and religious thinkers, al-Kindi, al Farabi, al-Battani, Ibn Sina and al-Ghazzali. It was from Muslim Toledo that Europe first learnt to understand that learning knows no frontiers, that it is universal, global, and 'human' ; it concerns mankind as a whole, without respect of race or religion. Entering Europe through philosophy Toledo Muslim philosophy exercised a profound influence on its theology. It provided an intellectual stimulus for the reconciliation of faith and reason leading to develoopments of far-reaching consequences over the centuries."

In the Islamic world on the other hand, doors were bolted against all breath of rational thinking, particularly in the realm of religious thought. In full possession of the entire corpus of

Aristotelian thought-categories though the Muslims were, they utilised it in setting the seal of immutability on the Quranic teaching as unalterable and final, instead of putting it to use as a means of bridging the gulf between religious dogma and intellectual activity in the world of Islam. What the learned interpretors of the *Quran* did, was to confer upon it absolute authority making Islam a fundamentalist religion. These guardians of the faith took all care against any reinterpretation of the Quran. Sensing danger of innovation, they rejected *ijma*, the principal of consensus, confining its relevance to the first century Islam. They gradually narrowed down the range of *ijtihad* the 'principal of movement' as Iqbal calls it, or 'freedom of judgment' as popularly understood, as fearing that individual reinterpretation and schism might ifringe the absolutism of the Holy Book, ultimately closed its gate. The consequence of this action by the custodians of theology was that "The code of conduct represented by *Sharia* was fixed and final in its terms and any modification was regarded as a deviation from the legitimate and valid standard. In other words, the religious code thus established was an all-embracing one, in which every aspect of human relationship was regulated in meticulous detail; the law having once achieved perfection of expression, was in principle static and immutable, for Muhammad was the last of the Prophets, and after his death in 623, there could be no further direct communication of the divine will to man. In the Islamic concept, human thought unaided cannot discern the true values and standards of conduct, such knowledge can be attained only through divine mediation, and acts are good or evil exclusively because Allah has attributed this quality to them. Modernity in Islam as an active principle of change forward which manifested itself in its Golden Age lasting a bare two centuries 900-1100 gives place to traditionalism, defined as the claim most religious systems have that they alone bear within themselves a deposit consisting of ceremonial, myth, dogma or ethic or of some of these elements, revealed by some ultimate divine or quasidivine authority, and meant to be handed down to posteritty by a succession of duly qualified trustees."

This rigid and inflexible attitude has confronted, in the past as much as it does today, the Muslim community the world over with the problem inherent in the very nature of Islam namely, the need to define the relationship between the standards imposed by the religious faith and the mendane forces that activate society. At the one extreme is the solution adopted by classical jurisprudence—a divine nomocracy under which religious principles were elaborated into a comprehensive and rigid scheme of duties to form the exclusive determinant of the conduct of society. The other is the adoption of secularism, which relegates religious principles to the realm of individual conscience and allows the forces of society unfettered control over the shape of its laws. The first solution must be rejected it dualism and hypocrisy in life are to be avoided in a world which is fast moving towards closer union not merely on material but also on the intellectual plane. It is unrealistic and totally unworkable in a technological civilisation. The second solution obviously is un-Islamic seen through the glasses of traditionalism, although it may be acceptable to the Westerniser, without a great deal of resistance as contact with Western secular philosophy has instilled in them an unconscious readiness for change. As Professor H.A.R. Gibb writes:

"Nevertheless, it is impossible for the Muslim who absorbs a secular education on Western lines to avoid some overlay of Western thought in his mental activity; and if it does not take a religious form, it creates an implicit tendency to adopt the values, humanistic or otherwise, that are manifested in Western civilisation and apply the concept of evolution without regard to Muslim theological limitations." Or in Renan's words:

"La jeunesse d'Orient, en venant dans les ecoles d'Occident puiser la science europeenne, emportera avec elle ce qui en est le corollaire inseparable, la methode rationalle, l'esprit experimental, le sens due reel, 'l'impossibilite de croire a des traditions religeuses evidement concus en dehors de toute critique."

But the seeds of modernity in Islam were already planted by

the first delibrate attempt at a westernizing policy by turkey in the early eighteenth century after the humiliating defeats the Ottoman Emppire sustained at the hands of Austrians and their allies. Turkey then decided to follow Peter the Great's policy of westernisation as a means of throwing off its weakness and of recovering its past military power. The person responsible for this bold imaginative step was Damad Ibrahim Pasha, deputy Grand Vizier 1716, and Grand Vizier 1718 to 1730. Damad Ibrahim instructed Turkey's ambassador in Europe to study thoroughly the means of civilisation and education, and report on those capable of application in Turkey. This step led to contact with French culture which, in turn produced impact on the cultural and social life of Turkish society. The beginning thus made of westernization as a reaction to military defeat proceeded apace during the decades that followed and brought Turkey deeper under the influence of Europe and widened that Gulf between those who desired to modernise Islam by ridding it of the accretions it had gathered over the centuries on the one hand, and the custodians of orthodoxy who opposed every change in this direction, on the other. It must be emphasised here that the modernists did not denounce Islam; all they wanted was to reject contemporary Islam as full of accidental growths and to return to the early Islam of the days of the Holy Prophet and his successors. They rejected, therefore, the validity and legality of the *Shari a* and advocated *ijtihad.* They stood for Islam free from the theological developments of later times.

The seeds of modernity planted in early eighteenth century came to full fruition after Turkey's sudden colapse in the first World War in October 1918. As a reaction again to another humiliating treaty—the Treaty of Severs, in 1920, which aimed at the partition of the "Sick Man of Europe," the Turks fought back the enemies under the leadership of Mustafa Kamal one of the most forceful figures in recent history, and established a Republic in which the state was separated from the Church for the first time in Islam. A series of reforms followed secularising the colleges and schools, the introduction of the Latin alphabet, the liberation of women, the discarding of the Friday in favour of Sunday, the abolition of polygamy and the introduction of the Swiss Civil Code and the Swiss Code of Obligations. The Muslim Private Law ceased to be law in the Turkish Republic. Thus took palce in Islam the most "incisive revolution in its history." The point to note is that modernity in Turkey, brought about by Mustafa Kamal, left the Turks as much Muslim as the Lutheran Reformation towards the end of the Middle Age left proteseants Christian.

A situation similar to the military defeat suffered by Turkey at the hands of a European power, early 18th century, roused Egypt from traditionalism after its occupation by Napoleon about the end of the 18th century and led it on the road to modernity. The path, it followed too, was similar, namely, to turn to the West in search of means of self-preservation. It was felt that, as in case of Turkey, it was through the adoption of western methods that Egypt could maintain its political integrity. Thus, Muhammad 'Ali, the creator of modern Egypt realised, as did Ibrahim Pasha of Turkey in the preceding century, that it was an Egyptian army trained in Western skills and modern weapons alone which could repel the threat from the West and that this training could only be had from the West. He, therefore, sent his offers to Italy and France to study military science, mathematics and medicine. As a corollary to this step, he ordered the translation of works on these and other subjects by Western scholars into Arabic. Furthermore, he popularised education by opening schools all over the country. The intellectual awakening of the Arab community had started.

But little did the leaders of Egypt appreciate the fundamental fact that Europe's material progress had its root in a process of intellectual revolution which began with the 13th-14th century Renaissance; and that it was a mere outward manifestation of the culmination of a long-drawn out conflict between traditional beliefs and rational thinking, and most important of all, little could they imagine that in the words of Renan "the youth from the

East who acquired modern science could carry with it what is its natural corollary, the scientific method, the spirit of experiment, and the reluctance of accepting religious beliefs uncritically."

And that is what exactly happened. The impact of Western education led the Egyptians to re-examine traditional Islam in the light of modern scientific discoveries in order to close the rift between orthodoxy and secular thought by making palatable to the traditionalists the concepts of modern science which differ sharply from those Middle Ages which the Muslims cherished as their dogma. These concepts, in order to be accepted had to be brought into harmony with the scriptures.

The forms such attempts took are highly interesting to the student of the conflict between the advocates of liberalism and the custodians of orthodoxy in Islam. Like the young Ottoman liberals the young Egyptians who had come under the influence of European culture tried to justify the adoption of western institutions in Islamic terms, as being not the introduction of something new but a return to the true spirit of Islam. Thus, Tahtawi (1801-73), who was profoundly influenced by French Enlightenment and knew the ideas of Rousseau and Montesqieu as intimately as Islamic theology, held that Egypt must adopt the modern sciences and the innovations to which they would lead, and that she could do so without danger to her religion. For the sciences, then spreading in Europe, had once been Islamic sciences : Europe had taken them from the Arabs, and in taking them back, Egypt would only be claiming what was her own, that the secret of European strength lay in the cultivation of the rational sciences, and, that the Muslims fell behind as a result of their neglect. At the same time Tahtawi and others of his way of thinking were conscious of the problem facing the world of Islam of reconciling the claims of divine revelation and those of human reasoning proclaiming itself the only adequate path to knowledge—how to become part of the modern world while remaining Muslims?

A significant, and at the same time of far-reaching relevance to the steady growth of a mind oriented to modernism was the conscious efforts made to evolve a medium in the Arabic language which would make its users feel citizens of the new world of science and invention. The name associated with this subtle attempt at injecting modernism in the Arab mind is that of a member of the Maronite community of Lebanon, Butrus-al-Bustani (1819-83).

The mind of the Egyptian youth, already stirred into vigorous thinking over the problem of adaptation to the changes resulting from contact with European culture came, at this stage, under the influence of a strange personality in Jamalu'ddin al-Afghani (1839-97). Althogh much has been written about him, little is known for certain about his origins. The fact, however, remains that he exercised chastening influence on the whole Islamic world in the last quarter of the nineteenth century. "He became the guide and unofficial teacher of a group of young men, mainly from the Azhar, who were to play an important part in Egyptian life and were never to shake off the influence of al-Afghani. Besides "Abduh, the group included Sa'd Zaghlul who, fifty years later, was to become the leader of the Egyptian nation. He taught them mainly in his own home, what he conceived to be true Islam: theology, jurisprudence, mysticism, and philosophy."

During a life of long travels through India, Persia, Turkey, France, England and Russia, al-Afghani devoted his learning in persuading Muslims to understand their religion aright and live in accordance with its teachings. He believed that the Muslims would be able to face the rising European powers which threatened their freedom only if they organised their life in pursuance of the precepts of the *Quran* and united. Al-Afghani was a staunch pan-Islamist and a savage anti-West. His Islam could be reduced to a belief in a transcendent God to the finality of prophethood in Muhammad and the *Quran* as the world of Gou uncorrupted. Described as the 'Wild, man of genius," al-Afghani left an enduring impression on the burgeoning progressivism of Egypt. Of the many who came under his influence, Muhammad 'Abduh was the most outstanding.

Like al-Afghani, his guru and preceptor, 'Abduh's starting point was the problem of inner decay in Islam and the need for an inner revival. The orthodox believed that the Prophet was sent not merely to preach a way of individual salvation but to establish a virtuous society. This belief implied that there were certain ways of acting in conformity with the Prophet's message and the will of God, and certain others which were not. But as time passed, the Islamic society was faced with problems not foreseen in the prophetic message and found itself acting in ways which might even be interpreted as contradicting it. How then to bridge the gap between what Islamic society should be and what it had become. This had been the problem which confronted the Muslim thinkers in the later Middle Ages but it assumed a graver form as the movement of westernisation advanced.

The solution of the problem, according to 'Abduh was to interpret God's commandments rationally and in the light of general welfare. Islam be held is true sociology, the science of happiness in this world as well as the next. The ideal Islamic society once existed during the Golden Age of Islam the first generation of obedience, and was rewarded by political success and intellectual development without parallel in the speed and manner of its flowering. This society decayed when alien elements crept into it: "the philosophers and extreme Shi'ism brought in the spirit of excess and a certain type of mysticism obscured the essential nature of Islam."

It was 'Alduh's conviction that the Islamic society would not be able to regain its past strength and become prosperous until it acquired from Europe the sciences and this it could do without abandoning Islam, for, Islam taught the acceptance of all the products of reason. This acceptance 'Alduh held involved changes in Islamic institutions—its legal system, its schools, and its methods of government. Muslims in his opinion, must do what they always have done, that is, to re-interpret their law and adapt it to modern problems, 'Abduh stood for a bold re-interpretation of Islam in the interest of the Islamic society holding that "God's purpose in Making his revelation was to promote human welfare" and, that "the judge should choose that interpretation of the law, regardless of whether it was derived from his own legal code or not, which best fited the circumstances." 'Abduh aimed at producing a synthesis of the four traditional Sunni legal systems which can have the good points of all the creation of a unified and modern system of Islamic law.

The significant service 'Abduh rendered to the cause of modernism in Egypt was to stir into active thinking, on the problem, a number of younger men who, after his death, pulled the lead he gave in different directions. If, for example, his insistence on the unchanging character, in essentials of Islam led to fundamentalism, his emphasis on the legitimacy of social change resulted in a *de facto* division between the two realms, that of religion and that of society, each with its own norms. Others again worked out the principles of a secular society in which Islam was honoured but was no longer the guide of law and policy. There were others among his students who refused to confer upon Islamic law its position as the moral basis of society. These would not concede to Islamic society any superiority over a non-Islamic society. The world, they held is standing forwards an ideal socity in which reason will reign supreme.

Post-'Abduh Egypt seethed with intellectual stirrings all striving for closing the rift between orthodoxy and secular thought. Thus the belief that the Muslims have received from the past an unchanging norm of wisdom which should for ever regulate the organisation of society has been shaken. The *Sharri' 'a* has been abandoned, with astonishing speed and completeness. And all this happened imperceptibly. Despite al-Azhar, modern Egypt has become increasingly secular-minded. It is a modern state based more on a strong faith in nationalism rather than on religion.

Turning to India we witness a scene at once baffling and perplexing. It is axiomatic with scholars writing on modernism in Indian Muslims to hail Syed Ahmad Khan as the father of a 'movement' directed to this end. Thus, we have Professor II. A.

R. Gibb in his brilliant Haskell lectures, delivered before the University of Chicago in 1945 and later published under the title *Modern Trends in Islam* :

> The most remarkable feature of the first Indian modernist movement, led by Sir Sayyid Ahmad Khan (d. 1898), was its organized character. That it owed mainly to the foundation of a college at Aligarh in 1875, now (since 1920) the muslim University, with the object of combining religious education with modern scientific studies."

and Wilfred smith in his first highly informative and challenging book *Modern Islam in India,* published in 1943 and since repudiated by him :

> "It was he around whom the entire movement gathered, as it grew from small and much opposed beginnings to permeate the whole of the growing Indian Muslim middle-class life."

and The Lichtenstadter in her *Islam and the Modern Age, 1959:*

> "Western learning and the curricula designed for western needs and interests were introduced to enable the eastern student to hold his own against, if possible to complete with, the foreigners. Gradually, the luminaries of western thought took the place of the great Muslim thinkers in the curricula of eastern universities. The founding of the Anglo-Muslim Collge (now the Muslim University) in Aligarh, India, in 1875 is the best example for this process."

and many others in similar vein. With due respect to these scholars for their learning and sympathetic interest in contemporary Islamic world the present writer hesitates to share their views on the role the M.A.O. College founded in 1870 is credited to have played in the propagation of its founder's attempts to modernise Islam. Indeed, he is inclined to reject the claim that there was a movement which "gathered around Syed

Ahmad Khan" engaged in giving a rational interpretation of the *Quran.* And his doubts are rooted in his close association, first with the College, and then with life in the University since its inception in 1920. The college, as he found it on his arrival welnigh fifty years ago, was, to quote again Rev. Wilfred Smith "pro-British through and through" and "one of the objects of the College was to make the Muslims of India," not modern in outlook but, "worthy and useful subjects of the British Crown."

It is a fact of history that Syed Ahmad Khan was forced by his co-religionists to abjure all he had been preaching through the pages of the *Tahdhibu' l-Akhlaq* for seven years as a price for the founding of the College. His successors, everyone of whom was a British protege and in receipt of pension from the later's "faithful ally" the Nizam of Hyderabad, were small men as far as intellectual perception, breadth of vision and contemporary western education were concerned. They were appointed as Secretaries of the College by the British with the deliberate purpose of protecting the middle class Muslim youth against the breath of change in Islam which Syed Ahmed Khan had been trying to breath into Islam. Such an intellectual revolution the British knew, would lead inevitably to political awakening as it did in the case of Bengal in early nineteenth century and was behind the burgeoning national movement. The Honorary Secretaries of the College served their masters faithfully and wiped out all traces of progressive thinking from the College. They kept out of its Board of Trustes the few forward looking young Muslims who were trying to rescue the Muslim youth from the grip of these obscurantists. The Imam brothers and the Ali brothers were the pioneers in this conflict, but being in a hopeless minority these good men never succeeded in reversing the reactionary trends in the College.

As for the period, beginning with the transition from the College to the University as a recoil to the attempts of nationalists among the Muslims to free the College from the reactionary elements controlling it at the time, no change in basic character of the Institution took place. The University, from the day it saw the light in 1920 to 1947, was under the control of an individual whose one concern, with the support of the British, was to perpetuate the policy of the trustees of the College in subordinating the academic objectives of the University to the loyal service of the rulers by ruthlessly suppressing all trends towards modernity within its four walls. The gemtleman was an avowed enemy of progressive thinking on the one hand and an unblushing opponent of the nationalist movement in the country on the other. True, the University could not live in a glass house. Surviving repression, a group of young men were able to build up an opinion in favour of modernism. They went to the extent of defying public opinion and inviting official opprobrium. But, as professor Gibb has so eloquently observed, "But what is more serious is the effect among modernists themselves of this unwillingness to think out and to define their position clearly. Instead of a broad current of soundly based and rationally acceptable arguments, modernism, lacking the discipline of controlled thinking, often loses itself in a maze of subjective impulses and is ever liable to the danger of plunging headlong over some unseen precipice."

Freedom of the country has brought about little change in the situation. It may sound paradoxical but it is a fact that a secular government has been protecting the traditionalists in control of the University on political considerations. The manner of dispersal of the annual meeting of the University Court in 1965 is a case in point. Any slightest move by an enlightened individual to cause the slightest ripple in the stagnant pool of obscurantist thought in the Institution, is threatened with direct consequences. It will be carrying the debate to undue length to attempt an analysis of the situation as it obtains today at the University. I shall, therefore, content myself by quoting below a melancholog but revealing extract from a "question" Rev. Smith has posed in the Aligarh number of the Aligarh magazine published in 1955:

"Sir Sayyid saw the need for modern education in his community, and devoted his energies to seeing to it that this need be met. He also recognized that the community would not be willing (and rightly!) to have modern education, if this meant abandoning Islam. He, therefore, was careful to provide a college in which both modern secular education and Islamic religious instruction would be simultaneously provided. Yet he also sensed that his own views on religion, his own interpretation of Islam, the endeavours which his own mind was making to synthesize and harmonize his religious tradition with the spirit and knowledge of modernity, were unacceptable to most of his fellow Muslims.

"Accordingly, he conceded that in the new college, Islamic instruction should be provided by the recognized—that is, the traditional—religious leaders of the community, in the traditional way. These, of course, were the proponents of the traditional interpretation of Islam. He himself felt that this traditional interpretation was in fact an outworn interpretation; that pure Islam in its original pristine form was simpler and more relevant, was less tied to the social decaddence of the immediate past. However, he made it clear that he would not force his religious views on the students of the college; that the Department of Theology would be quite autonomous and not the source of propaganda for the new views.

"Probably it was necessary to make this concession in order to have his English education accepted in the other departments, and in order to have parents send their sons at all. However, is it not possible to question the wisdom of this decision? Or at least, to speculate about what might have been the result had the concession not been made. How far is it true that the resulting dichotomy of religious versus-secular learning has infected the Aligarh Movement and its attitude to life ever since? The fact that all other studies were in the English language, while the study of Islamics was in Urdu, seems to have had an important psychological effect. Graduates of the College, and of the university since, appear to have adopted an attitude towards the intellectual problems of religion which is very special and isolated. The College itself made apparently no attempt to integrate the science, philosophy modern history, and other matters taught in the college, with the tradition of the *`ulama.'* And since the College did not do so neither did the students; and indeed they were induced to feel that to do so was unnecessary.

"Not that the Aligarh Movement quite segregated religion from the rest of life Muslims have never done that; and the recent political history of the sub-continent has illustrated the continued tie between the two. Yet one may ask whether perhaps the situation has resulted in an emotional rather than intellectual attachment to religion, and in an understanding of Islam which is more traditional than contemporary.

"Nowadays not a great deal of attention is paid to Sir Sayyid's religious views. Is this because they were not sound, were not interesting, were not very relevant to the problems and situations confronting modern Indo-Muslims? Or is it simply because they were neglected, in the college which otherwise is a memorial to his vision and his insight? If his *Tafsir,* for instance, had been studied alongwith (not instead of !) the other earlier commentaries; if his interpretation of the prophet had been examined alongwith other biographies; would the results have been bad or good? No doubt, some would have disagreed; but might this have led to more critical study, to argument and counter-argument, to constructive new theology for the future instead of a return to or maintenance of the old? Would the use of English for religious instruction as well as other instruction have led to more synthesis and integration between the whole world of knowledge, sacred and secular?

"The above is in no way meant to suggest that the teaching of religion at Aligarh has in itself been inadequate. It would be absurd for an outside to criticize. Sir Sayyid for his decision, to question the instruction that human fact been offered. Our concern is not really with the teaching of religion which has been available, but rather with the lack of co-ordination between that teaching and the teaching of other things. It may indeed be that the result of the dichotomy have been good. My only real question is to wonder what those results are."

Rev. Smith has put a pertinent question to Aligarh in his characteristic manner of deep understanding, modesty and humility. Will Aligarh provide a reply? Weighed in the scale of what succeeded Syed Ahmad Khan's readiness to abandon his crusade against *taqlid* in favour of *ijtihad,* it would appear that the step led to most unfortunate results for the Muslims of India. By his action Syed Ahmad Khan left the coast clear for the traditionalists to entrench themselves in the M.A.O. College against any basic change in the Muslim approach to the problem of the conflict between old beliefs and modern world. The effect of this set-back in the intellectual evolution of the Muslims of India found expression in the worst tragedy that ever befell the community in the unnatural division of the country. No wonder Pakistanis hail Syed Ahmed Khan as the first to conceive the idea of Pakistan.

Other names usually referred to in connection with modernism in India Islam are those of Ameer Ali, Khuda Bakhsh, Iqbal, Yusuf Ali and Azad. If by modernism we are to understand "the necessity of intellectual response within a religious faith to the pressure of circumstances and ideas as they bear upon traditional dogma and behaviour" hardly one in the list stands the test. As for Ameer Ali, "not content as some, merely to assert that Islam is not illiberal or unscientific, he turns the tables and claims that Islam and progress are synonymous. In a most assured *tour de force* he harmonises the mosque and modernity." Describing him, Proffessor Gibb says. "But he (Ameer Ali) presents practically the whole range of modernist apologetic argument on the subject, and more persuasively than most of the later writers and pamphleteers, who repeat his assertions in every Muslims language in more violent or more restrained tones." Ameer Ali lacked the intellectual integrity of Syed Ahmed Khan and instead of judging Islam and its teaching against its historical background, used his intellectual skill in rationalising it.

In Khuda Bakhsh we meet "one of the earliest thinkers to claim a right to use the *Quran* so to speak idealistically, whether or not the interpretation was, by historical criteria, fictitious". He is remembered more for his translations into English of important Dutch and German works on Islam than for any significant contribution to the understanding of Islam. Reading him one feels one is in the presence of an individual who allows himself to be swayed more by emotion than by logic and historical data. Here is a quotation in illustration:

"There is one thing which Profesor Hell has not done. He has not accounted for the collapse of a civilisation which united striking material prosperity with distinctive intellectual greatness, which stood out for light amidst deep and deepening darkness, which was a beacon into it own and succeeding ages, and which at one time seemed, like Roman civilisation, firmly planted, secure of permanence, scornful of the waves of time. But lively intellectual activities, rise of religious sects, disturbing doubts and scepticism, political chaos-these lossened even the one remaining tie of a common faith," etc. etc.

Reading the above one finds it hard to differentiate the scholar from the propagandist. Apart from the faulty logic and fulsome verbiage, little regard has been bestowed upon facts of history.

One is tempted to bracket Iqbal with Khuda Bakhsh in their disregard of history and the tidal wave of emotional upsurge in the presentation of Islam. Of the two, Iqbal decidedly had a more vigorous intellect and deeper learning; he was more sensitive and better informed by problem facing Islam today. All these natural gifts notwithstanding, Iqbal failed in his impact on the Muslim mind of contemporary India in solving the perennial problem of reconciling faith with reason. This was so because he preferred a highly charged emotional weapon of poetry instead of well-reasoned prose to rouse his co-religionists to activity. Secondly, despite a keen intellect he could not allow his vision to transcend in its sweep the limitations of a rigid outlook. Age, instead of broadening narrowed his vision further.

He found fulfilment in prescribing the creation of a separate homeland for Muslim by dividing India as a solution of the conflict between the old and new in Islam. Commenting on the medium Iqbal adopted, Kenneth Cragg observes: "And the medium was well-chosen since the very form of poetry absolves the writer from necessities of logic, consistency or argumentation. He could be dynamic vehement, outrageous, satirical, sugggestive, passionate, trenchant and allusive, by turns, without the obligations of consistency or justification to which prose is bound. He turned his fire on Western materialism and Mulla ignorance with equal zeal."

Describing the essential Iqbal Professor Gibb comments: "Iqbal spoke more truly than he intended when he implied that Muslims were only taking back from Europe a further development of some of the most important phases of culture of Islam'. He was thinking of physical and psychological theory; but what the Muslim intellectuals did take back from Europe was, above all, the imaginative legacy of romanticism, which had indeed been stimulated in Europe by the influence of Arabic literature in the Middle Ages and again by the popularity of the Arabian Nights in the eighteenth century. The unconscious irony of Iqbal's claim is rendered still more striking by the fact that he is himself the most conspicuous example of this process, since the ideas expressed in his lectures on religious reconstruction are (as we have seen) the product of the intuitive reasoning of the Sufi attracted into the orbit of the high priest and prophet of Romantic antirationalism, Henri Bergson."

'Abdullah Yusuf 'Ali, despite his labours in re-interpreting Islam in modern terms was rejected outright alike by the educated and the Mulla. His over-enthusiasm to equate Islam with modern thought had the opposite effect of repelling the Muslims from his method of Quranic interpretation. Even his competence as a translator from Arabic into English was doubted.

Next in our list is one of the most brilliant men of our age anywhere. He was a child prodigy having mastered medieval learning while yet in his teens. He used to hold his elders in awe by his intellectual reach, by the subtlety of his mind, by his amazing memory and by the depth of his knowledge. While owning indebtendness to Syed Ahmad Khan as his intellectual mentor, Azad rejected the former's thesis that the redemption of the Muslims of India from social, economic, and religious backwardness lay in total acceptance of the British rule, Azad became an ardent believer in Hindu-Muslim unity as the corner-stone of Indian nationhood. As a corollary, he was convinced that freedom from foreign rule could only be achieved if the two communities were persuaded to believe that "God created all men as human beings, but they adapted varying names and labels and broke the unity of mankind to pieces". To this end, he utilised his exceptional gifts of prodigious intellectual prowess, his felicity of expression and his boundless learning. The *Tarjumanul-Quran*-his *magnum opus*, was the product of Azad earnest efforts to bridge the gulf between the two communities. He believed that the rigidity of outlook of his own community would be dissolved if he demonstrated that "the *Quran* declares that human nature is so constituted that outward forms will differ, and everyone thinks that his way is superior to that of other; he cannot look at his own way from the point of view of his opponents. But even as your way is excellent in your own eyes, even so in other people's eyes their way is excellent. Toleration is therefore the only way".

This may be regarded Azad's efforts towards modernising Islam; in harmonising it with changing situations. Why these efforts failed is a different question and can be answered at a different level. For our purpose it will suffice to point out that Azad's method did not take into consideration the fundamental of the problem of modernity in an established social tradition; it was pseudo intellectual in that it had no permanence or continuity about it. As already stated above, the only effective method of solving the problem is the historical method. Maulana Azad was too shrewd a man not to have understood this, but an excess of enthusiasm for the forging of Hindu-Muslim accord seems to have withheld it from the focus of his attention.

So far in my treatment of the central theme of the seminar vis-a-vis Indian Islam I have found non-except Syed Ahmed Khan who can be said to have approached the problem of bringing about the intellectual revolution in Islam which would lead to modernity in its interpretation. But the community not only rejected him but has forgotten his original mission altogether. Azad, a greater intellectual was best qualified for the work. His dedication to the cause of the country's freedom led him to an approach which his community will never accept. The scholar who has treated the subject scientifically and with courage, however, is Mr. A.A.A. Fyzee. An eminent writer on law he has advocated all his life fundamental change in the basic concept of Islam in order to provide a rational interpretation of the *Quran.* I can do not better than end my survey of the problem with a quotation from his "*A modern Approach of Islam*":

"Religion should place emphasis on devotion to God, cleanliness of spirit, orderliness of life, and not be enmeshed in the minutiae of particular do's and don'ts. Apart from everything else the Islamic virtues of generosity, humility, brotherliness, courage and manliness should be targht by examples drawn from early Muslim history. Additionally, the ethics and morality of Islam should be fortified by the teaching of the ethical and philosophical teachers of the modern world. We must keep our hearts and minds open to the thought of Barth, Tillich, Kierkegaarde and Radhakrishnan. We cannot make the *Quran* a book `which imprisons the living word of God in a book and makes tradition an infallible source. . . .' The Rabbis `do not listen to their conscience, they consult law books. So do the religious mentors of Islam. " He also asks for a re-examination of *sharia and Kalam.* He says:

"The theology of Islam must be re-examined in all its aspects, and modern philosophy metaphysics, ethics, psychology and logic should be applied to formulate an drestate its essential dogmas. The scholastic theology of Islam (*Ilmu'l-kalam)* in its various aspect has not been substantially reformed since the days of Ghazali. The current stream of European thought; the great advances made by Protestant thinkers from Luther downwards, and by the scholastics from St. Thomas Aquinas and Suarez down to Maritain and Berdyaev; and the speculations of Jewish and other thinkers of the modern world must be used with discrimination to fortify and re-shape Islamic theological principles.

None of the personalities cited as exponents of different approaches to the inner conflict in modern Islam succeeded in showing the way out of the intellectual impasse the thinking section is encountering but evading its logical consequences. This attitude has led to unblushing opportunism, even if mildy put. Some seek refuge in Iqbal quoting some verse or other as it suits the occasion. Other prefer to evade the issue altogether and behave as if no problem exists. Is this a desirable state of affairs, at least judged at academic level? For possible way out I shall only quote Professor Gibb and close:

"But what is going to happen when the technological processes of Western civilization penetrate more deeply into Muslim society, with more and more disturbing effects? Outwardly, the alternatives would seem to lie between an increasing secularism or a more violent Mahdist reaction—the choice depending in part upon the relations which develop between the Muslim peoples and the Western countries. But, given time and a world at peace, the result may just as well be gradual reassimilation of the intellectuals, a closing up of split created by modernism in the forces opposed to both seculatism and Mahdism, a reassertion of the cultural values for which Islam has traditionally stood, and the development of antitoxins to counteract the virus introduced from the West.

"If this is to be realized, however, the Muslims faith will have to show that it possesses the strength and vitality to generate these antitoxins, mainly out of its own resources, but bot excluding the possibility of adapting some of the constructive elements in Western thought in place of its destructive romanticism. The future of Islam rests where it has rested in the past-on the insight of the orthodox leaders and their capacity to resolve the new tensions as they arise by a positive doctrine which will face and master the forces making for disintegration."

8

Islam and Women in India

From the time of the Aryans, we have record of invasions of India by many warlike races but most of them settled down in the country, accepted the Indo-Aryan cultural and religious hegemony, and became Hindus or Buddhists. When they adopted Hinduism, their gods were incorporated in the Hindu pantheon and they themselves were given a caste status in keeping with their power and prestige; in course of time, they lost their individuality and were absorbed in the vast Hindu fold. But with the arrival of the Muslims, for the first time in Indian history was introduced an element which Hinduism could not digest. The social and religious conceptions of Hinduism and Islam were so different that it was found impossible for the two to merge.

If Hinduism could not assimilate Islam, the latter could not annihilate the former either. In the eventful history of Islam, it had completely wiped out, in regions it ruled, all ancient religions like Zoroastrianism and the faiths of Syria, Asia Minor and Egypt; Christians and Jews were allowed a precarious existence as Kithabias or the People of the Book. Islam, as is well known, partially recognises the validity of the Old and New Testaments and as such was less intolerant towards Christianity and Judaism than towards non-Kithabias or People without the Book. In India, however, Hinduism, in spite of its reverses in the battlefield, showed unexpected vitality in its determined resistance to Islam; it put up almost as much resistance as European Christianity. And this, in spite of the fact that practically the whole of India was conquered by Muslim arms, and the Muslims ruled the country for well over half a millennium. In the end, the impossibility of either sub-duing the other was recognised, and the country was divided into Hindustan and Pakistan.

The prolonged Muslim rule, however, produced a composite culture in India. While the Hindus have all along remained the majority community in India, even during the heyday of Muslim power, Muslims, after the establishment of their suzerainty, became the second biggest community, numerically: this position they have retained in Hindustan or Bharat even after the partition of the country.

There was, thus, close contact between the two peoples for centuries; though neither lost its individuality and distinctive characteristics, both the communities influenced each other considerably in their long and continued co-existence. Further, even during the early stages of Muslim rule, only the upper classes were foreign immigrants; the vast majority of the Muslim population of India was of indigenous extraction, and their customs, manners and social life remained largely rooted in Indian soil while their beliefs were but partially modified by Islam.

The Muslim dominance of India falls into two clearly marked periods. The earlier phase started with the annual raids of Mahmud of Ghazni (eleventh century); this invader made no effort to extend his empire into India but was generally content to plunder the great cities of India, with the ostentatious object of destroying idolatry and furthering the cause of Islam. Mahmud made some seventeen such raids but his activities did not extend farther than the Doab.

The real invasion of India by the Muslims started some hundred years later by Mohammad Ghori who defeated Prithwiraj Chawhan of Delhi in 1192, and appointed his able general Kutub-ud-din Aibeck to look after his Indian dominions. Both the Sultan and Kutub-ud-din extended their conquests, and by 1206, the date of Mohammad's death, the whole of northern India from the Punjab to Bengal came under Muslim sway.

The earlier Muslim period may be said to have ended with the defeat of Ibrahim Lodi in the battle of Panipat, in the year 1525, by Babar who founded the Moghul empire in India. The absence of a sound principle of succession, which had been a distinctive feature of Islam in the early days of its expansion, often led to many wars of succession in India too; the most competent person was considered the proper person to lead the faithful, and what with every one near the court claiming to be the most competent, and the quarrels of slaves, and sons of slave-girls (who were not debarred succession) intriguing for power, the death of a reigning monarch was invariably an occasion for fractional wars of succession in the early Muslim world.

With the arrival of Babar, things changed. The Moghuls though Muslims, brought with them many of the laws of Chengiz Khan, and followed the Mongol tradition of succession. Their empire flourished in India for full two centuries with extra-ordinary vigour under able rulers, and the name of the Grand Moghul became a byword for greatness and splendour throughout the world.

Further, with the Muslim period, the regular written history of India began. The history of pre-Muslim India was mainly based on archaeological finds, ancient inscriptions, and on passages of dubious value in the religious and secular literature of the country, and on stray accounts of travellers like Fa Hien and Huien Tsang. But after the Muslim conquest, regular historical works on India by Muslims were written; travellers like Ibn Batuta too added considerably to our knowledge of Muslim India. During the Moghul period, Europeans too came to India in large numbers, and we have their very valuable accounts which were free from any leanings towards Islam or Hinduism.

All told, our knowledge of the Muslim period in India is much more thorough and reliable than the previous Hindu period.

Legal Status of Muslim Women

To the Muslim, marriage is not a sacrament as understood by the Hindus and Roman Catholics, but a secular institution mainly based on the theory of contract. Certain broad outlines are clearly defined within which the term of contract operates. A man cannot marry more than four wives at a time, though he is allowed to keep concubines and slave-girls if he could afford them. The Koranic injunction is: "If ye fear that ye cannot do justice between orphans, then marry what seems good to ye, of women, by two's three's or four's; if ye fear that ye cannot be equitable, then only one or what your right hand possesses". The text is not very clear, but the generally accepted interpretation is that limited *polygyny* is permitted. It must be borne in mind that the Arabs of the Prophet's days had very lax matrimonial laws, and the rule regarding a maximum, of four was a restraining piece of legislation. In no case, however, is polyandry permitted. Further, "ye are also forbidden to take to wife, free women who are married, except those whom your right hand shall possess as slaves". A Muslim woman cannot marry a non-Muslim, while a Muslim male may marry not only Muslim women but also Kithabias.

> Marriage being essentially a civil contract, the essentials are that there must be a proposal by one party, and acceptance by the other. Such a proposal and acceptance must be made in clear terms and in the presence and hearing of two male or one male and two female witnesses, who must be sane, adult Muslims. Both the offer and the acceptance must be at one meeting and no other writing or religious ceremony is essential for a valid marriage. There is optional registration for Muslim marriage, and divorce in some districts of Bengal and Assam, but it is expressly provided that the registrar shall not be authorised to be present at the marriage ceremony unless invited. The usual form given by the Hedaya for proposal is: 'I have married myself to you', and the acceptance is 'I have consented'. The Shia law, however, does not consider the presence of witnesses essential for marriage.

Normally, a marriage is contemplated as between adults, as they alone are capable of forming a regular contract. But the marriage of minors is valid, if performed with the consent of the father or the guardian. But if it can be shown that the guardian or father had acted in bad faith or fraudulently or negligently, the marriage is voidable on the option of the minor attaining majority.

The contract generally involving economic obligations, a woman is entitled to claim from her husband a sum of money as the dower. This dower is usually of two kinds: (1) The amount settled on the wife at the time of marriage, and (2) what is known as the 'deferred dower' she is entitled to receive if and when divorced. This deferred dower often works as a wholesome deterrent against frivolous divorces, especially as men can, under Muslim law, divorce their wives at will.

The duties of a wife, according to Muslim law, are residence in the house of her husband, obedience to him in his reasonable orders, and "performing her marital functions whenever required by the husband at reasonable times and places with due regard to health and decency and observing strict conjugal fidelity and refraining from undue familiarity with strangers and all unnecessary appearance in public".

The duties of the husband are to maintain his wife, in accordance with his means, to eschew cruelty, to provide, if he has more wives than one, each with a separate sleeping apartment, give each an equal share of his society and equal treatment, and to allow the wife to visit her parents or relatives once a year. He has the right of physical correction but not of assault or cruel thrashing. The husband is under no obligation to observe conjugal fidelity, and a wife cannot leave him on that account.

Among the Shia's, what is known as Muta marriage is also prevalent; according to this form, a couple are married for a stipulated period after which the marriage becomes null and void without any divorce proceedings.

Divorces are permitted under Muslim law and they generally fall into three categories:

(1) At the will of the husband without any legal proceedings. In this type of divorce, all that a man has to do is to repeat the word 'Talak' (divorce) three times and send his wife away. Though apparently very simple, the procedure can be made very difficult if a big amount has been stipulated in the marriage contract as the deferred dower;

(2) By mutual consent of the husband and wife without any legal proceedings;

(3) By the intervention of a court of law at the instance of the wife.

As a rule, unless it forms a specific stipulation of the marriage contract, a woman cannot divorce herself, but she may obtain a divorce in a court of law under certain conditions. According to the Distribution of Muslim Marriage Act of 1939, for instance, a Muslim woman can claim divorce in case her husband takes another wife, on the ground that "there is unequality of treatment either psychologically or economically".

All told, though the Muslim law, as in all patriarchal communities favours the stronger sex, the marriage contract can be, if well drawn out, as advantages to the wife, in many respects, as to the husband, but unfortunately social conventions and the general disabilities of women usually prevent them from taking full advantage of the law of the Prophet.

The Muslim law of succession and inheritance is equally humane. "A woman is as much an heir as a man under Muslim law, and the son does not exclude a daughter from a share of the father's property." Marriage does not give the husband any rights over the property of his wife during her life-time, which she can administer in her own right and even alienate without the permission of the husband.

Thus the position of medieval Muslim women, in law, had been, in certain respects, better than of contemporary Hindu women, but in actual working it fell far short of its aims because of the rigidity of the Purdah system and the ignorance of women.

Yet, India produced some outstanding Muslim queens who inherited their parents' titles and governed kingdoms efficiently and wisely. Hindu queens could not reign in their own right; the most they could do was to act as regents for their sons in their minority or rule jointly with their husbands.

Sultana Rezia (thirteenth century) was a notable example of a Muslim Queen who ruled the vast empire of her father with remarkable energy and ability. Chandbibi of Ahmednagar (Moghul period) was another important Muslim queen of medieval India. Coming to more recent times, "the three successive rulers of the Bhopal State were women; it was a common saying in the state, that the state had enjoyed justice and prosperity under her queens, and there was a prediction that once a male became a ruler, the state would perish". And strangely enough the state was merged into the Indian Union at the time of the Nawab who succeeded the three Begums.

Though, under Muslim law, marriage is not a sacrament, it generated, in India, conjugal fidelity in males at times even more lasting and passionate than in sacramental forms. Jehangir's attachment to Nur Jehan became proverbial in India; Shah Jehan's passion for his devoted wife Mumtaz gave the world the Taj Mahal.

It may also be mentioned that *polygyny* has been prohibited in Pakistan under the regime of Ayub Khan; in India, however, while *polygyny* has been prohibited among the Hindus, it is still lawful for the Muslims.

Muslims and the Purdah System

We have seen that from very early times, there was a tendency among kings in India to protect women from the gaze of the vulgar. The twin fear of the evil eye and of intrigue seems to have been the inspiring force for this royal passion for seclusion of their women. As a rule, the custom was confined to kings, nobles and merchant-princes in pre-Muslim India, but with the advent of Muslims it spread to the genteel and the middle classes too. Even now, Purdah among middle classes of Hindus is generally confined to those places in India where Muslim rule had been prolonged and prominent as in the north, and seldom obtains in southern India.

We may now give some thought to the origin, development and prevalence of the institution of Purdah among the Muslims.

The Arabs at the time of the Prophet were mostly nomads and possessed many of the simple virtues of a nomadic race. Woman played an important role in their camp life; she had even to take part in the tribal brawls, and as such keeping her as an ornament in the harem was foreign to the spirit of the Bedouin.

The Arabs, like the Jews, were a patriarchal community practising polygyny, and with them there were no strict laws as to the number of wives a patriarch could have; as a rule, it was limited only by his economic resources. Prophet Mohammad, as we have seen, advised his followers to exercise restraint in the matter of marriage. Mohammad himself, it is true, married several wives, but in most cases, he had recourse to *polygyny* out of a sense of duty towards friends fallen in battle in his cause. When he wooed Illead, for instance, she told him that she would not make him a good wife as she was of a jealous disposition, had a son, and was no more young Mohammad did not deny these disqualifications but proved his case by telling her that she was, at any rate younger than he, that he would be a father to her son, and as for her jealousy, he would pray to Allah to cure her of it. Such *polygyny* was hardly meant for pleasure.

Mohammad had a profound respect for women, inspired partly by his own innate sense of chivalry and partly by Kadija's devotion and services to him. Unlike certain other religious teachers, who followed the celibate life, Mohammad took a legitimate interest in sexual joys and domestic life, but never did he treat woman as an article of pleasure as some of his misguided followers did later. Nor could the Arab of his days afford the luxuries of a harem filled with pleasure-girls. The richest Arab of the time counted his wealth in camels, horses and a few tents. Streams flowing wine and palaces filled with Houris existed only in his Paradise.

But before long the Arabs changed the history of the world. With a suddenness that took the Arabs themselves by surprise, from the obscurity of the desert they poured forth armies that began to dictate terms to Byzantian emperors. The banner of Islam was carried into far places, and Muslim arms swept all before them. The men who inspired this movement were rulers like Caliph Umar "who owned one shirt and one mantle only both conspicuous for their patchwork, slept on a bed of palm leaves and had no concern other than the purity of the faith, the upholding of justice, and the ascendancy and security of Islam and the Arabians."

But the days of such austere Caliphs soon passed away. The later Caliphate became the wonder of the world, and Baghdad, its seat, a legend for wealth, splendour and luxury. Persian and Byzantian vices were imported into the city and improved upon. Arabs did not consider it necessary to wait till death for the enjoyment of the pleasures of Paradise; the wealthy and the powerful excelled the promises of Paradise, in the number and quality of the Houris of their harem. Nor was the Commander of the Faithful lacking in zeal. He counted the Circassian and Persian slave-girls of his harem in hundreds if not in thousands. Trading in slave-girls was the most profitable and fashionable commercial enterprise of the age, and palatial establishments were kept by wealthy merchants where princes and nobles retired for pleasure and seductive Greek girls ruined promising young men. Some of these singing girls were sold for fabulous sums to infatuated voluptuaries.

Nor did the search for pleasure end here. All legitimate means of sexual pleasure were soon exhausted and homosexuality became the pet vice of the age. The Caliph often set the example. We are told the story of a boy who became the object of jealousy between a reigning Caliph and his brother; "the boy was shut up in the seraglio, the Caliph fearing his abduction". Nobles often prided themselves on the number of boys and pages in their entourage as much as they did on the number of their mistresses. The `beloved of the poets of these degenerate days was a male and not a female. The scandal is brought forth to us with particular force by Alberuni who noticed that "when Kabul was conquered by Muslims and the

Ispahbad of Kabul adopted Islam, he stipulated that he should not be bound to eat cow's meat or commit sodomy (which proves that he abhored the one as much as the other").

With such flaming vices running in their veins, men were insisting on the fidelity of their women; and what they could not get by love they decided to force by the cudgel; the development of the Purdah, particularly its more undesirable features, was in no small measure due to this masculine effort to break the spirit of woman.

In the earlier days of Islam when the Purdah was first introduced among the Arabs, spirited ladies objected to it. Ayesha (a niece of Ayesha, wife of the Prophet) never wore the veil, though her husband insisted; "on me", said she, "God has set the seal of beauty, and I rejoice when my beauty is seen and the mercy of God therein acknowledged. Never shall I cover my face, for no flaw or fault finds a place in God's work". But women of this spirit were few and their voice was heard only in the beginning, and men did not find it difficult to stifle it.

Nor did theologians and moralists fail to take notice of the levity of the fair sex. In the earlier days of Islam women, it would appear, were free to visit the mosque and pray. This practice was, later, condemned, as good men found it difficult to concentrate their mind on prayers in the presence of women; by the third century of the Muslim era, the practice of letting women attend the mosque generally fell into disuse, though among certain sections of Muslims it has continued to the present day.

> The disgrace of having lowered the position of women, belongs, in the first place, to the morose fanatical theologians of Islam. It was not due, to be sure, to the fact that they were indifferent or insensible to feminine charms—for they had their own well-stocked harems—but outside that little Paradise, they loved to affect a thorough contempt for the things of the world and the levity of the fair sex. For this reason perhaps, one of the oldest traditionalists had collected, with apparent

relish, several traditions which purport to say that women for the most part will go to hell.

It is unfortunate that the Islam that was introduced into India was not the simple dynamic religion of the Arabs of the Prophet's days, but the religion of the half-converted Turks, who brought with them many of their wild traits, and of decadent Persians who had earned a reputation for refinements in vices. The Muslim society introduced into India had developed its own conception of the two-fold division of women into the bond wife and the free woman of the city. So rigid was the seclusion of women as conceived by this society that all women who had any claim to respectability, including women of the lower middle classes, had to don the veil while moving out-of-doors. So strict was the convention in Muslim India, that any woman found in a public place without veiling her face was taken for a 'shameless' woman and molestation of her was considered no serious offence as much a woman was reckoned outside the pale of decent society. As a result, even non-Muslim women, under Muslim rule, took care to veil their faces when they went out. Hindu women did not put on a tailored veil like the Burkha of the Muslims (the Burkha covers a woman from head to food; it hangs from the crown of the head, and has two eye-holes for sight), but usually covered their faces with the end of the Sari or wrapper.

While the middle class Hindus thus observed in Purdah in regions ruled by Muslims, Hindu kings and chiefs imitated the ways of the conquerors, and laid out their harems after the fashion of Muslim Sultans and noblemen.

As the Purdah became stricter, prostitution became more popular. Courtesans seemed to dominate the social life of Delhi; their number became so large and influence so widespread that Allauddin Khilji had special orders issued to control them, and a good number were forced to marry and lead domestic lives. All Sultans, however, did not consider them an unmitigated evil. Kutubuddin Mubarak (fourteen century) for instance, practically lived with them. "He often dressed himself in female attire, and with his body adorned with trinkets, he went out in the city in the company of harlots and danced at the houses of nobles." Muslim kings, as a rule, did not behave in this manner, but the very possibility of such a public exhibition of imperial patronage of fine arts is a said reflection on the power the prostitute held over the court and the aristocracy. In the reign of Kutubuddin Mubarak, "so eager was the demand at the court for mistresses that the price of a pretty girl who could be bought in the last reign for a couple of pounds ran up to as much as £200/-".' It must, however, be mentioned to the credit of Muslim divines that they never allowed the courtesan access to religious shrines, and throughout the centuries, in spite of depraved kings like Mubarak, prostitution in Muslim India remained strictly secular.

But to revert to the Purdah. The feelings of the Muslim nobility in the matter of the Purdah are best illustrated by an incident narrated about the lady Sahibji, wife of Amir Khan, a noble of Shah Jehan's court. She was, one day, being carried in a litter through one of the lanes in Delhi, when a state elephant broke loose and rushed into the lane. The men who were carrying the heavily curtained litter dropped it on the ground and ran for life, and the lady saved herself from the fury of the beast by jumping out of the litter and rushing into a shop near by.

But this was an unpardonable sin on the part of the lady; she had broken the aristocratic conventions of modesty, and her husband sent her away to her father's house as she had exposed her face to public gaze; as a noblewoman she should have died rather than suffered such humiliation. Shah Jehan, however, interceded on behalf of the lady; if, instead of rushing to the shop, he argued with his outraged noble, the lady had remained in the litter, the elephant, that had broken the litter, would have trampled and killed her, in which case, it was pointed out, her body, perhaps naked, would have been exposed to public gaze, a disgrace more painful than her appearance without the veil. Under the circumstances the action of the lady was the lesser evil, the emperor maintained; this argument is said to have soothed the nobleman who took his wife back.

The incident and the argument show how touchy the nobles were in the matter of feminine modesty. The worst disgrace that could possibly befall a nobleman was the exposure of the face of his wife in public. It was because of this that when a medieval Muslim monarch wanted to award exemplary punishment to a treacherous or rebellious subject, he paraded his womenfolk through the streets without the veil. A man whose women were subjected to this humiliation was as good as dead to society; failing revenge, he could just as well go and hang himself.

It must, however, be mentioned that while the Purdah was more strict on the women of the nobility than on the middle classes, its adverse effects were less marked on the former because of their affluence. Royal and aristocratic households had extensive pleasure parks and sports grounds where women could divert themselves and Poly was a favourite game with the Moghul ladies. They had the benefits of education too, and lady teachers gave instruction to young ladies. The main disadvantage of the Purdah, among these upper classes, was that they were denied knowledge of the outside world and the pleasures of a mixed society.

The middle classes could afford none of these luxuries and seclusion made their women, anaemic, narrow-minded and victims of many physical ailments. Within middle class households. Purdah, however, was less strict. While noblemen and kings never gave access to their harem even to intimate friends and relatives, among middle classes, women could appear without the veil before visiting friends and relatives and converse freely with them. The French traveller Bernier, while he was in Kashmir, wished to see the famed beauties of the valley and had, according to his own accounts, recourse to a ruse by which he was enabled to see many middle class Muslim women and converse freely with them; he made friends with a Muslim school master, well known in the locality in which he lived, and the genial teacher took him round to many families, introduced him as a Muslim friend seeking a bride, and the women, both young and old, came out from the inner apartments, and freely discussed the stranger's eligibility for matrimony.

Bernier noticed that Indian Muslims had a preference for Kashmiri girls, and many of them married in Kashmir "in order to get fairskinned children." In the outlying areas of Kashmir, however, nobility of blood was considered more important than the pigmentation of skin, and Bernier has left us the story of a Moghul nobleman who fell out with Jehangir and was obliged to wander in the hills of Kashmir where he had to live among two different tribes; in one, the men brought their daughters to keep him company in order to obtain for their community noblemen and noblewomen, but when the other tribe heard this they exclaimed what fools the men of the first tribe were, to obtain children in their daughters since they were either married or had to be married, which would alienate the progeny from the family; hence they asked their wives to sleep with him in order to retain the nobility of Moghul blood in their own households.

How much truth there is in the story cannot be ascertained. Rumours of this nature have persisted in India, and travellers to the hills of the north have regaled, down the centuries, the dwellers of the plains, with strange stories of the boldness of the daughters of the Himalayan hills and of highland hospitality reminiscent of the days of Uddalaka Swetaketu of Vedic fame.

The Moghul Harem

We have plenty of information about the way of life of Moghul ladies, mainly from independent accounts of European travellers many of whom had spent several years in different parts of the Moghul empire. Of these travellers, Bernier and Manucci were the more important. Manucci was an Italian who travelled extensively in Moghul India, but his accounts were marred by a love of scandal. The Frenchman Bernier, on the other hand, was a man of letters and a physician of considerable skill; he was attached to the staff of a Moghul nobleman and had access even to the seraglios of the gentry. Above all, he had an objective outlook and a sense of proportion; as such his accounts are more trustworthy and dependable.

According to Bernier, Moghul princesses usually remained unmarried as their parents considered sons-in-law a possible danger to succession. Shah Jehan's two daughters, Jahanara and Roshanara, we are told, grew into spinsters, which led to a good deal of talk in the town. Jahanara was a partisan of Dara, Shah Jehan's eldest son, while Roshanara was a staunch ally of Aurangazeb, the youngest. While Aurangazeb was the viceroy of the Deccan, it was Roshanara who kept him informed of all that was happening in the imperial capital. It would appear that there was an agreement between the two that when Aurangazeb would ascend the throne, Roshanara was to be married as a reward for her services; an agreement, by the way, respected by Aurangazeb in the breach rather than in the keeping.

Anyway, several stories were current in Delhi about intrigues in the harem, in which one or the other of these princesses was the heroine. One story tells us how Shah Jehan boiled alive a lover of Jahanara; the gallant used to visit the princess stealthily, smuggled in by her maid-servants and eunuchs; the emperor came to know of it and set a trap. When the lover was in the princess's apartments, Shah Jehan surprised them, and Jahanara made her lover hide in a bath-tub, kept for boiling water, and covered it with a lid. The old fox saw what was happening and casually started an inspection of the apartments; seeing the bath-tub, he was seized with a desire to have a hot water bath immediately and asked the menials to boil the water straight-away. He stayed in the bath-room till the water was well boiled, and then left to attend to important state affairs without taking a bath.

Aurangazeb, it would appear, was less cruel to the lovers of Roshanara. Bernier, who was friendly with a Portuguese lady in the seraglio, has left us a tale of two lovers of the princess as narrated to him by the lady. On one occasion, it would appear, the young gallant, after his dalliance with the princess, was being smuggled out of the seraglio by her slave-girls who, taking fright on hearing some untoward noise, left him in the garden. The eunuchs on water saw him prowling, caught him and produced him before Aurangazeb. He was asked by the stern emperor how he got in, to which the culprit replied that he came scaling the walls; on this, the emperor ordered him to be thrown over the walls.

Another young man, on a different occasion, was found prowling in the garden, caught and brought before Aurangazeb; this man, however, had come by the gate and not over the walls. So he was let free and the sentinels were punished.

It is significant that on neither occasion Aurangazeb sent for Roshanara. The emperor, perhaps, had in mind the Koranic injunction that it was the duty of every Muslim to get his daughter or ward married when she came of age, and he was possibly of the opinion that Roshanara alone was not to blame for these affairs.

Bernier, as a physician, was at times taken to the seraglio of Aurangazeb, when the emperor was not present, as European physicians were considered great wizards by Moghul ladies, and there was always some important lady or other ailing in the harem. He could not have seen much of the harem as he was always blindfolded or put in a veil. "I have sometimes entered it", says Bernier, "when the king was not at Delhi, and I think pretty far upon the occasion of a great lady that was so sick that she could not be carried to the gate according to custom, but I had always a covering of Kashmere over my head which, like a scarf, hung down to my feet, and an eunuch conducted me by the hand, like a blind man."

The women of the imperial harem and the nobility had many diversions, and occasions for social intercourse which was, however, strictly confined to women. A very important social function was the mock fair, held occasionally in the imperial seraglio, in which the ladies of all the grandees took part. The fair was held in the park attached to the seraglio, and any lady was free to open a stall, stock wares and sell them. The buyers were generally the ladies of the seraglio; on occasions, the emperor himself appeared in the market of the fair and struck a deal. "The wares are fine purified gold, rich embroideries of the new fashion, rich ribbons well wrought upon cloth of gold, or pieces of that fine cloth which is worn by great ladies, and other merchandise of great price." New feminine fashions and styles were introduced in these fairs, which were open for the better-known courtesans of the city who were the leaders of fashion in those days. The ladies of the nobles took care to bring their young daughters of marriageable age to be seen by the Begums of the court and by other noblewomen, who assembled in the fair, and many a marriage proposal started its wandering career from here.

"The jest of the fair is that the king comes to bargain with these fair merchants, like a petty merchant, penny by penny, contesting that they are not in earnest, that it is too dear; that he would not give more than so much; that the merchandise of such a one is far better, and the like". The sales girls on their part, treated the mean bargainer and his wives with the contempt they deserved, told them that they could not appreciate a good thing when they saw one, that they were at liberty to go to cheaper stalls since they did not appear to possess enough cash to buy merchandise in respectable stores. Anyway, when bargains were struck, payments were made on the spot in cash, and at times it happened that His Majesty and his Begums slipped into the palms of the sales girls gold coins instead of silver ones as agreed upon, and the whole market was filled with an atmosphere of hilarity, pleasant raillery and innocent liberties with the mighty.

Akbar initiated these fairs which continued till the Moghul empire broke up. During the reigns of Jehangir and Shah Jehan, the better classes of courtesans, as already noticed, were invited to open their stalls in the fair, but Aurangazeb prohibited their entry into the seraglio.

Jehangir and Shah Jehan were particularly fond of the company of the dancing girls, and during their reigns the girls had to attend the palace once every week; Shah Jehan, we are told, often diverted himself in their company till late at night. Bernier has related an amusing incident that had happened in Jehangir's time during one of these weekly visits of the dancing girls to the court, as illustrating the eccentricity of the emperor. A Frenchman named Barnard, who was supposed to be good at medicine and surgery, was a friend of Jehangir and a regular companion of his drinking parties to which, for obvious reasons, he admitted preferably Christian foreigners.

Barnard had a good practice at the court and among the nobles of Delhi, but was perpetually in need of cash especially as he was very fond of music and dancing, and patronised the more well-known of the dancing girls of the city. One of these was a very young and accomplished girl, whose mother resisted all attempts of Barnard to approach her, as the lady thought that association with the debauched Frenchman would rob her daughter of her beauty and charm. The Frenchman, biding his chance, one day, found her making obeisance before the emperor in the court, along with other girls; the time was opportune, as Jehangir was in a jovial mood and was going to give him a present before dismissing him. Barnard, on seeing the girl, begged Jehangir to be excused for declining the present, and requested that he should be presented with the dancing girl instead, and he pointed her out to His Majesty. The assembled dignitaries could not suppress their smile, nor could the emperor; the latter promptly ordered the sentry on duty to bodily lift the girl and place her on the shoulders of the Frenchman, which was immediately done. And Barnard, to the merriment of the whole court, walked away, the girl riding on his neck.

Bernier once travelled from Delhi to Kashmir in the entourage of his employer when Aurangazeb went on a pleasure trip to the happy valley, and he has left us a detailed description of how the ladies of the seraglio travelled on these occasions. "Some are carried, like the king, in litters borne by men, painted, gilded and covered with great and costly network of silk of diverse colours, enriched with embroidery, fringe, and thick, pendent tufts." Roshanara was the first lady of the seraglio, during Aurangazeb's reign,

> . . . and nothing more stately can be imagined than to see her march first, mounted upon a stately elephant of Pegu, in a Mik-dember, all shining of gold and azure, attended by five or six elephants with their Mik-dembers, almost as splendid as hers, filled with the principal female officers of her house; some of the more important eunuchs, richly adorned and advantageously mounted, riding on her side each with a cane in his hand; a troupe of Tartarian and Kashmirian maids of

honour about her, oddly and fantastically dressed, and riding on very pretty hackney horses; and lastly, many other eunuchs on horseback accompanied by scores of pages and lackeys, with great sticks in their hands to make a way far off.

After Roshanara Begum, I saw pass one of the principal ladies of the court, mounted and attended in proportion; after this a third, in the same fashion; and then another, another and so on to fifteen or sixteen, all more or less bravely mounted and accompanied according to their status, pay and office. Indeed this long file of elephants, to the number of fifty or more, thus gravely marching with paces, as it were, counted, and with all this gallant train and equipage, does represent something great and royal; and if I had not beheld this pomp with a kind of philosophic indifference, I know not whether I should not have suffered myself to be carried away to those extravagant sentiments of most of the Indian poets, who will have it, that all these elephants carry as many hidden goddesses; it is true that one can hardly see them and they are almost inaccessible to men.

The guards were particularly insolent and mercilessly used their sticks on any unfortunate man who happened to come within striking distance of the mobile seraglio. Bernier himself on one occasion, strayed too near the ambit of the harem and had to fight his way back to safety; fortunately he was on a fleet horse and escaped without major injuries. Yet conditions in India, he says, were better; for in Persia, the Purdah was more strict, and any one found near the seraglio was immediately put to death, even if he were within half a league of the seraglio. Further, in Persia, "it is required that as many as there are in the villages and boroughs, where they pass, do all abandon them and retire afar off."

Hindus and Muslims

During the pre-Moghul Islamic period, the ruling classes were mostly Muslims of foreign extraction, Turks or Persians. Indians were generally looked upon as an inferior race; while Indian Muslims who proved worthy were, at times, given positions of trust, Hindus as a class were generally made to feel that they were a subject race whose salvation lay in absolute obedience to the Muslim.

We have been favoured with the view of a Muslim divine who, when consulted by Allaudin Khilji on the point, laid down the code of conduct for the Hindus as follows: "They are called Khiraj Guzars (payers of tribute), and when a revenue officer demands silver from them, they should, without demur, and with all humility and respect, tender gold. If the tax gatherer chooses to spit into his mouth, he must promptly open his mouth. The meaning of doing such a thing is that the Hindu, in acting this wise, shows his meekness, humility, obedience and respect". The injunction of this fourteenth century divine was, no doubt, stricter than the code of conduct laid down by Indo-Aryan law-givers for Sudras and other non-Aryans; but while these were offered some compensation for their obedience by way of better rebirth, the Hindu found no advantage in accepting this humiliating position under the Muslims, as in spite of the acceptance of the most humiliating condition the Hindu was offered, after death, hell and heaven; as such, though the Muslims found little difficulty in defeating a Hindu army, when it came to the question of consolidating and ruling the conquered territories, they met with determined opposition from the ill-treated Hindus who, together with rival claimants in succession, made early Muslim rule in India a continuous state of war or threat of war.

With the arrival of the Moghuls, there was a welcome change. In the matter of succession, as we have seen, they followed the traditions of the Mongols and not of the Arabs. In their religious policy too they tended rather to the liberal Mongol tradition than to Islam. All told, though converted to Islam, the Moghuls in India prided more on their Mongol ancestry than on Islamic traditions, and were, with the exception of Aurangazeb, rulers first and Muslims afterwards.

Akbar, by all accounts, was the greatest of the Moghuls. Like Kubilai Khan of China, he was a wise ruler and astute statesman; from the history of Islamic rule in India he learnt that no permanent peace was possible in India without conciliating the recalcitrant Hindus, especially the Rajputs to whom the leadership of the Hindu community had passed on the Muslim conquest of India. Akbar, while in no way compromising his paramount claim to the sovereignty of India, initiated a policy of conciliation; he abolished the Jezia or poll tax levied on Hindus under previous Muslim rulers, and appointed Hindus to positions of trust.

One of the main principles of Hindu polity, from time immemorial, had been that the king, whatever his personal religion, ought to patronise all recognised religions of his subjects. Akbar accepted this principle and refrained from persecuting the Hindus and destroying their temples; he invited to his court learned men of all religions, Brahmins, Jains, Zoroastrains and Christian priests and held philosophical conferences in which all of them were at liberty to discuss their view points freely in his presence.

These measures found immediate response. Conciliated or defeated Rajput chieftains took service under him and some of his most able administrators were Hindus. And what is more important to our subject, he initiated inter-communal marriages, and himself gave the lead by marrying ladies from Rajput clans. This innovation, however, did not prove very popular; it never spread to the common people, and even among royalty it fell into disuse after a generation or so.

Anyway, since the Hindus and Muslims lived together, there were cases, among ordinary folk, of inter-communal love affairs and resultant troubles. Under Muslim dominance, in such cases the Hindu was often converted to Islam, conversion to Hinduism being prohibited.

A peculiarly intriguing scandal of this nature happened in Delhi which Bernier has narrated. A Muslim eunuch, by name Didar Khan, highly placed in the seraglio, had a suburban Bungalow to which he often repaired during holidays and his neighbour was a Hindu scribe who had a pretty young sister. The girl often visited the eunuch's establishment and gradually gossip started and began to spread. Anyway, because of the sex or rather lack of sex of the eunuch, the Hindu gentleman ignored these malicious rumours; but pressed by his friends, he kept a watch on his sister and caught her sleeping with the eunuch. The infuriated scribe stabbed the eunuch to death. This murder led to an uproar in the city; the eunuchs of the seraglio petitioned the emperor demanding the execution of the Hindu, but Aurangazeb, who had always had an eye on spreading the faith, had the Hindu converted, and let the matter drop at that.

In the bitterness of the earlier periods of Muslim expansion which had come on the Hindus with particular severity, the Rajputs produced some remarkable cases of feminine heroism. We have already noticed the Rajput women's preference for Sati to capture by the invaders. In Rajput legend lives the memory of many remarkable ladies who fought the invaders heroically and preferred death to subjection. One such heroine was Padmini, wife of Bhimsi, the Rana of Mewar. When Allauddin Khilji invaded the fort of Chitor, it was defended by Bhimsi then acting as regent for his nephew who was a minor. If Rajput accounts are to be believed, Allauddin was not so much after Mewar as after Padmini whose fame as a beauty had reached him; the Sultan could not storm the fortress, and started negotiations with the defenders. If the Rajputs were to grant him the mere sight of Padmini, he sent word, he was prepared to raise the seige and go back to Delhi. Bhimsi was reluctant to show his wife to Allauddin, but in order to avoid unnecessary bloodshed, he agreed to allow him entry to the fort and see a reflection of Padmini in a mirror. The shadow was better than nothing, and Allauddin with a picked bodyguard went to the fort, trusting on the Rajput's code of honour; after seeing the reflection of Padmini, Bhimsi, like a good host conducted his guest back to the foot of the hill where he fell into an ambush; the treacherous Sultan took him to the camp from where he sent word to the fort that Bhimsi was held as hostage for the surrender of Padmini.

A plot was now hatched in the fort to redeem Bhimsi. The Rajputs sent a message to Allauddin agreeing to surrender Padmini, but wished her to be carried in a litter, accompanied by her ladies-in-waiting as befitting her station; this was agreed to, and Padmini started with her train of heavily curtained litters which were, in reality, carrying not ladies but Rajput warriors armed to the teeth; the litter-carriers were, likewise, the pick of the defenders of Chitor. On the entourage reaching Allauddin's camp, these redoubtable warriors created panic in the Sultan's camp, released Bhimsi, and escaped to the fort with Padmini, fighting the column that came in pursuit of them.

The story of another spirited Rajput lady, who rejected a husband because of his cowardice, illumines Rajput legend. She was the wife of Maharajah Jaswant Singh. In the war of succession that followed Aurangazeb's rebellion, Jaswant Singh fought against Aurangazeb and, in one of the battles, he was defeated by Aurangazeb's forces and he fled to his own city, where he found the gates of the fort closed against him. His queen sent word to him that her husband, because of the dishonour he brought to his clan by his flight, was, for all intent and purpose, dead to her and she was going to become a Sati.

For a Rajput there were only two ways of conducting himself honourably in a battle; he had either to win or to die. While this code of honour produced much romance, in a war it often led to the ruin of the Rajputs. The art of running away, when victory is impossible, is as much part of military strategy as heroism, and till the leadership of the Hindus passed into the hands of the Mahrathas, who were generally free from many of the superstitious heroics of the Rajputs, the Hindus had steadily lost ground to the Muslims in the war of the two communities for the rulership of India.

Sati in Muslim India

The Muslim conquest, as we have seen, led to large-scale immolation of women, especially among the Rajputs who considered it a lesser evil than capture by the invaders. But the Muslims themselves, with their secular notions of marriage, were against the institution of Sati and did what they could to abolish or discourage it among the Hindus whom they ruled. But due to various reasons they could not stop it by law in their dominions.

By the time the Muslim rule was well established in India. Sati had become equally well-established among the Hindus who came to look upon it as a religious institution with all the sanction of hoary tradition. The later muslims, as already noticed, found it difficult to rule the country without the cooperation of the Hindus and were reluctant to interfere in the religious observances of the Hindus especially when this, in no way, helped the Muslim cause. Hence, though many Muslim rulers tried to abolish Sati in their dominions, the institution, for all practical purposes, flourished without much hindrance.

Forcible Sati was abolished by law in most of the kingdoms ruled by Muslims and the widow, who wished to burn herself with her husband's body, had to obtain the permission of civil authorities of the place in which she lived; in practice, however, this led to no serious impediment as the permission, in course of time, degenerated into a mere legal formality. The trouble about the question of willingness or reluctance of the widow depended upon a peculiar circumstance in the institution. A strong convention had risen among high caste Hindus that a widow, unencumbered by pregnancy, infant-in-arms or old age, should voluntarily announce her intention to become Sati immediately on the death of her husband; in most cases, the decision so announced was genuine as the woman was in extreme distress. And once the decision was announced, it was irrevocable. In some cases, it did happen that reflection, or the sight of the flames unnerved a widow and she wanted to retract. But this was not permissible, and a widow who feared to proceed to the cremation ground or ran away during her journey brought disgrace on the whole family and was abandoned; to prevent her escape, she was usually surrounded by men armed with sticks who goaded her on to her destination by physical force. In spite of such precautions there were cases of escape and if a widow was young and attractive, there were gangs of outcastes prowling around to carry her off in case she managed to escape.

Bernier mentions a case in which a Hindu clerk attached to his employer's establishment died and he, Bernier, was sent by the Muslim nobleman to dissuade the widow from becoming a Sati.

When the Frenchman broached the subject to the wailing widow, she roundly refused and threatened to bash her head against a pillar in case she was not permitted to mount the funeral pyre. Finding his mission not very easy, Bernier announced to the widow that the employer of her husband had settled a pension on her for the education of her children in case she refrained from committing herself to flames. Even this information did not have the desired effect, when Bernier, in all indignation, shouted at her: 'Then take your children, you unhappy creature, and cut their throats and burn them with you. I am going back to my master to tell him that you have refused his offer and he may cancel the pension". This worked especially as all the relatives of the lady joined him in his denunciation of Sati; she looked dazed and passed into a swoon, we are told, and in the end consented to live.

Bernier during his travels witnessed many instances of Sati in India. On one occasion while journeying from Ahmedabad to Agra, he saw, in Rajputana, a Sati seated on the funeral pyre of her husband with stoic courage while flames started raging round her; even when her clothes caught fire, she sat unperturbed. Five slave-girls were noticed dancing round her, and one after another these too jumped into the fire without any show of reluctance.

Again, while travelling from Surat to Persia in the company of certain other Europeans, Bernier saw a middle-aged woman who immolated herself. Her calm, amounting almost to cheerfulness, astonished the travellers. After mounting the pyre, and taking her dead husband's head into her lap, she herself, with the torch in hand, kindled the pyre, while Brahmins all round the pyre did the same, and in a moment the woman was engulfed in the flames.

Bernier also witnessed some cases of Sati in which the sight of the funeral pyre completely unnerved the widow whom men with long poles pushed into the flames; also of widows who fled the flames and ran for refuge to the outcastes who made away with her. At Lahore, he beheld a pitiful case of a child widow, hardly twelve, being pushed into the flames by an elderly woman. The sight so infuriated the Frenchman that he wanted to strangle the hag and the priests who presided over the horrible ride. But he did not dare interfere, and had to "content myself with detesting this horrid religion".

The Italian traveller Manucci was bolder. He tells us that once he, with an Armenian youth, charged into a Sati procession and carried off the widow; the two Christians were on horseback and very soon escaped into safety. The Armenian, later, married the girl and lived happily with her.

Both Manucci and Bernier report a strange case of Sati which took place in Bengal while the former was travelling in that region. A married Hindu woman, it would appear, was in love with a Muslim musician and they decided to marry after doing away with her husband. This man was accordingly poisoned, but his death changed the mind of the paramour who refused to elope with her. According to custom, however, the widow declared her intention to become Sati, and this decision so moved her paramour that he wished to possess a relic of her. It was usual for people to gather on either side of the road by which a Sati procession passed, as well as at the cremation ground, in order to pick up any relic the Sati might throw away, as such relics were supposed to possess miraculous powers since a Sati was a living saint. The widow's paramour followed the procession, and appeared at the cremation ground; the Sati saw him and held her necklace up as if offering it to him. The pyre was kindled and as the paramour approached to receive the relic, she caught him in a vicious grip and both perished in the flames.

With the disruption of the Moghul empire, even the small influence Muslims exerted against Sati as dissipated, and the custom spread all over India, even among the Sikhs to whom it was expressly forbidden by their religious teachers.

The Vijayanagar Empire

For about two centuries from the time of Mohammad Ghori, the Muslims were fully busy extending and consolidating the conquest of northern India, and the regions south of the Vindhyas were free from their incursions. The Hindu kings of the south seem to have imagined that the Muslim outburst would spend itself up in the north; oblivious to the threat from the north, they were busy fighting, among themselves, their age-old feuds, and remained as disorganised and weak as the Rajput kingdoms of the north at the time of the invasion of Mohammad Ghori.

But soon they were made to feel the Muslim impact. Allauddin Khilji sent his able general Mallick Kafoor for the plunder of the southern kingdoms, and without encountering much opposition he advanced as far as the Pandyan kingdom and returned to Delhi with trains of caravans laden with booty. Allauddin was not interested in consolidating his conquests but was content with the loot. Later, Mohammad Toghlak made further incursions to the south.

South India was now roused to the danger, and a kingdom rose to resist the attack. It was the Vijayanagar empire which not only resisted the Muslim onslaught for about two centuries, but rose as a first class power in India. The rise of the Vijayanagar empire was coeval with the expansion of the Portuguese power in the east, and the opportunities for commerce with the Portuguese, who considered the Muslims their natural enemies, made this empire one of the richest in India and the wonder of many a medieval European traveller.

We are here concerned not so much with the history of Vijayanagar as with the social life in this medieval Hindu empire. We have been favoured with many accounts of Vijayanagar by Muslim and European travellers who visited the kingdom at the height of its power, and most of the accounts read strangely like Megasthenese's accounts of Chandragupta Maurya's court, which show how little the Hindus had changed during 1800 years in their ideas of statecraft and government.

Nicolo Conti visited the kingdom in 1420 and wrote about the king and his women:

The inhabitants of this region marry as many wives as they

> please who are burnt with their dead husbands. Their king is more powerful than all the other kings in India. He takes to himself 12,000 wives of whom 4000 follow him on foot wherever he may go, and are solely employed in the kitchen. A like number, more handsomely equipped, ride on horseback. The remainder are carried in litters, of whom 2000 or 3000 are selected as his wives on condition that on his death they should voluntarily burn themselves with him which is considered a great honour for them...
>
> At a certain time of the year their idol is carried through the city, placed between two chariots in which are young women, richly adorned, who sing hymns to the god, and accompanied by a great concourse of the people.

Conti seems to have imagined that every woman he saw near the palace was a wife of the king. The narrative of Paės who visited Vijayanagar in 1537 is more reliable. "The king has twelve lawful wives", he wrote, "of whom there are three principal ones, the sons of each of these three being heirs of the kingdom, but not those of the others. This is the case when there are sons to all of them, but when there is only one son whosoever he may be, he is the heir". Of his twelve lawful wives, eleven were princesses of neighbouring kingdoms or of his own vassals, and one a dancing girl "whom in his youth he had for mistress before he became king, and she made him promise that if he became king he would take her to wife."

Paes describes the harem life of the Vijayanagar king in considerable detail.

> Each one of his wives has her house to herself with her maidens and women of the chamber, and women guards and all other women servants necessary; all these are women and no man enters where they are, save only the eunuchs who guard them. These women are never seen by any man, except perhaps by some old man of high rank by favour of the king. When they wish to go out, they are carried in litters, shut up

> and enclosed, so that they cannot be seen and all the eunuchs with them, fully three or four hundred; and all other people keep a long distance from them. They told us that each of these queens has a very large sum of money and treasure and personal ornaments, namely armlets, bracelets, pearls and diamonds, and that in great quantity, and they also say that each of them has sixty maidens adorned as richly as could possibly be with many jewels.

Paes, like Conti, noticed that there were in all about 12,000 women in the king's harem.

> For you must know that there are women who handle sword and shield, others who wrestle, and others who blow trumpets and other pipes; in the same way they have women as bearers and washing folk, and other offices inside their gates, just as the king has officers of his household. The three principal wives have each the same, one as much as the other, so that there may never be any discord or ill-feeling between them; all of them are great friends and each one lives by herself. It must be gathered from this what a large enclosure there must be for these houses where so many people live and what streets and lanes they must have.

The king's establishment and the harem constituted a city by itself and the wealth, mainly derived from foreign commerce, enabled the court to put up a show as splendrous as that of the Sultans of Delhi.

Paes has also given us some idea as to how the Vijayanagar king conducted himself towards his wives.

> The king lives by himself inside the palace and when he wishes to have with him one of his wives, he orders a eunuch to go and call her. The eunuch does not enter where she is, but tells it to the female guards who make known to the queen that there is a message from the king, and then comes one of her maidens or chamber women and learns what is

> wanted, and then the queen goes where the king is or the king comes where the queen is and so passes the time as it seems good to him without any of the others knowing. Amongst the eunuchs the king has some who are great favourites, and who sleep where he sleeps; they receive a large salary.

Though we have detailed descriptions of the royal harem, we know little about the life of ordinary folk. Purdah, though strict in the palace, does not seem to have been prevalent among the middle classes. Anyway, women of the common folk do not seem to have considered life in the king's harem, even as queens, an unmitigated blessing. We are told in this connection the story of a beautiful peasant girl who rejected the proposal of marriage by the king himself. When the royal messengers came with the proposal and presents from the king, the spirited young girl told them that she did not wish to be a queen as this meant virtual captivity in the harem, but was content to marry a man of her own status so that she could have freedom to visit her parents and relatives and live the normal life of a woman. The king, who was not used to such refusals, took this as high treason and marched at the head of an army to capture the girl; but the girl happened to belong to a border village situated in the territory of a neighbour who opposed the Vijayanagar monarch, and this led to a war.

About courtesans the same old story is repeated. We have already noticed their presence in the temples of Vijayanagar. The cities too had their full complement of them. "Who can describe fitly to you the great riches these women carry on their persons"? Asks Paes. "They are adorned with collars of gold with so many diamonds and rubies and pearls, bracelets also on their arms and on their upper arms, girdles below, and of necessity anklets on the feet. The marvel should be otherwise, namely that women of such a profession should obtain such wealth; but there are among them who have lands given to them, and litters, and so many maid-servants that one cannot number all their things."

The Muslim envoy Abdul Razak, sent to Vijayanagar by the Shah of Persia, was equally impressed by the courtesans of the city. "The splendour of their houses, the beauty of these heart-ravishers, their blandishments and ogles are beyond description", he says.

The Vijayanagar empire eventually succumbed to Muslim expansion under the Moghuls.

The Sikhs

The never ending enmity between Hindus and Muslims made many rightminded Indians work for the unity of the two communities. Akbar, as we have been seen, approached the problem from a political angle and his conciliatory measures were eminently successful in creating better understanding between Hindus and Muslims. He even had ideas of founding a new Indian religion through a synthesis of Hinduism and Islam but in his attempt to work it out, he failed; his social approach to the problem too had but limited success and was in effect confined to his marrying some desirable Rajput ladies, which did not bring him much popularity either with the Muslims or the Hindus.

Guru Nanak who lived in the fifteenth century tackled the problem from a purely religious angle. He could not, as he wished, convert all Hindus and Muslims to his way of thinking, but founded a sect known as Sikhs (disciples) who followed his teaching in which he combined what he thought to be good in Hinduism and Islam. The Sikhs, originally, were a pietist sect and their main tenets were monotheism and a dislike of idolatry. They rejected caste, but accepted the Hindu doctrine of metempsychosis.

The Sikhs received the patronage of Akbar but Aurangazeb, whose policy was to establish a Muslim empire in India, a Sunni empire at that, viewed the innovations of the Sikhs with suspicion, and he imprisoned Teg Bahadur, the ninth Guru, and had him put to death "for presuming to gaze from the roof of his abode upon the apartments of the ladies of the royal harem". The result of this unwise action was bitter opposition to the Muslim rule by the Sikhs who were already showing political ambition. From comparative obscurity they emerged as a martial people and under their able leader Ranjit Singh built up an empire which became the most important political power in the Punjab.

But the Sikh empire was short lived. It rose to power in the beginning of the nineteenth century but was subdued by the British who defeated the Sikhs in the battle of Sabraon in 1849 and annexed the Punjab to their spreading colonial possessions in India.

Thus, the Sikhs did not have time to build up laws and social theories and the *Granth,* their Bible, is not comprehensive like the *Koran* or the Old Testament; it was mainly compiled from the sayings of the Gurus and does not contain detailed injunctions concerning codes of conduct. Besides, the Sikhs, as a class, though good soldiers, were poor scholars, and often neglected the study of their scriptures which were, however, highly venerated.

All told, the matrimonial laws of the Sikhs were not very clearly defined, and a good deal of traditions and customs came to be recognised as the main deciding factor in social matters. Most of the Sikhs were of Hindu extraction and followed the traditional usages of their castes, and there was no attempt, at any time in the history of the community, at unification of social codes. Sati was expressly forbidden to the Sikhs by the third Guru Amardas, but kings and nobles who imitated the Rajputs, practised it. Four queens of Ranjit Singh died with him; Suyjet Singh was less powerful but he had a bigger harem and three hundred women were burnt alive with his body. In the turbulent days that followed the death of Ranjit Singh, it was not often the widow who decided about her immolation but the soldiery. In 1845, for instance, when Jowahir Singh, suspected of treachery to the nation was killed, his wives, who refused to become Satis, were dragged by the soldiers and consigned to the flames. On the other hand, there were also cases of high born ladies who thought it their duty to perish with their husbands. This, at least, was the case of the widow of Sardar Sham Singh of Attari who swore he would not return from the battlefield of Sabraon, and died fighting.

As a rule, Sati was confined to the women of kings and nobles and among the middle classes the widow was not only allowed to live but to remarry. Among those Sikhs who were of Jat extraction (the Jats were peasants who claimed Rajput ancestry), it was customary for the widow to marry the brother of her deceased husband; in the absence of the brother-in-law the widow could marry a man of the same community. Widow marriage was, however, considered inferior, and was known as Karehui (already married) as distinct from regular marriage which was known as Shahdee.

"The Sikhs did not avowedly abandon the Hindu codes of law which, from time immemorial they had obeyed, and neither Nanak (first Guru) nor Gobind (tenth and last Guru) laid down new rules by which their followers should be bound in matters of marriage and inheritance". As such a wide variety of marriages, ranging from the sacramental forms to casual unions difficult of proof, was prevalent among the Sikhs; similarly, both child-marriage and adult-marriage were practised.

A peculiar form of Sikh marriage, resorted to in times of trouble when the tedious formalities of a regular marriage ceremony could not be gone through, was the Chadar Dalna (blanket-throwing). In this, there was no witnesses or priests, and the man took to wife a woman without asking anybody's leave. The marriage was, however, valid, and children could inherit, and it often happened that, on the death of a prince or chieftain, rival claimants for the dead man's estate appeared on the strength of a Chadar Dalna marriage.

Some kind of legal recognition of certain forms of marriage was considered essential, and in 1909 what was known as the Anand Marriage Act was passed. But as the Act did not reject the authority of customary law it was not of much help in litigation. The Hindu Marriage Act of 1955, which is applicable to the Sikhs, has now superseded all customary law and has brought the matrimonial laws of the Sikhs in conformity with those of the Hindus.

Islam and women with stand to gain if the role and status of muslim women in Indian society is brought at par with other communities in the Indian sub-continent and become an integral port of the popular Indian cultural milieu.